IN SEARCH OF DONNA REED

In Search of
Donna Reed

BY JAY FULTZ

University of Iowa Press Iowa City

University of Iowa Press, Iowa
City 52242. Copyright © 1998
by the University of Iowa Press.
All rights reserved. Printed in
the United States of America.

Design by Richard Eckersley

http://www.uiowa.edu/~uipress

Printed on acid-free paper

98 99 00 01 02 C 5 4 3 2 1

Library of Congress Cataloging-in-Publication Data
Fultz, Jay   In search of Donna Reed / by Jay Fultz
p.   cm.   Includes bibliographical references and index.
ISBN 0-87745-625-9
1. Reed, Donna, 1921–1986.   2. Motion picture actors
and actresses—United States—Biography.   I. Title.
PN2287.R285F86 1998   791.43'028'092–dc21 (B) 97–48310

Dedicated to my mother,

Dorothy Sawtelle Fultz,

and to the memory of my father,

James R. Fultz

Contents

Acknowledgments

A biographer is a detective, delineator, diplomat, a bit of a daredevil. And a debtor because beholden to many people. For the priceless gift of time and memory, I'm grateful to Donna Reed's family— to her widower, Colonel Grover W. Asmus; to her children, Mary Owen, Timothy Owen, Penny Owen Stigers, and Tony Owen Junior; to her siblings, Keith Mullenger, Lavone (Heidi) Flynn, Karen Moreland, and the late William L. Mullenger. And grateful to her relatives in Iowa and elsewhere—to Donald and Roberta Yankey, Frederick and Opal Whiteing, Earl and Delphine Shives, Clyde Shives, the late Leona Rollins, Sandy Mullenger, Violet Mullenger, and the granddaughters of Aunt Mildred Van Kampen Hostler, Nanette Linden and Michela Grant.

I'm grateful to Donna's friends and associates everywhere—to Doris Cole Abrahams, Steve Allen, the late Barbara Avedon, the late Professor Jerry Blunt, Ann McCrea Borden, Fred Briskin, U.S. Representative George E. Brown, the late Virginia Christine, Jeff Corey, the late Mary Lou (Mrs. Delmer) Daves, Rosemary DeCamp, Danny Desmond, Nancy Dillon, Kathleen Freeman, Jimmy Hawkins, Jeffrey Hayden, Claude Jarman Junior, Marian Drake Justice, Deborah Kerr, the late Alexander Knox, Harvey Korman, Angela Lansbury, John Philip Law, Carl and Friday Leonard, Alfred Levitt, the late Helen Levitt, Former Senator Eugene McCarthy, Andrew McCullough, Betty (Mrs. Charles) Massman, the late David Miller, Robert Ellis Miller, Patti Petersen Mirkovich, the late Nate Monaster, Anthony Moreno, Virginia Patton Moss, the late Gene Nelson, Gigi Perreau, William Roberts, Norma Connolly Rodman, Pat (Mrs. Randolph) Scott, the late Anna Schneller, the late Ann Straus, Jody (Mrs. Rex) Watkinson, Paul West, Esther Williams, Marie Windsor, Freddy Young.

I'm also grateful to Donna's high school classmates, including Arden Amman, Harold Auld, Margaret Anderson Carbee, Arlen Gemeroth, Dr. Thomas Hutcheson, Donald Jensen, Kenneth Langer, Ervin Mohr, Erma Jensen Monson, Joyce Ely Nebergall, Virginia Richard Powell, Vernette (Mrs. Lilburn P.) Taylor, Lucille Kepford Toney, Ila Bledsoe Wiebers; and to her college classmates, including Eugene Dow, Jane Fisher Engleman, Elberta Casey Hunter, Mary Huston Jaco, Mendie Koenig, Ardath Atkinson McLean, Helen Katz Mann, Sam Sebby, Harvey Tietzell.

And grateful to many archivists and librarians, among them Samuel Gill and Kristine Kreuger, Margaret Herrick Library, Academy of Motion Picture Arts and Sciences; Ned Comstock, Cinema Library, University of Southern California; Audree Malkin, Theater Arts Library, University of California at Los Angeles; Bob Boyce at the Bennett Martin Library, Lincoln, Nebraska; and the women at the Norelius Community Library, Denison, Iowa. Also valuable to me in my research was *Donna Reed: A Bio-Bibliography* (1990) by Brenda Scott Royce. Individuals who provided specialized help were Adelaida Martinez and Christy Hargesheimer.

I'm especially indebted to a number of people who, perhaps without knowing, kept me going: Colonel Asmus first of all; Joyce Anderson Fisk, who saved and made available to me half a century's worth of Donna's letters; William Tuttle, the dean of Hollywood makeup artists and Donna's first husband, who was unfailingly helpful and fatherly; the late Moria Turner Bruck, who with her husband, Charles Bruck, welcomed me to their home in Los Angeles and gave affectionate support; Virginia Ricks Hill and Marie Legér (Kelly Quinn), who also befriended Donna at Los Angeles City College; the late Sarah (Sukie) Mergener, sister of Tony Owen, whose charm warms my memory; Betty Massman, who shared letters from Donna and straightened me out on some genealogy; the late William Graf, a former producer at Columbia Pictures, whose interest in my project testified to his habitual generosity in aiding others; Paul Petersen, who was every parent's dream son and has matured into a man who looks out for others, while retaining Jeff Stone's robust spirit; Shelley Fabares, kindness personified, who encouraged me to write my own book when I was worried about pleasing everyone. I must also thank Lillian Burns Sidney, Donna's drama coach at MGM. Although she did not approve of every aspect of this book, I'm grateful to her for vivid early glimpses of Donna in Hollywood. Other benefactors could be added to this list, and I'd like to mention again Mary Owen, who is a true aristocrat in her honesty, humility, and humanity.

So many dear personal friends sustained me over the months and years that I can only name a few: the Yankeys, Mickey Willroth, and Mearl and Lillian Luvaas in Denison; Patricia Murphy, a second sister, who was by my side at the beginning; Avis Burnett, also very special and a biographer of Gertrude Stein, who read the manuscript and made suggestions; Aileen Fisher, the doyenne of writers for children, who did the same; Kay Graber, a confidante and one of the world's great editors; Robert Nott, whose experience in writing a biography of actor John Garfield made him kinsman of a kind; Harry Decker, commiserator and author of a haunting movie script about Donna Reed; James Cavanaugh, who shared tidbits about Donna that popped up during his research for a book on Van Heflin; Ronald Nelson, a pal from graduate school days; James P. Ronda; Timothy Bryant; Pat Bayles; Nancy Rosen; Ann Bardens; the Rev. Rob Gadeken; Douglas Clayton; Dika Eckersley; Sandra Johnson; Clayton Bruster; and, not least, Elaine (Lainey) Jenkins, whose wisdom helped me gain perspective in some discouraging times.

Finally, many thanks to Bob Thomas for giving me access to his papers at UCLA and to Charles Maland for his valuable suggestions in revising the manuscript. Holly Carver, Sarah Walz, and others at the University of Iowa Press know how to treat a first-time author, and I thank them for their friendly professionalism.

I'm proud that *In Search of Donna Reed* has been designed by my good friend Richard Eckersley.

From Iowa

D onna Reed probably came closer than any other actress to being the archetypal sweetheart, wife, and mother. In January 1986, Dan Rather and his competitors interrupted their nightly intonement of mayhem, murder, and political muddling to announce her death. On *Cable Headline News* an hourly filmclip chronicled her country Cinderella story. For a week in midwinter the print media echoed *Time* magazine in noting that she "symbolized the heartland virtues of American womanhood."

I was stung by the news, having followed the career of Donna Reed since my pimply adolescence in rural Kansas. That glow of hers, those striking hazel eyes, first did me in when I saw *Saturday's Hero* in the early fifties. Soon I was borrowing the family car and driving thirteen miles to the Bijou whenever she played.

What was so special about an actress who, to my friends, was just another actress? There was that translucent face, subtly expressive, refined by sympathy—the eyes reflecting intelligence and everything else. There was that voice—in my hungry range of reference, it suggested deep-dish apple pie, sweet and crisp, and lightly dusted with hauteur, a new word from some book. My interest was piqued because Donna Reed seemed distinctly underrated, unpromoted. I thought no one else liked her so much. Seeing *From Here to Eternity* or *The Far Horizons* or *The Benny Goodman Story* for the tenth time, I looked at the movie patrons looking at her, for they *had* to grant her the space of those extraordinary close-ups.

Real life was intervening, but the variable image of Donna Reed assumed a mysterious permanent place in my psyche. By the time her television series began in 1958, I was in the army and seldom able to watch. Influenced by critics, I dismissed it as unworthy of her. Only in the late eighties and early nineties, through daily reruns on Nickelodeon Network, did I really discover *The Donna Reed Show*.

Several decades earlier, at some sleepless hour in a fraternity house, I had caught snowy telecasts of *The Picture of Dorian Gray* and *They Were Expendable*. Now movie historians rated them classics, along with *Eternity* and *It's a Wonderful Life*. Overnight, it seemed, Donna Reed was the leading lady in more classics, televised more often, than the vaunted Crawford and Stanwyck. One December I gave a *Wonderful Life* party, before reading in the *New Yorker* that friends everywhere were gathering by the TV to view, not for the first time, Mary Hatch and George Bailey, the otherworldly Clarence, and the despicable Potter.

Most dead actors live only in the flicker of an electronic eye. But years after her death Donna Reed is referred to as if she were still living, in contexts that go far beyond the movies and television episodes that made her famous. Fixed in time, oddly timeless, she is an icon of popular culture. Her name is bandied in movies, books, songs, poems, magazine articles, and comic strips.

For many, Donna Reed epitomizes the deeply domestic woman of another era—to be revived or scorned. A journal reporting on the force of working women in the fall of 1995 carries the headline "Sorry, Boys—Donna Reed Is Still Dead." Another magazine feature, describing a return to the fifties tradition of eating at home, is illustrated with her photo and claims that "women still want to be Donna Reed." A 1993 issue of the sophisticated *New York* magazine examines the revival of mid-twentieth-century furniture, with "the Donna Reed armchair" representing the fifties. After the sexual revolution, good Donna Reeds are back, bemoaned the feminists. They might be surprised to know where the real Donna stood with them. Years before the resurgence of the women's movement, she "had a feminist consciousness without the vocabulary to go with it," said her friend, the writer Barbara Avedon.

Like the typical fan, that Kansas farmboy of long ago felt he *knew* Donna Reed. Her uniqueness, as sensed from afar, has proved out—but, of course, the woman was more complex and richly interesting than her screen persona. The real story of Donna Reed has never been told. It is a mystery because she was passionately, almost pathologically, private. The director David Miller found her "intriguingly covert," compared to those scandal-bitten actresses who were "overtly banal."

On one level, the story of Donna Reed is a gloss on the situation of many women stars during and after the studio period. On another, it is about strength of character, to use an unfashionable phrase. How she tried to keep her head while surrounded by corrupting influences; how she survived personally intact in a brutal profession, only to be humiliated at the last; how she grew, intellectually and politically, in a town devoted to the ephemeral and trivial—these are matters of consequence. Finally, this story is due, past due, because the life of Donna Reed continues to touch and inspire so many other lives, as the angel Clarence would say.

It begins in rural Iowa, somewhere between the bluffs of the Missouri River and the covered bridges of Madison County.

The population of Denison, Iowa, just under seven thousand, has nearly doubled since 1938, when Donna Mullenger left the family farm seven miles southeast of town. Nonetheless, there still exists, to paraphrase Gertrude Stein, a there there that any returning Mullenger spirit would recognize. The strip along Highway 30, formerly the historic Lincoln Highway, the first to link both coasts, has changed superficially. Flags along the street now proclaim "Denison: It's a Wonderful Life." New-fangled places have names like Cottonwood Square and Breadeaux French-Style Pisa. But Cronk's Cafe has been operating since 1929, and across from it the Park Motel rents out suites that were fit for a movie queen. To the south is the Northwestern Railroad depot, which is slightly smaller than it was when Donna boarded a streamliner for Los Angeles that Depression summer sixty years ago.

The prospect of a railroad line influenced Jesse W. Denison to found, in 1856, the town that bears his name. He was a Baptist minister and agent for the Providence Western Land Company, composed mainly of Rhode Islanders interested in Iowa property. Blessed with an aesthetic sense, Denison platted the town on the hills between the forks of the Boyer, a river that was already named in 1804 when Meriwether Lewis and William

Clark crossed it farther west. Donna Reed grew up among these nameless hills formed by ancient glaciers.

To go up the steep incline from Highway 30—up past blocks of trim houses with walled-in lawns—is to return to the town Donna knew as a girl. Gone is Chris Otto's Cigar Store with its wooden Indian; but the Candy Kitchen, where Donna sometimes shared a soda with a beau, has been restored. The adjoining Ritz Theater, where she paid a dime to see Jimmy Cagney and Bette Davis, has been refurbished and renamed the Donna Reed Center for the Performing Arts. On Broadway the Crawford County Courthouse, constructed of Bedford limestone and sandstone and dedicated in 1906, suggests the kind of civic stability and permanence that wars are fought for. Catercorner stands the old real estate office of Donna's youngest brother, William L., always called Billy by relatives living nearby. He mainly won his long battle with alcoholism before dying in 1993.

A few blocks east and partway down a hill made for sledding is the Norelius Community Library, which was built in 1979 on the site of the house occupied by Donna's parents, Hazel and William R. Mullenger, after they left the farm in the mid-fifties. On the grounds are two red oaks that William planted on the centennial of his father's birthday. Across from the library is the First Methodist Church, worship place for generations of Mullengers. Several hundred old neighbors, friends, and cousins gathered there for a memorial to Donna in 1986. A simple stone bearing her name has been set between the graves of her parents in Oakland Cemetery, although burial was on the West Coast.

An overlooked monument to Donna's early years is the frame house on Sixteenth Street where she stayed with her Grandmother Mullenger while attending high school. Essentially unchanged, this modest but comfortable house in front of the water tower, or standpipe, symbolizes Donna's social background—far removed from that of the McHenrys, Balles, Plimptons, Laubs, and Hestons, whose Victorian, Italianate, and Greek Revival mansions were, and are, hard by. Ironically, Donna's Academy Award is on display at a house whose interior she probably never saw while growing up. The Victorian structure, built in 1895 by the cattleman

W. A. McHenry and now a museum, boasts imported wood and a third floor that was originally a ballroom.

Denisonites have always found that strangers are more interested in hearing about the star of *The Donna Reed Show* than about corn and hogs and other local products. But they have taken Donna's fame in stride, partly because she discouraged fuss during her visits home and partly because they are too close to the earth and its uncertain bounty to be overly impressed by celebrity.

Besides, they had grown used to renown long before Donna was ever noticed. On June 4, 1927, Clarence Chamberlin, the son of a jeweler, left Roosevelt Field, New York, in his Bellanca monoplane, the *Columbia*, and forty-two hours later landed in Germany. A Denison boy had made the longest nonstop flight to date while introducing airmail service to Europe. Donna was six years old when several thousand Denisonites gave him a parade. Another native son, Bob Saggau, was a highly publicized halfback for the Fighting Irish of Notre Dame when she was still in high school.

Not that townspeople are indifferent to the attention brought by Donna's name. Mention of the cornfed beauty who was one of them is the beginning of a bond. The genuine sociability of Denisonites is an anachronism in a Midwest grown less friendly over time. Cronk's Cafe, which still serves the Belgian waffles Donna loved, and where coffee cups never reach empty, is only the most conspicuous haven of hospitality. Farmers still meet there every morning before the roosters crow.

Yet behind the relaxed and congenial exterior is a fear known to other Middle Americans. Denison's economy was hurting in the spring of 1990, after the closing of a meat-packing plant. Since then, developers have attracted some industry, but the young are still leaving Crawford County. The local opportunities for them are hardly better today than they were for Donnabelle Mullenger and her classmates in 1938.

Ironically, Donna, whose bright promise could not be realized in Denison, is now, after her death, the means by which hundreds of talented young people are brought to Denison every June. The Donna Reed Festival for the Performing Arts, supported proudly by the town, has expanded since 1986 to offer substantial scholarships in her memory and workshops taught by Hollywood and Broadway veterans. Not Pioneer corn, not Poland China hogs, but that unique festival is putting Denison on the national map.

Western Iowa was barely on the map when Donna Reed's ancestors started coming to it in the 1860s. They were of English, German, and Irish stock.

Donna's great-grandfather, William Reform Mullenger, was a bricklayer and blacksmith in the Chiltern Hills near London. His dreams could hardly be hitched to low wages and high rents. Although he might eventually inherit land, there was none to be had in England at midcentury. In 1857, with the Crimean War ended, emigrant ships were crossing the Atlantic again. William Reform and his wife, Mary Tyler Mullenger, were among the more than 250,000 foreigners who arrived in the United States that year.

Their timing was not propitious. Milwaukee, Wisconsin, where the Mullengers settled, was experiencing an economic slump like the rest of the country. If local reports didn't cause them to look south to Iowa, letters from England surely did, for the new state was being advertised abroad. According to one guide, Iowa much resembled the "finest portions of south of England counties."

William Reform and Mary, along with several of the English Tylers, started for Audubon County, Iowa, in 1862. They were lured by the recent Homestead Act, promising 160 acres—a quarter section—to anyone who occupied and improved the land. Iowa was filling up quickly, except for the western part, which was rumored to be prey to Indian raids and grasshopper plagues. Although the black soil was rich, homesteading was no cinch. The prairie grass grew as high as a horse's head and fires were dreaded, the wolves howled at night, and there were no herd laws or fences to protect and contain livestock.

William Reform and Mary Tyler Mullenger were the kind of sturdy pioneers described in Emerson Hough's novels but rarely in history books. She died in 1871, and he moved to other frontiers, always seeking a bend of river reminiscent of the Thames, exerting the enterprise that might cushion his old age. In 1918 he was buried in a pauper's grave in

Salem, Oregon. Donna Reed came to feel affection for the defeated adventurer who died three years before she was born. "He was always reaching for something unattainable, or unworkable if attainable," she wrote to a newly discovered English cousin.

The firstborn son of William Reform and Mary Tyler Mullenger, named William George, moved to Crawford County in 1877 at the age of nineteen. Finally he saved enough money to buy an isolated farm in Nishnabotny Township southeast of Denison. The future Donna Reed would grow up on that 120-acre farm, and it would remain in her family for nearly a century. William George brought to the place his bride, Mary Ann Johnston, the daughter of pioneers who had come to Iowa from Randolph County, Illinois, in 1869. A portrait of Mary Ann's mother, Elizabeth Herner Johnston, hangs today in McHenry House in Denison. It is possible to see the lineaments of Donna Reed's beauty in Great-Grandmother Johnston's finely modeled brow and intelligent dark eyes.

If Mary Ann Mullenger's beauty was mainly spiritual, it served her well; she needed to be as steady as a saint to live with William George. He was hotheaded, dyspeptically restless, and devilishly handsome. The mismatched couple raised three children: Mildred, who would figure importantly in Donna's life; Ruby, who died violently and mysteriously in 1917, six months after her marriage to a Nebraskan named Earl Law; and William Richard.

Still another William in the family! William Reform begat William George who begat William Richard. Born on the Fourth of July in the Depression year of 1893, William Richard inherited his father's good looks and his mother's gentleness. He grew up on a farm near the one that his daughter Donna would call home. It was a country visited by severe blizzards and droughts, cut off by bad roads, beyond the reach of mail delivery until 1901 and the possibility of telephone service until 1903.

In spite of local diphtheria and scarlet fever epidemics and a certain bleakness that drove out some neighbors, it was an exciting time to be young. By 1899, after Edison's invention of the kinetoscope, the first motion pictures were being shown at the Denison Opera House, and within a decade teams and wagons were sharing the streets with automobiles. No fifteen-year-old boy would have missed the Great New York to Paris Auto

Race, which passed through Denison in 1908. Then, as later, the Lincoln Highway and Northwestern Railroad brought circuses and celebrities to town.

Even if William Richard never saw President Theodore Roosevelt and other public men whose trains stopped at the depot, or heard the Chautauqua speakers in Washington Park, he developed an avid interest in current events. More than anything—pitching horseshoes, playing mathematical and word games—he loved to argue. Like his father, he devoured newspapers for topics, but unlike him he argued them goodnaturedly, probingly, often assuming the opposite point of view, like a good Republican being a better Democrat.

For William Richard Mullenger, the greatest pain and happiness came close together during and after World War I. The influenza epidemic of 1918 coincided with his army duty at Camp Dodge in Des Moines, where he helped care for hundreds of dying soldiers. That experience marked him permanently. His subsequent stint with the Coast Artillery in Florida was, by comparison, a winter sojourn. After returning home in March 1919 he took a job with a Denison seed company, the only time he was ever to work for someone else.

One day William Richard and his father went to the nearby farm of Charles Shives to borrow some item (no one remembers what). They came to the kitchen door just as a slight, dark-haired girl was fetching wood. On glimpsing them, she ducked her head into the deep woodbox, effectively hiding the top half of herself. "I thought she would never come back out," the younger William used to say, laughing. When she did, he faced his future wife.

Hazel Jane Shives would never lose her shyness. Small-boned, she weighed barely a hundred pounds. Her large brown eyes, pretty auburn hair, and delicate features reminded some of the actress Janet Gaynor. In middle age, even as illness began destroying her physical grace, she would look like a particularly patrician, though unpretentious, American Mom, the kind that World War II magazine photos showed in the kitchen baking chocolate cake for a soldier son. But at the moment Hazel met William R. Mullenger she was clerking at the Boys Department Store in

Denison and still comfortably obscured by three less retiring sisters and five live-wire brothers.

Hazel was born in 1899 to Charles and Mary Etta Petty Shives. Like the Mullengers, the Shiveses had farming in their blood; but they seem to have been somewhat more prosperous. Charles was an adolescent when he came with his father, Charles Alexander Shives, and three siblings from Montgomery County, Illinois, to Iowa in 1873. Shortly before, his mother, Eliza Coffin Shives, and teenage sister, Laura, had been killed when mules ran away with a wagon on a trail in Alabama near the Black Warrior River. They were taking a southern route in wintertime, traveling between home in Illinois and (probably) North Carolina, where relatives lived.

The Shives forebears of Donna Reed had followed a common hop-scotch pattern of immigration, reaching Iowa by a circuitous route that began in 1733 when Martin and Anna Scheib left the Steinweiler-Rohrbach area of the Rhineland-Palz. Sailing on the ship *Samuel,* they disembarked at Philadelphia, the principal port of entry for Germans before the American Revolution. Their five children, including Jacob (whose line would produce Donna Reed), settled in Bucks County, Pennsylvania, where many descendants still live. Among Jacob's issue migrating to North Carolina was Charles Alexander Shives, who would move to Illinois with his Quaker wife, Eliza Coffin, about 1857. Sixteen years later, newly widowed, he jumped to Iowa.

Charles Alexander Shives stands in the same relation to Donna Reed as William Reform Mullenger, and is another recognizable type. Her great-grandfather Charles bought a farm in Crawford County near the town of Boyer, where he helped build a Methodist Church. He voted Republican, supported the temperance movement, and generally exemplified the virtues of the Pennsylvania Dutch that would be passed on to Donna: thrift, industry, domesticity, and a love of land, which was to be kept in the family forever. His end was even sadder than William Reform Mullenger's. On a February morning in 1905, despondent because he could no longer work, Charles Alexander Shives positioned a shotgun so that the barrel was pointing toward his forehead and pulled a string attached to the trigger. Although suicide was not uncommon among pioneers, and the *Denison Bulletin* spared no details in its account, the manner of his death was never mentioned in the family.

His youngest son, Charles, is remembered as short and balding, witty, and devoutly religious. The father of Hazel Jane was a nurturer, a trustee and steward of the Methodist Church, and organizer of the annual Old Settlers' Picnic. He developed some fine farms in Crawford County and, with Mary Etta Petty Shives, raised a large, close-knit family. The Bible was read aloud every night after supper; anyone who giggled got sent outside, no matter the temperature. During meals Charles might regale his brood with comic stories and poems. Just as often he was an irresistible target for the jokes of his five strapping sons, Raymond, Harvey, Ross, Jesse, and Leslie. As a child, Donna Mullenger listened to her grandfather and uncles hold forth on Sunday afternoons while the women washed dishes in the nearby kitchen, muffling their laughter as they worked. "My memory is that they were much funnier than most entertainments one sees today, purporting to be funny!" she wrote fifty years later.

After Charles's death in 1936, Mary Etta lived on another eleven years, long enough to see her granddaughter become a screen star. Like most of the Petty and Shives women, Mary Etta was quiet and strongly domestic—Donna retained an image of her standing at the cookstove frying potatoes. In her prime she was quite beautiful, the member of the family whom Donna would most resemble. Mary Etta was also the link to some delightful surprises Donna would find in her genealogical searches. After the role of Mary Bailey in *It's a Wonderful Life* had given her cinematic immortality, she discovered, in the Petty branch of her family tree, an Irishwoman named Mary Bailey, who lived in the Ohio River valley early in the nineteenth century. When the Petty bloodline turned up a forebear named John Reed, Donna finally felt comfortable with the name that had been hung on her by a Hollywood publicist.

"So we beat on, boats against the current, borne back ceaselessly into the past," wrote Scott Fitzgerald. For Donna Reed, a dedicated genealogist, the truth of that was intensely personal. Two pioneer lines began to converge on the day the shy daughter of Charles and Mary Etta Shives, Hazel Jane, met young William Richard Mullenger, discharged from the military. They were married in the summer of 1920 in the Methodist parsonage at Sac City. "The bride was charming in a gown of flesh-colored georgette, embroidered with beads, and a hat to match. Following the ceremony the young people departed for Lake View, where they are enjoying a honeymoon at the home of the bride's brother, Jesse Shives," reported the *Denison Review*.

The decade associated with jazz babies and high-steppers began depressingly for rural Iowans. Saddled with heavy mortgages incurred for overpriced land during the war years, many farmers felt pinched as crop surpluses and tariffs kept market prices low. As early as 1921 there were signs of the hard times ahead. Some stores in Denison closed; others did business on a cash-only basis. On February 9 a local newspaper editorialized that "many who used to eat sirloin steak are getting along very comfortably on corned beef." That same day the *Bulletin and Herald* announced on an inside page: "January 25—Born to Mr. and Mrs. William Mullenger, a girl."

Donna's very first press notice, like so many that would eventually follow, contained an error; in fact, she had arrived on January 27. No kindly doctor had to plow through country roads during a blizzard, for she was born in Denison on a fair day. Leona Rollins, whose father was Mary Ann Mullenger's brother, recalled going to an apartment at 1725 Second Avenue North to see Baby Donna Belle. It is said that she got her middle name from Belle McCord, the midwife who assisted Dr. Carr at her birth. However that may be, the first child of Hazel and William Mullenger always answered to Donnabelle while growing up.

Donnabelle was barely a month old when Hazel and Bill moved to his boyhood home in Nishnabotny Township. The irascible William George and long-suffering Mary Ann had sold it at the bargain price reserved for an only son—$35 an acre—and retired to Denison. On a March day the new Mullenger family carted their possessions over a dirt road southeast of town. Along with them went an antique organ and several volumes of poetry—the bequests of William Reform to Bill's first-born, and gifts that Donna would treasure.

Today the route is named Donna Reed Drive and is paved to the north corner of the old Mullenger farm. From there a gravel road leads south up a hill and past the site of the homestead, easily overlooked because all that remains is a ramshackle corncrib with a horseshoe over the door. The trees that Donnabelle's father planted still stand, and weeds among foundation stones suggest a forgotten cemetery. Cars raising dust on the road can't dispel the trespasser's sense of remoteness. It is easy to imagine that buffalo once wallowed on the dished-out hills to the west; harder to realize that a large, happy family lived here.

But more than seventy years ago the place was alive with the sounds of chickens and cows, children, and calls to dinner. Old photographs show several barns, a feedlot, and a two-story white farmhouse, boxy and (like so many in Iowa) built on a high foundation, incongruent with the horizontal lines of the landscape.

Except for the convenience of a Chandler car and later a Dodge, the Mullengers lived pretty much as their parents had. There was no electricity until the late thirties, about the time Donnabelle left home. Butter and cream were cooled in a cistern during the summer. Bill read the *Des Moines Register* and *Pathfinder*, a weekly magazine, by the light of a kerosene lamp. Hazel's chief link with the world was through a crank-up, battery-powered telephone. She carried water from the outside cistern into the kitchen and cooked three meals a day on a wood-burning Proctor stove. The only other heat in the house was supplied by a living-room furnace fired by corncobs, coal, and chopped branches; it was capable of sending warmth to an upstairs bedroom through a floor register. Comfort went only so far: The outdoor privy was no place for lingering in sub-zero weather.

Furnished with filmy white curtains at the long windows, overstuffed sofas backed by antimacassars, and solid oak tables and chairs made by prisoners at the state penitentiary, the farmhouse was intended for a sizable family. In time Donnabelle was joined by a brother, Keith, and a sister, Lavone. She was old enough to help care for her siblings when another brother, Billy, arrived. Very early, it seems, she began looking out for others—some relatives noticed and called her "Little Mother." In one memorable snapshot Donnabelle stands protectively among neighbor children who appear windblown and grimy. Her chubby face, slightly upturned and framed by blonde bangs like a little Dutch girl's, shines out of the general dinginess.

Donnabelle was no angel, of course, but her position as firstborn imbued her with a sense of responsibility and seriousness beyond her years. From the Mullenger side, William George excepted, she inherited a steady calmness and optimism. Many years later, she would realize how much of her father's upbeat attitude and emotional resilience she had drawn on for *The Donna Reed Show*. From the Shives side, she got her extraordinary sensitivity. The Shiveses were nervous and high-strung, inclined to worry about their own problems and everyone else's, and also apt to get their feelings hurt. Hazel, whose refinement concealed a certain grit, was a feminine model. She was, an adoring daughter recalled, "fearfully maternal." One day old neighbors would be reminded of Hazel, moving about quickly and efficiently in her kitchen, when they watched Donna's show.

By the time that window on family life opened to television viewers, Hazel and Bill were living in town and proudly recalling how hard their children had worked on the farm. Donnabelle rose early to milk the Holstein cows (a fact that Hollywood would exploit). She gathered eggs, collected corncobs, picked corn, pitched hay, fed the livestock, and took her turn operating the windmill, which pumped water from a well to the cistern by the house. On hot summer days she bent over rows of potato plants, knocking off bugs into a pail of kerosene. She was all over the place. While still a lass, Donnabelle felt proprietary toward the land in a way that those who merely reside on it never do. Inside, she helped Hazel prepare meals and can tomatoes and peaches in a kitchen without any modern facilities. She also played a part in the great Iowa tradition of cooking for thrashers, who consumed platters of crisp fried chicken, roasts with real brown gravy, mounds of mashed potatoes dripping with home-churned butter, succulent sweet corn, and mile-high apple and cherry pies.

During the school term Donnabelle escaped the grueling ritual of washing and ironing clothes, which took an entire day. Hazel began by fetching water, heating it on the stove, lugging it to a Cushman wooden tub powered by a gasoline engine—and proceeded with washing, putting the clothes through a wringer, hanging them on a line to dry, and finally pressing them with flatirons heated on the all-purpose kitchen stove. Lavone, who can still see her mother carrying in water and hear the click of her heels on the sidewalk, did her share of the chores. Although more of a tomboy than Donnabelle, she pulled house duty, scrubbing and oiling the hardwood floor every week. The boys were kept busy in the barns and fields, Keith developing the kind of know-how that would make him a 4-H champion and Billy playing catch-up.

When they weren't working, the Mullengers mixed mainly with scads of relatives who lived nearby. It hardly mattered that farmers didn't fit into Denison society—Hazel was happiest when surrounded by her family. Donna's need in later years to make and maintain family connections surely owed something to nostalgia for long-ago picnics and dinners with the Mullenger and Shives clans.

Donnabelle saw a lot of Aunt Mabel and Uncle John Yankey and her cousins, Opal, Donald, and Curtis. At the Yankey farm she could look forward to hand-cranked ice cream and Aunt Mabel's famous banana-nut cake. Grandmother and Grandfather Shives often hosted holiday dinners. Because space was limited, the men ate first, the children next, and the women last. That arrangement didn't hold for smaller Sunday dinners, after which the women talked and sewed while the men practiced target shooting with a Winchester .22 or played horseshoes. A winner of local tournaments, Bill Mullenger made ringers every chance he got.

If Sundays were for visiting relatives, Saturday night was for going to town. During the summers it was about the only time Donnabelle, Keith, Lavone, and Billy saw outsiders. The family would pile into the old Dodge and head for Denison to buy staples like sugar and flour. Occasionally they took in a double-feature at the Opera House; more often they chatted with neighbors on street corners or watched people from their parked car. Donnabelle would share a sack of candy with the younger ones, and ice cream cones might be handed around, but dining out wasn't expected. Restaurants drew mainly workingmen, and fast Happy Meals were the arch of the far future.

The family's German shepherds—Rex, Ace, and Phoebe—were omnipresent and overfriendly. But Lavone's Shetland pony, Daisy, disliked Donnabelle. The future actress who would ride in horse operas was always greeted by Daisy's lowered ears and skittish sidestep. Before long, Donnabelle's interest began to shift from home-ground play to a larger arena of personalities and ideas. She corresponded with a Pennsylvania penpal and exchanged comics and magazines with a neighbor boy, Arden Amman. A lifelong love of reading began with a card from the Denison library that allowed her to borrow biographies of Florence Nightingale and Abraham Lincoln (who once owned property six miles north of Denison) and the novels of Bess Streeter Aldrich. And she discovered the movies. Opal Yankey Whiteing remembered Donnabelle's upstairs bedroom, where the walls were lined with photo cutouts of Greta Garbo, Clark Gable, and other Hollywood luminaries. The only fan letter she ever wrote was to Anne Shirley, the youthful star of *Anne of Green Gables*.

One charming diversion illustrates the closeness of the Mullenger children—in this case Donnabelle, Keith, and Lavone. As school made inroads on their shyness, they formed a singing group, performing first at family get-togethers and then at box suppers, corn shows, and church picnics. Keith played guitar and the girls joined in singing sad, sweet songs that made the women in the audience cry. Their repertoire included "Babes in the Woods," "Dear Old Southern Home," "Silver-Haired Daddy of Mine," and, most affectingly, "Put My Little Shoes Away."

Mother dear, come bathe my forehead,
For I'm growing very weak.
Mother, let one drop of water
Fall upon my burning cheek.
Tell my loving little playmates
I no longer more will play.
Give them all my toys, but Mother,
Put my little shoes away.

By this time—the twenties had tumbled into the thirties—all three children were attending a rural school, Nishnabotna Number 3, only a quarter-mile from their house. Donnabelle, who had started in 1926, helped carry water from the Mullenger cistern to the white schoolhouse, where Marian Drake taught eight grades in one room. Its furnishings were standard: a recitation bench and desks, small library, blackboard, pull-down map, and picture of a girl looking up at a robin. On winter mornings the twenty or so pupils hovered around a coal furnace, which also served to heat pans of soup at noon. Miss Drake, later Mrs. Earl Justice, recalled that Donnabelle suffered from chilblains. In tears, she would go home and return to school after her mother had applied kerosene to the swelling caused by extreme cold.

Although the conditions seem primitive now—both sexes shared the outhouse, and a nearby cyclone cave attracted snakes—the children were well taught. Rural students often surpassed town ones in the eighth-grade examinations required by state law. Donnabelle studied the Elson Basic Readers, which were used in Iowa for generations. She was smart without being smarty, determined to excel.

And, for one so young, very meticulous. One day Donnabelle took a test and Miss Drake checked her answers against a printed key. Thinking an answer marked wrong was really right, the girl consulted with her busy teacher, who quickly referred to the key. Not satisfied, Donnabelle took the problem home to her parents, who drove into town to ask Grandmother Mullenger, a former schoolteacher. Yes, she too said Donnabelle's answer was right. And indeed it was; Miss Drake happily corrected the key.

High principles entered into the air breathed. Report cards bearing the motto "Honor Lies in Honest Toil" alloted as much space to conduct as to performance in subjects. Keith painstakingly copied maxims into a homemade booklet, including the Dutch proverb "When two quarrel, both are in the wrong." Enveloped by Miss Drake's gentleness, the pupils formed a family. When the teacher stayed late to prepare lessons, Donnabelle, having finished her chores, returned to the schoolhouse to keep her company. Miss Drake never forgot the farm girl's big smile, or her first public performance, a recitation titled "Betty at the Baseball Game." Incongruously, Donnabelle impersonated a self-absorbed socialite unfamiliar with strikes and home runs. Miss Drake recalled: "She had special gifts in English—charming enunciation!"

Whatever Donnabelle lacked in material goods was made up for by the moral support and encouragement of her parents. Bill Mullenger never spanked the children. When they were naughty, he would say, "Now, let's talk this over." The Mullenger girls never felt less valued than the boys. Donna's strong sense of fairness and equality, fostered at home, would make her sharply aware of the advantages enjoyed by men in Hollywood. Bill's formal education had ended at eighth grade, but his continuous reading and zest for knowledge set an example. After a day in the fields he sat by a coal-oil lamp and helped Donnabelle, Keith, Lavone, and Billy with their geography, science, and math lessons. Close by, Hazel paused in her knitting or mending to contribute. She saw schooling as the means to an easier, more secure livelihood.

If Hazel experienced moments of dissatisfaction, so did other farm-wives who met for lunch and needlework once a month. These women endured isolation and went without some of the modern conveniences taken for granted by Omahans and even Denisonites.

Yet the Mullengers managed. Progressive-minded, they were involved in 4-H. Keith would go farthest in the farm club aiming "to make the best better." In the late thirties, after electricity came to the countryside, he wired the chicken barn so that an alarm clock turned on lights at three o'clock in the morning. That 4-H project, which increased egg production, won him a Westinghouse college scholarship. In time all the Mullenger offspring took prizes for their purebred hogs, sheep, and colts. Donnabelle, who belonged to the Nimble Fingers 4-H Club, made her own uniform, a middy with a long pleated skirt that she later thought unattractive. At age thirteen she won a blue ribbon at the Iowa State Fair for her wholewheat yeast rolls—not for the biscuits preferred by Hollywood legend makers.

Meanwhile everyone was busy and still young and apparently healthy. On the cusp of the Great Depression, the Mullengers might have passed for an All-American farm family.

In the mid-twenties a sign on the Commercial Bank in Denison had read: "A boy with a bank book, a Bible, and a dictionary is well fortified for life." Although sexist by today's standards, it summed up the values instilled in Donnabelle Mullenger. Showing ambition and planning carefully were moral imperatives. That simple faith in progress through hard work and right living was about to be severely tested for the Mullengers and other Americans.

By 1927 thirteen banks had closed in Crawford County. Several years later a delinquent tax list occupied three columns of fine print in the *Denison Bulletin*. Farm foreclosures increased as prices dipped—in 1932—to ten cents a bushel for corn and less than a cent a pound for hogs. Even farmers who rented saw their possessions sold out from under them. Bill Mullenger was better off than many because he owned his land, but the clay soil wasn't uniformly productive.

The drought that began in 1930 and lasted nearly a decade brought with it dust, insects, disease, desperation. The Mullengers lost entire crops to the grasshoppers. They had to slaughter their dairy cows when they failed the mandatory tuberculosis tests. With lingering pain, Keith recalled: "Cows that otherwise looked healthy were sentenced to early death in order to minimize the risk of spreading TB through milk-drinking children in Iowa. Some wondered why state laws didn't require children to be as carefully tested as cows." When most of the hogs came down with cholera, Bill Mullenger had to kill and burn them. The only time he cried, according to Billy, was when one of the horses died from eating sweet clover, all the feed that was available.

No one was more deeply and permanently marked by the Great Depression than the farm girl who became Donna Reed. Witnessing adversity early, she could never quite believe in her fame and fortune. From Hollywood, she testified to "the drought that withered crops and parched the earth only to be followed by the wind that swept the dry topsoil into great, dark, choking dust storms." To the end of her life she was haunted by the sound of livestock "crying for water" and by the sight of neighbors moving out in rickety automobiles holding a few belongings. One day a little girl from a nearby farm came to tell Donnabelle that she would not be playing with her anymore because her family was going away. "She didn't know where they were going; they were simply leaving, giving up."

In refusing to yield to bad conditions, Bill and Hazel Mullenger passed on to Donnabelle and the others a lesson about Iowa backbone—or just plain "Iowa Stubborn," as the song in Meredith Willson's *Music Man* calls it. But their courage cost something. Overwork and worry put Hazel in a Council Bluffs hospital in 1930 for ulcer surgery, then considered a serious operation. Donnabelle took care of four-year-old Billy during that period. It was the beginning of her life-long anxiety about her mother's health. Although Bill Mullenger fit the image of the farmer drawn by the editorial cartoonist J. N. Darling, he was in some respects ill-suited to be one. The omnipresent dust affected his lungs and caused headaches. Donnabelle, strongly attached to both parents, suffered with them as the Depression wore on. Later she wrote about her "anguish" in seeing them rise early and retire late every day, "laboring hard with no returns."

Yet Bill Mullenger's quiet optimism wasn't lost on Donnabelle. His resourcefulness abetted her own. When the drought killed trees in the yard, she and Keith helped him plant more: walnut, Chinese elm, evergreen, white ash, blue spruce, a mulberry by the cellar door. As Bill fussed over the seedlings, carrying water to them, Hazel joshed, "They won't grow, you loon!"

Bill's experimental attitude and playfulness distinguished him from most of the furrow-browed, dog-tired daddies. He introduced lean-bacon Tamworth hogs to the neighborhood and raised Shropshire sheep (Donnabelle liked to watch the shearing) and German shepherds (until some dogs transported sixty miles to Oakland found their way back home in two days). Despite his vulnerability to dust, he was energetic, always raring to play horseshoes or wrestle younger men. "Bill did a little jig when he walked," recalled Earl Shives.

Reverses might have reduced the jig to a stagger by 1932, but Bill Mullenger rejected government aid—payments for keeping "Roosevelt acres" unplanted. Even less did he approve of the "radical" Farmers Holiday Organization, whose action in barring the foreclosure of a farm near Denison in 1933 brought out the state militia and put Crawford County in the national spotlight. Bill's allegiance went, instead, to the Civilian Conservation Corps, which established a camp at Denison in 1935 for instruction in erosion control. His experiments with strip farming and contouring, adaptable to the hilly land, were fairly advanced for the time. Because his interest in saving and improving the soil seemed obsessive, he was a bit of a laughingstock, according to his children.

Though more prone to discouragement, Hazel also set a tone for the family's survival. A fragile but active Demeter, she kept the larder filled. Potatoes and canned goods from the half-acre garden were stored in the earth-floored basement. From wild plums she made a memorable jam and, for a special treat, fried doughnuts. She taught the girls kitchen skills, but neither was able to duplicate her yeast-risen bread. Years later, in California, Donna would be homesick for the smell and taste of that fresh-baked bread. From the ubiquitous patterned feedsacks Hazel sewed tea towels, housedresses, and underwear or "Omar panties." Donnabelle followed her example and by adolescence was running up her own clothes on the old Singer.

If the Mullenger farm was not a country manor, it was not a poor place out of *Grapes of Wrath* or *Tobacco Road* either. During the Depression, Bill and Hazel superintended a cottage industry. Three-quarters of the family's needs were supplied by the farm. No one went hungry or naked. Hazel served well-balanced meals and the children wore warm coats, although hand-me-downs were in style. Quality possessions had accumulated through years of married life, from Hazel's Spode bone china to Bill's farming equipment.

Of course, the more the Mullengers owned, the more they risked. Donnabelle, already schooled in notions of getting ahead and putting something aside, saw that the rules might count for little in a time of general distress. She loved the farm but never romanticized growing up there, saying much later, "It may have been good training for life, but we had rough times."

If Donnabelle was stamped by the Depression, never able to feel secure, her younger sister, Lavone, was not so shadowed. Perhaps more sheltered, Lavone recalled no real deprivation during the thirties. She spoke her own truth in 1990: "Poverty as we know of it today is a far cry from the wonderful wholesome life that we knew in Iowa."

Donnabelle took a tentative step out of that 120-acre world in 1934, when she started high school in Denison. Because no buses ran and the roads were often impassible in winter, she boarded during the week with Grandmother Mullenger. William George had died in February and

Mary Ann was lonely in the house by the water tower. She had grown stout and preternaturally quiet during a succession of deaths in the family. A pleasant-faced woman with a strong chin and gray hair combed into a bun, she stayed close to home, weeding the garden, sewing quilts, writing penpals, and playing Chinese checkers. One of her few indulgences was going to the movies (anything with Kay Francis), usually on Bank Nights. Mary Ann was a second mother to Donnabelle, and no less strict for being gentle. She set a nine o'clock evening curfew that Donnabelle chafed under when boys began noticing her good looks.

At this time she wore the plainest homemade clothes, no makeup at all, and her hair simply arranged and curled at the ends, for Hazel wouldn't allow a permanent. Being from the country was a strike against Donnabelle socially. The town girls, who had gone through grade school together and were better heeled and dressed, snubbed her. Feeling left out was a new experience after growing up in a large extended family. It amounted to a personal crisis, the first to challenge her sense of worth. For a year or so Donnabelle retreated into shyness almost to the point of invisibility. Although she finally won acceptance for qualities hard to ignore, she was never part of the faster "in" crowd.

A block away from Grandmother Mullenger's house lived a vivacious blonde who became Donna's life-long friend, Joyce Anderson. From their porches the girls signaled to each other in a high whistle. They walked uphill and down to school, and in the evening to the library because neither had any money to go elsewhere. The Andersons had moved to Denison from the hamlet of Boyer after losing their lumberyard. So Joyce was, like Donnabelle, an outsider. They exchanged girlish confidences and tried to crack the secret code of popularity. Each promised to name a future daughter Nancy (and never did).

More serious concerns linked them. As members of the Youth Temperance Corps, Donnabelle and Joyce signed pledges not to drink alcoholic beverages or smoke. The YTC was an arm of the WCTU, which had always kept Denison more or less dry—a miracle, considering how the German farmers loved their beer. Now in 1934, with Prohibition ended, one of the first liquor stores in Iowa was about to open in Denison and the churches were mobilizing. Even then, Donnabelle, a true Aquarian, was interested in causes. She was attuned to developments because the Shiveses, particularly Grandfather Charles, had preached against repeal. Her parents had never served alcohol at home and, for health reasons, had also banned coffee, tea, and aspirin. When the WCTU sponsored a declamatory contest at the Methodist Church, Donnabelle represented a good sister of sobriety and Joyce a baddie besotted with drink. The outcome was never really in doubt.

Donnabelle's first boyfriend was Tom Hutcheson, who would become a doctor in Denison and eventually retire to California. Like most young people then, he and Donnabelle didn't own cars, so they walked everywhere—rarely to the Ritz Theater, occasionally to the Candy Kitchen, often to the Northwestern depot to watch the trains come in. Tom remembered Donnabelle as "my favorite girl, my timid little Irish farm girl," and as more petite than she later appeared to be on the screen.

Although Tom was a husky running back for the Denison Monarchs football team and not so timid, he went no further with Donnabelle than pecklike kisses and hand-holding. Sex wasn't a complete mystery to a healthy country girl, no matter how virginal, but neither was it a subject of conversation. In those more innocent days, skinny dipping at the gravel pit west of town seldom included girls. Equally off-limits to Donnabelle was the Uwana dance pavilion, where drinkers glided to a seductive whispering jazz and got their cars tangled in the oak trees outside—until one night a high wind blew the entire structure across a field, much to the satisfaction of some citizens.

For Donnabelle and Tom the town wasn't completely dead. Something was always going on—spelling bees, rooster derbies, cornhusking contests. Interesting people strayed through: Hairbreadth Harry, King of the Hoboes; Captain Jack Lloyd, immortalized as Burning Daylight by Jack London; and Bette Davis, who one October day in 1934 arrived in a Packard and ate at the Denison Hotel. Anyhow, evenings were for studying.

At Denison High the teachers were demanding, proud that Iowa led the nation in literacy. Donnabelle was required to memorize details of Civil War battles and the names of generals on both sides. She mastered enough algebra and geometry to be able to help others pass those subjects. Joyce Ely was struck by her intelligence and seriousness, and Margaret Anderson by her "beautiful eyes." But other classmates retain only a generalized impression of an ordinary, pretty girl. "The most unusual thing that I can say about Donnabelle is that she was nice," said Arlen Gemeroth. "Any time you were around her you had that nice feeling." Hardly anyone would have predicted Hollywood fame for her—or anything except homemaking and, possibly, taking shorthand in some Des Moines office.

Two teachers encouraged her in different directions. Edward Tompkins, who taught chemistry and would later work on the Manhattan Project, advised the shy Donnabelle on "how to win friends and influence people." She read Dale Carnegie's bestseller and, with characteristic diligence, applied its precepts to the stratified society of school and town. Another mentor was Hilda Catron, remembered as a wonderful teacher of Latin and drama. Mrs. Catron cast Donnabelle as the feminine lead in *Night of January 16th*, the sanitized version for amateurs that Ayn Rand disowned.

Play production brought Donnabelle and John Roy Nau together. Tall and debonair, Jack was a former Californian who seemed lost in Denison. He lived with his divorced mother and her father. Jack Nau is remembered as "Jack Armstrong, the All-American Boy," and as a character whose elegance barely concealed his roughness. By all accounts, he was a possessive fellow. Jack and Donnabelle were inseparable during their junior and senior years, off by themselves in the halls when Principal Harold Welch wasn't monitoring. Saturdays would often find him bicycling the seven miles to the Mullenger farm.

Jack apparently fell in love with Donnabelle. Whatever her feelings, she was flattered by the attention of the best-looking boy in school. And frightened by his jealousy. Tom Hutcheson recalled standing with Donnabelle on Grandmother Mullenger's porch one night when Jack began pelting him with rocks. That led to a man-sized fistfight and Jack's retreat. "You were the only one outside the movies who ever fought over me," Donna used to tell Tom.

Any kind of human action seemed puny set against the fury of nature in 1936. The coldest winter, which often closed Donnabelle's school, was followed by the hottest summer. Drought continued for the sixth year, and the worst epidemic of grasshoppers in the county's history led the government to dole out poison and bran. In western Iowa fifteen major dust storms in four months shrouded the sun. Ervin Mohr retains a small image of the universal dirt: one day he stepped outside with an open-faced cheese and onion sandwich that was blackened within minutes. Destitute farmers met at the courthouse in Denison; and Arden Amman's parents, who lived near the Mullengers, lost their land.

Surrounded by despair, Bill and Hazel tried to maintain a normal family life. In the evenings she might sit at the piano and play "Josephine" and "Missouri Waltz" as a cue for singing. Somehow, money was found for the children's music lessons. Lavone got weekly dancing instruction; and, borrowing a formal from her friend Virginia Richard, Donnabelle joined Rainbow Girls. Picnics were Depression-proof, and at one Donnabelle and Joyce Anderson performed a mock wedding.

Bill still drove the family to Shenandoah for Henry Field's variety show, heard over Radio Station KFKN but more fun to see. In those days before the REA transformed rural living, the Mullengers listened to programs on a battery-powered receiver made by a Denisonite. The menfolk favored the news and market reports, while Hazel tuned in "Kitchen Klatter," aired by Earl May's KMA. Joyce Anderson Fisk remembers that Donnabelle sometimes listened to a young sportscaster named Dutch Reagan on WHO in Des Moines. Had the farm girl been able to foresee a future that included Ronald Reagan as a friend, she would have been astounded.

In the summer of 1936, Donnabelle participated in an event that seems portentous now. The Majestic Motion Picture Company of Los Angeles was touring towns in the Midwest, shooting documentaries and story shorts with local casts. A unit came to Denison in August with the announced intention of showing how sound movies were produced. Donnabelle auditioned at the Ritz Theater and was excited to get a part in *Runnin' Wild*. According to her cousin Donald Yankey, she rode through Denison in a convertible, a delectable target for a thief who jumped on the running board, grabbed her jeweled necklace, and ran toward the

Northwestern tracks to hop a freight. Yankey was among the pursuers who wrecked a Model-T Ford at an intersection and spilled out onto the street. A nimble hero, coy flappers, and determined crooks added to the pandemonium. The silent version shown at the Ritz must have seemed like a mishmash of Keystone Kops and Floradora Girls. No print survives.

The once-mousy girl from the country was finding herself on display more often. Donnabelle entered the declamatory contests popular in that era. And, like the Iowa heroine of Ruth Suckow's novel *Odyssey of a Nice Girl*, she was talented enough to win. In one countywide competition, she placed for her rendition of a piece called "Mothers of Men." Donnabelle's looks undoubtedly contributed to her growing self-assurance, as Hazel's never had for her. Though not mirror-struck, she would be drawn to many beauty contests. The first occurred in the summer of 1937, when, sponsored by Nelson's Shoe Store, she was named runner-up for the title of Miss Denison.

Increasingly, Donnabelle was attracted to the performing arts. The movies belonged so wholly to commonplace fantasy that she couldn't aim for them. Instead, she entertained thoughts of a career in radio. The field was wide open—almost, since a prejudice against women announcers kept their number few in the thirties. Supposedly, women lacked the stamina to face the microphone for long hours—and other women, the bulk of the listening audience, preferred male voices. Donnabelle, whose quietness belied her ambition, thought of the big stations in Chicago and beyond. Lying in bed at Grandmother Mullenger's house, she heard the new streamliners pass through and, like George Bailey in *It's a Wonderful Life*, dreamed of faraway places.

There was little time for daydreaming as she finished high school in 1938. Donnabelle sharpened her study skills to graduate in the top ten of a class of eighty-five. Finally allowed to date, she went out more often—once with Jack Nau, Joyce Anderson, and Ken Langer to a big-band dancehall in Carroll, where Betty Hutton was singing. Langer borrowed his father's Model-A Ford. During those last busy school days and moonlit nights when the world seemed to end at Carroll, the young people hardly took note of Hitler's invasion of Austria and the movement of Japanese troops into Canton and Hankow.

Unlike some of her classmates—such as Lucille Kepford, who went from door to door selling homegrown fruit for a dime a bucket, and Arlen Gemeroth, whose spare time was filled clerking in a grocery and delivering bread and newspapers for a total of $2.50 a week—Donnabelle didn't work after school, although she helped her grandmother and still did farm chores on weekends. Having to count every nickel and dime made her prudent when money did come.

Outwardly cheerful, Donnabelle was not immune to the pervasive sense of hopelessness among her peers. She breathed the same air as Ervin Mohr, who all through high school worried about how he was going to make a living; the same as Don Jensen, who felt the interminable drought was bringing the world to an end; the same as Ila Bledsoe, who considered the best wedding gift a bin of fresh clean corncobs.

Because of the Depression, the senior class had to forgo a yearbook, but pictures were taken. A demure Donnabelle wore a high-necked dark dress for hers. She was, during one breathless fortnight in May 1938, a star on two small stages.

On Friday the 13th, Donnabelle was crowned Queen of the May at the gymnasium. Outfitted in an evening gown, a present from her parents, she knelt on a silk pillow as Pat Powers, the runner-up in the voting, placed a tiara on her head. Among the seven hundred spectators were a lot of proud Mullengers and Shiveses. Then a hundred schoolgirls danced in elaborate formations à la Busby Berkeley and executed difficult figures on bicycles. The event was an artistic if not a commercial success. The *Denison Record* reported a take of only thirty dollars because so many relatives were admitted free.

Donnabelle was in the spotlight again on May 24, with more to do as the leading lady of *Night of January 16th*. She portrayed a woman on trial for the murder of her boss, a financial titan modeled on the real Ivar Kreuger, the Swedish Match King who died violently in 1932. Jack Nau played the prosecuting attorney. The jury, selected from the audience, acquitted Donnabelle's Karen André. As a proud Karen, at once chilly and smoldering, Donnabelle registered strongly. "Her ability to sustain the mood of the drama was unusual for a high school student," recalled

Margaret Anderson Carbee, a cast member. But at that time only Hilda Catron, the director, predicted any kind of stardom for Donnabelle.

Whatever illusions the farm girl had about an acting career were dissipated by daylight. Her immediate worry was getting a college education when there was little money to spare. Hazel and Grandmother Mullenger had attended a special school in Denison, but no one on either side of Donnabelle's family had gone to college. After high school graduation, a girl was expected to marry and perhaps work somewhere before submitting to her biological destiny.

Then the unexpected occurred: Aunt Mildred offered a home to Donnabelle in Los Angeles. She was ecstatic to discover that for five dollars a semester she could enroll in radio and secretarial courses at Los Angeles City College. The irony of fate has never seemed sharper in retrospect. If money had been available, Donnabelle undoubtedly would have matriculated at the University of Iowa, which offered an exemplary curriculum in radio, and thus bypassed fame and fortune.

Sometime before she headed west there must have been a scene with Jack Nau. He was intent on marrying Donnabelle, according to Harold Auld, who was close to the situation. Even after his folks moved to Carroll, Jack remained in Denison in order to be near her, supporting himself by working in a restaurant. But their serious romance was about to be cut off by geography and changing circumstance. Marriage and motherhood were not Donnabelle's top priorities, and her parents adamantly opposed any course that might deny her a college education. "Jack was very unhappy about the way things turned out," said Auld. "He was so bitter that he never returned to Denison."

Jack was not at the Northwestern depot when Donnabelle left for California on a late summer day in 1938. Legend persists that she drove a jalopy to the West Coast, with sixty dollars in her pocket. *The Lion's Roar*, published by Metro-Goldwyn-Mayer, would say that she rattled into Los Angeles in an old sedan, its radiator boiling. Not true. She took a train west, probably with less than sixty dollars. Reportedly, Hazel said on leavetaking, "Continue to be yourself, Donnabelle. I know we can rely on you always to be a lady." That has the ring of truth.

Keith remembers the family huddled forlornly at the station. Eleven-year-old Billy broke into tears as he said good-bye. Although happy for Donnabelle's opportunity, Bill and particularly Hazel were worried about their seventeen-year-old going so far away. It was the beginning of Hazel's great sadness in seeing the family scatter. "I can still see my mother crying as the train pulled out," says Lavone.

Donnabelle waved from the window as the little group at the depot receded. Surely she felt drained—and then increasingly excited as she passed beyond the state line and Omaha for the first time in her life.

CHAPTER TWO

To California

D onnabelle Mullenger seemed predestined to head west instead of east. Since the end of the nineteenth century so many Iowans had migrated to Southern California that it was known variously as Caliowa, New Iowa, and the Seacoast of Iowa. Starved for real estate and winter sunshine, midwesterners had diluted the Spanish character of Los Angeles, boosted the rolls of Rotarians and Republicans, and installed Aimee Semple McPherson as the priestess of Four-Square religion. The former Iowans, lonely amid the palm and jacaranda trees, congregated for state picnics at Long Beach.

Well over a million souls lived in Los Angeles when Donnabelle arrived in 1938. From the train depot, she ventured out into a city still checkered by country and innocent of freeways, although the Arroyo Seco would be christened a year or so later. Without a car or much coin, Donnabelle was far from home. Aunt Mildred was here, swallowed up in the anonymity of a southeastern suburb, but the wherewithal of Donnabelle's survival was not yet clear. She would need more than the advice of Dale Carnegie's book!

She went to South Gate, where Aunt Mildred owned a clapboard bungalow on Virginia Avenue, near the tracks of the Southern Pacific. Today South Gate is semi-seedy, and gangs spill over from nearby Watts and Compton. During the time Donnabelle stayed there it was a quiet manufacturing center somewhat isolated from the rest of Los Angeles. Mildred's husband, Charles Van Kampen, worked in the General Motors plant. Her little daughter from a previous marriage, Joyce, helped give some semblance of a family, but it was a strange household that Donnabelle had come to. For Mildred was, by Mullenger standards, eccentric, not at all the drab, self-effacing aunt out of central casting. Striking was the word for Aunt Mildred. In photographs she appears statuesque. Her dark hair is swept back from a finely sculpted face and fixed in a braid at the top. Donnabelle found her as settled as she was ever to be.

The gypsy in Mildred had surfaced early. She fled Iowa in 1921, lighting first in Omaha, where she worked for a hatmaker and lived at the YWCA. Then she married Lowell Ison and, after his death, Van Kampen, who was her vehicle to La La Land. It is tempting to connect Mildred with one or two of the cults and bizarre movements that flourished in Southern California during the thirties, the "golden age of crackpotism." But she seems to have gone her own way, consuming only organically grown fruits and vegetables (and no Iowa beef), engaging in elaborate beauty rituals, walking miles until she was flushed by fresh air, touring nearly every state by bus. She thrived on a fantasy that put her just a little beyond kin. Her nephew Bill remembered that she was "always searching for something she wasn't going to find." To Donnabelle and Lavone she was a model of fashion, chic on a limited budget, and the source of second-hand clothes.

The perch that Aunt Mildred offered Donnabelle was to prove uncomfortable. For the time being, however, the Iowa farm girl experienced a kind of thawing out in Los Angeles. In her letters to Joyce Anderson during the fall and winter of 1938–39, Donna (no longer burdened by the *belle*) reveals her exhilaration at going to Ocean Park for dancing, to the Inglewood race tracks, to Big Bear Lake in the mountains, to the new CBS studio for a Burns-Allen broadcast, to the Mayan Theater to see a stage hit called *Alien Corn*. One night Aunt Mildred took her to the follies where Mickey Rooney's father, Joe Yule, performed. "The whole show," she reported, "was one big filthy mess." Then, to continue an evening of unaccustomed "slumming," she and her aunt soberly watched and mingled with "the soaks" at the Paris Inn in downtown Los Angeles. To her friend in Iowa she wrote, "Gosh, if you were only here with me, going to school and going places, we'd have a swell time."

In fact, Donna's schedule left little time for frolic. The next two years would be rigorous. Those who knew her at Los Angeles City College still marvel at the stamina she showed in studying and working more than eighteen hours a day.

Aiming at a career in radio, she found herself in a drama department that was considered one of the best in the United States. Its fame was due to a distinguished cadre of teachers headed by Harold Turney and Jerry Blunt. In 1938 they made the most of humble facilities. The Little Theater in ivy-covered North Hall no longer had spotlights set in large tomato cans, but there were enough physical barriers to test the ingenuity of student actors and directors. Endless rehearsals were held in an airless space that had once been a women's gymnasium, and a loyal public came to the plays even during the Depression.

Jerry Blunt's introduction to Donna Mullenger came when she walked across the stage, her thick-soled brown joggers clunking with every step. Later he kidded her: "You've spent too much time following the plow." Donna's voice betrayed her midwestern background; in a recording the broad *as* and hard *cs* came through. She certainly didn't stand out among the supercharged drama students whose obsession was "to act or die!" But Blunt recalled that she was intelligent and responsive—and something else. "Part of her charm was a sweetness that wasn't cloying because it was too easy."

Classmates retain an image of Donna as wholesomely pretty, rather chubby, and unpretentious. Hazel (she later called them lion) eyes and difficult medium-length light brown hair. Thin and tilted nose, more Garboesque than junior-miss pert. A close friend named Marie Legér, who became known in radio as Kelly Quinn, envied that nose and found it a pleasure just to look at Donna's classic profile. She had the professional beauty's face that was slightly large in proportion to the rest of the body. Standing only five feet, three and a half inches, Donna reached 125 on the scales, but lost five pounds during the unusually hot summer and fall of 1939. Unlike another student in the drama department, Alexis Smith, who dressed in fashionable clothes made by her mother and owned twenty sweaters, Donna had only a few outfits. She wore out a gabardine skirt and several silk jersey blouses. A letter at the beginning of a school year reveals her low spirits at not being able to buy a "darn new stitch." Generally, she was cheerful. What is often remembered about the collegiate Donna is her almost childlike enthusiasm, breaking through an ingrained shyness.

Donna survived a course called Analysis of Dramatic Construction, which was used to weed out the weak. Forty percent of entering students quit by midterm. She read to the verge of eyestrain, shelling out $6.50 for a temporary pair of glasses. In a day when students were expected to write literate papers, she proved perceptive. Analyzing the film *Foreign Correspondent* when it appeared in 1940, she observed that director Alfred Hitchcock "takes an audience so fast that factual mistakes are covered up and never noticed."

Mind and body were required to work together in ways never signified by the 4-H Club motto of Donna's childhood. She learned how to move on stage, expressively and economically. In pantomime classes she spent hours opening imaginary doors and windows. Voice exercises called for her to stretch, sigh, pant, yawn, hiss, spit, chew, and gag. A particularly convulsive routine went: "*Up* came the oysters! *Up* came the ham! *Up* came the marmalade! *Up* came the jam!" The doyenne of speech teachers was Vocha Fiske, who was certainly outside Donna's experience. In trying to get students to project more powerfully from the diaphragm, the elegant but earthy Miss Fiske analogized, "Just remember this: Queen Elizabeth could fart and blow her skirt up a foot from behind!" With so much bidding for attention, Donna wasn't alone in feeling unnecessarily burdened by classes in anatomy (actors had to know their bodies) and physics (they had to know the nature of sound).

Like so many others, Donna later appreciated the discipline instilled by Jerry Blunt. But keeping up was, she confided to Joyce Anderson, "a struggle, and I do mean a struggle!" Her friend Beulah (Moria) Turner, whose father ran the United Artists commissary on Formosa Avenue, remembered that the coeds used to cry in the rest room because "it was all so hard." The demands couldn't be taken lightly by anyone with Donna's diffidence, sensitivity, and pride.

In the drama department's caste system, beginners spoke only to other beginners and advanced acting students spoke only to Mr. Blunt, whose approval was a benefaction. It's fair to say that Donna didn't experience the warm validation enjoyed by the tested talents who dominated the Little Theater. Her feeling of being somewhat outside can be discerned in this, as in nearly every other, phase of her life. She was both feverishly attracted to and repelled by the self-contained world of the department.

If Donna and her young women friends were anxious about making the grade, so were many of the young men. Harvey Teitzell, who passed a test in emoting with Donna's help, would navigate a B-24 bomber over Italy in World War II. In the midst of flak from the enemy, he repeatedly said to himself: "I'm prepared for this. It's not as bad as acting in front of Jerry Blunt."

Donna worked backstage, learning all those things that eat up the time of every aspiring thespian. A program for *The Taming of the Shrew* lists her as rehearsal secretary, misspelling her name. She never played a leading role, but one event must have filled her with *déjà vu*. In a 1940 production of *Night of January 16th* she was on stage as a court reporter while her old high-school part of Karen André was taken by Alexis Smith. The polished Miss Smith was seen by a talent scout in the audience and signed by Warner Brothers. For Donna that illustrated the close call and far remove of starry fortune.

Unlike Alexis, Donna had to work for her room and board. Early in 1939, after her first semester, she moved out of Aunt Mildred's house in South Gate, ostensibly because she had to spend three hours a day riding buses to and from the campus. There seems to have been some trouble with Mildred, but Donna never reveals in her letters what it was. A friend sensed that Mildred looked down on the farm girl as a poor relation. It was a pattern for Mildred, who was generous to outsiders but often simply "not there" for blood kin.

The eighteen-year-old Donna, really on her own now, took a job between classes in the drama department's library. Under the auspices of the National Youth Administration, a New Deal program, she earned thirty-five cents an hour. Boarding with the Baumeister family on Alexandria Street, she scrubbed floors, ironed shirts, and helped with the cooking after a long day of classes and NYA duties. Then she studied until midnight or after. By the fall of 1939, Donna was enrolled in fifteen and a half academic units and, on top of that killing schedule, was working thirty-eight hours a week. In the morning she dressed in twenty minutes and for the next eighteen hours never slowed down, she reported to Joyce Anderson. What was the secret of her stamina? A country-bred physical constitution, certainly. "And Donna was totally focused," recalled Virginia Ricks Hill, who saw her on campus every day.

Circumstances left Donna no choice but to succeed. She couldn't run home. It was two thousand miles away. There was no money to catch a train or fly to a town in Iowa that former classmates were trying to leave and getting stuck in. There was no letting down parents who were counting on her to make the most of an opportunity denied previous generations of Mullengers. Having come so far, there was no letting *herself* down. The face of economic depression seemed less grim in California than elsewhere, but there was no likelihood of getting a decent job if she quit college. There was no going, with hand out, to her one relative in Los Angeles unless she wanted to be turned into a full-time housemaid. There was nothing to do but everything.

Donna's drive had a playful dimension. "I work like a fiend all during the week and then on Friday and Saturday nights tear loose," she told her closest friend in Iowa. Predictably, she attracted young men, but her locket on a chain still carried a photo of Mom and Pop.

On arriving in California, she was "horrified" to see the kids jitterbugging—ballroom dancing was all she knew—but soon a self-declared German baron was teaching her how. With Jack Marshal, the proud owner of a $350 guitar that he played at theaters, she gravitated to Angeles Harlem. In a back room of the Ritz Club bandleaders and their musicians jammed all night, after their regular gigs. Donna was entranced. "It would cost a fortune to hire some of the groups that get together," she wrote. Another Jack, named Williams, who was the University of Southern California's star polo player, took Donna to his games, but she didn't like his spoiled rich-boy ways. Most of her escorts were as cash-poor as she was, and going dutch was unheard of then. When Earl Carroll's dazzling theater restaurant opened late in 1938, Donna couldn't pass through its portals because the price of admission was five dollars a couple.

These outings may seem like heady stuff for a girl who shortly before had been limited to a picture show and a soda in Denison, Iowa. But they were only occasional and driven more by curiosity and a receptive spirit than social ambition. Mainly, Donna moved around on the Big Red streetcars, sometimes riding out to the beach at Santa Monica.

Everything around her afforded excitement. Los Angeles inspired a cleansing of the doors of perception in that era before freeways strangled it and smog settled in. Virginia Ricks, a classmate whose trademark was pigtailed hair, took Donna downtown to introduce her to the exotic fabrics at Bullock's and to the fine silver and china and crystal on the ninth floor of J. W. Robinson's. Their excursions ended at the Comet, where twenty cents bought all the fresh orange juice one could drink.

A few miles away was the separate sphere of the campus. Donna attended a costume party dressed as Snow White in a long cape and stand-up collar and had the best time of her life. She went around with Lou Hurwitz, an older student in the drama department who directed and acted in Shakespeare plays, presented in an open court without microphones. They made an unlikely couple—the stocky, unhandsome, sophisticated Jew and the comely, golly-gee ingenue.

Lou, always protective, helped Donna adjust to a place where late fall brought hot Santa Ana winds instead of snow flurries. "I have a terrible cold; living out here is just one big cold," she wrote to Joyce Anderson in November 1938. The frantic pace contributed to her indisposition, and overrode it.

That fall the big news in letters home concerned her first visit to a movie studio: Metro-Goldwyn-Mayer in Culver City. Donna was one of nine students at Los Angeles City College chosen by producer Carey Wilson to advise the makers of a new Andy Hardy picture. Like the others, Donna dashed off a brief autobiography (now lost), identifying herself with a member of Judge Hardy's family. She participated in a five-hour conference that was supposed to keep the Hollywood people in touch with reality. "The studio lot is so mysterious," Donna told her Iowa pen-pal. "All the buildings are white, tall, close together, with few or no windows. I felt sorta pinned in!" The players in the popular series treated the college students to lunch in the MGM commissary. "Gee, wasn't that fun. Mickey Rooney is so short, he isn't cute at all; he was awfully scared. Ann Rutherford was too sweet for words; she truly is a darb. She told us about herself, the schools she went to, etc. Cecilia Parker ate with us too. I don't like her; she smokes, and of course she offered me cigarettes, but I'm still a nonsmoker and intend to remain [one]." When Franchot Tone passed by the table, her heart "missed a few beats." That visit to MGM prefigured an unimaginable future. Only a few years later Donna Mullenger would be Mickey Rooney's leading lady in a Hardy picture.

Now as the Depression wore on, Donna would have welcomed the prospect of a stenographer's job paying fifteen dollars a week. At the beginning of 1939 she was looking ahead, hoping that Joyce Anderson could join her at Los Angeles City College. Rooming together would save them money, and by working through the summer in NYA they'd accumulate "a pretty good pile," Donna argued. In a few years her savings would help her sister attend college. "I'd like for Lavone to take up designing, clothes, etc. Yeah, I do lots of daydreaming. Doesn't hurtcha none I guess."

In the spring of 1939 Donna's homesickness was heightened by worry about her mother, who wasn't feeling well. "I wish I knew what to do," she wrote to Joyce. "Have you seen her lately?" She inquired about her brother Keith: "Has Casey grown up much? How tall is he now? Has his voice changed entirely?" Her hometown beau, Jack Nau, soldiering at Fort Dodge, wrote often, expressing his undying ardor while boasting of his appeal to the women there. A snapshot of him jolted her because he had changed so much. Donna wondered if she had changed, become Californized. "I really don't think I have. Are my letters different, Joyce?" By July she was suffering from record-setting temperatures in Los Angeles and almost nostalgic for the humid Iowa summers.

Donna wouldn't see her family for another year. The trip back home in the summer of 1940 was an adventure: She rode with a party from Iowa, taking her turn driving an old Ford that threatened eruption through endless miles under a fierce sun. But in the middle of 1939 Donna was getting around; she seemed to be repeating experiences on an escalating scale.

She won a beauty contest sponsored by the South Gate chapter of the Veterans of Foreign Wars. A photograph in the *Hollywood Citizen* on June 1 shows her being made up for the pageant by Perc Westmore of Warner Brothers. Wearing a one-piece bathing suit and smiling broadly, she looks soft and fetchingly milkmaidish. Her prize was twenty-five dollars, more than a week's salary, and a chance to represent South Gate in the Tournament of Roses. On the following New Year's Day, Virginia Ricks was surprised to see Donna gracing a float in the parade. She hadn't said a word, even to her good friends.

Not all was roses and peaches. Overworked and frustrated by missed opportunities for acting and directing assignments, Donna in the fall of 1939 considered transferring to the University of Iowa, where Joyce Anderson had started radio courses.

The powers in the drama department at Los Angeles City College clearly thought that Donna Mullenger would never succeed as an actress. Classmates might have predicted stardom for some of the theatrical spellbinders, but not for her. Mendie Koenig, who later appeared in movies with the East Side Kids, recalled rehearsing a one-act play with Donna, who was "a sweetheart." She tried valiantly, and failed, to master the dialect of a black itinerant worker. Some women classmates said Donna lacked the ethnic European spirit and tragic feeling of better stage actresses. But—unlike flashy performers who did brilliant turns at the Little Theater and quickly burned out—she had the capacity for steady development and the saving bourgeois quality of common sense.

A Swedish fellow who longed for character leads, Sam Sebby, remembered an incident involving Donna because it amounted to an epiphany. One day in 1939 three naive hopefuls piled into an old Chevy. Drama classes were over for the day and they were going to a tryout. "Jim Goddard positioned himself behind the steering wheel. He had a wonderful Irish face, was a southerner, best at comedy. Beside him sat Donna Mullenger, a serious actress, prettiest girl at LACC. Usually reserved, today this midwesterner was wholesomely boisterous. I climbed into the back seat. We were on our way to a reading—for a play or something with music that someone in the drama department had told us about. We left the college parking lot, drove north on Vermont Avenue to Hollywood Boulevard and turned west. Practicing vocals seemed a darned good idea, so with windows down we worked 'Row, Row Your Boat' and 'Down by the Old Millstream' into an extravaganza of hoots, squeals, and laughter.

We sang good and loud, made funny faces, and waved. Passersby laughed and waved back. We became less rambunctious on approaching the corner of Hollywood and Vine. I felt something vast, promising, and enticing. For a moment I became contemplative. That intersection was an access point to the World's Motion Picture Center. I glanced at my friends and thought: I hope at least one of us becomes an important film star. The next day we went back to classes. The so-called reading was a laugh at least. The producers wanted dancers!"

That year a guest lecturer, the actor John Carradine, advised students in Drama 60 *not* to go into theater. Times were rough and Donna had to think about supporting herself. The NYA and servant jobs kept her afloat now, but then what? Feeling increasingly anxious, she took up typing, shorthand, and stenography.

The wisdom of that decision sank in when she flunked a final examination in acting class. She had selected a speech from a Shakespeare play but forgot every word of it when she ran out on the stage. For all her staying power, she wasn't immune to simple fatigue—or rebellion. According to one observer, Donna began to read from the playbook (a no-no) and then threw it down, saying, "I can't do this old Shakespeare!" She stalked off stage.

By the fall of 1940 Donna seemed to be treading in a zone with no clear arrows pointing beyond. She assessed her situation in a letter: "This will be my last year at City College. If I can't go to UCLA, then I'll go to work."

In one respect Donna's situation improved somewhat. She had boarded with a family that exploited her by piling on the work. Then in late 1939 or early 1940 she moved to the house of a kindly older couple, George and Annie Johnson. George, a dealer in antiques and Persian rugs, had a glabrous head due to a medical condition; and Annie, who called herself Aunty John, was a fixy sort.

Again, Donna earned her keep by cooking and dusting, washing and ironing, and often took up her books late at night. Even though she slept in a closed porch, the surroundings were better. The house on Kingswell Avenue was well furnished, and George cultivated roses in a backyard where Donna sunbathed with Virginia Ricks, another roomer. Life there was properly ordered. Virginia remembered reaching across the dinner table once and saying, "Excuse my boarding-house manners." Aunty John responded grandly, "The day will never dawn that I run a boarding house. *This* is a residence for young ladies!"

Amazingly, Donna found the time to write letters and see movies. *Foreign Correspondent* was "the best all-around picture I've ever seen," she reported to Joyce. *The Long Voyage Home* was "an artistic masterpiece"; *Bittersweet*, "stinko"; *Thief of Bagdad*, "a work of genius" because of its Technicolor. One evening she went to a review for British Red Cross Relief and stood beside James Stewart and Olivia de Havilland "a long time" before recognizing them.

She might pop up anywhere. In October 1940 Donna was in the broadcasting studio that originated a program emceed by Horace Heidt. From the studio audience she rose to answer in the alloted seconds a question about how to tie a shoelace. She won ten dollars. Voices from out of the past rang up; her mother in Iowa spent the next day taking phone calls.

Then something big happened that owed nothing to her years of hard work, except indirectly, but everything to her good bones and eyes and teeth. She was elected Campus Queen at Los Angeles City College.

It was an era when feminine beauty reigned. The local newspapers heralded the Orange Queen, the Sun Goddess, the Princess of the Grapes, the Talk of the Town Girl, the Prettiest Girl on Horseback. Donna was escorted to a dance at the Biltmore Ballroom by a suave fellow named Bert Todd and during intermission was crowned queen with a wreath of gardenias. She wore a black taffeta gown with a white insert at the breast that held a flower. Milton Dobkin, a journalism student who knew she would win, had arranged for a photographer from the *Los Angeles Times* to be present. And sure enough, on the morning of December 2, 1940, a meltingly beautiful Donna Mullenger appeared on a front page. That photograph would quickly change the course of her life.

Donna-rella had shone at the ball, her likeness had been taken, and a pursuit of princely dimensions had begun. The story goes that two or three movie studios and four agents called within twenty-four hours after

Donna's picture was published. Paramount offered a screen test and Columbia wanted her to come by. She did what thousands of hungry hopefuls would *not* have done: She did not bite immediately. She chose to complete her secretarial course at Los Angeles City College before considering any Hollywood offers. "I might not be any good in the movies," Donna said. "Then what would I do? If I finish out this semester, I'll at least know how to be a secretary."

In February 1941 school was over and Donna was brought to the biggest and glitziest of the studios, Metro-Goldwyn-Mayer, by a representative of the Feldman-Blum agency, an Englishman named Bill Smith. There she met Billy Grady, the legendary talent scout who had "discovered" James Stewart and Joan Blondell. According to Grady in his autobiography, *The Irish Peacock*, Charles Feldman had called him in a panic. Would Billy at least go through the motions of interviewing this college contest winner? Her name was Donna Mullen or something like that. Feldman evidently felt that he had to approach the great Grady in a way that didn't presume too much on his time. So he presented the girl's visit to the studio as hardly more than a prize for being named campus queen.

Face to face with Donna, Billy Grady "was taken by her great beauty." She had a look of quality. To ease her visible tension, he told a story about the time he passed through Denison, Iowa, and stayed at the hotel. Amused, she smiled warmly. "Miss Mullenger said very little during our visit, but I found her personality commanding." To the astonishment of his associates, he ordered a screen test to be made. "It is seldom that a thousand-dollar test is arranged for a hopeful with absolutely no experience," wrote Grady. "But Miss Mullenger had all the requisites and with a little coaching she might come through."

Donna's view of MGM had been limited during her visit as a student to rap about the small-town world of Andy Hardy. Now, with Bill Smith, she went past the colonnaded main gate and farther into the fifty-three-acre concrete city, arriving at a spacious office outfitted like a living room. It was the domain of Lillian Burns, a diminutive, stylish woman with dark hair. The quintessential drama coach, she was highly disciplined and demanding, formidable in her emotional intensity, precise and emphatic in her manner and speech.

After more than a half-century Lillian Burns Sidney remembered Donna from the very first day: "She was brought in and she wore a little tan skirt and white blouse and had a tie on and white socks and brownish brogues and of course all you could see were those beautiful eyes and that face which was tense and shy." Miss Burns gave some material to Donna, who reported back at the appointed time to begin preparing for her screen test. Trembling a little, she sat in a green chair, against which her white socks were more conspicuous than socks should be. When the coach suggested a break for lunch, Donna said softly, "Oh no, I'm not hungry. May I just stay here?" Miss Burns, realizing that the girl didn't have enough money for lunch and bus fare too, ordered sandwiches for them both, and they got down to work.

For some weeks in the early spring of 1941 Donna, under the tutelage of Lillian Burns, did dramatic interpretations that tapped her inner resources and tested her natural range of expression. Miss Burns saw possibilities in the quiet girl who appeared every day in the same tan skirt and white blouse that were always freshly ironed and immaculately clean. But she held up Donna's screen test until the right material and partner could be found.

Meanwhile, the Feldman agency had moved Donna to the Studio Club on Lodi Place, a sort of sorority (more often a heartbreak hotel) for women trying to crash show business. Finally, Bill Smith, a nice man but an agent nonetheless, confronted Lillian Burns, demanding to know when Donna's test would be made. "We're paying her rent, you know," he said. To which Miss Burns replied, "Look, it will be ready when I say it's ready and not before. I'll pay that $12.50 a week out of my own pocket. So don't pester me." As it turned out, the wait proved her wisdom.

Almost as if on cue, a stage actor named Van Heflin entered. He was fresh from playing on the boards with Katherine Hepburn in *The Philadelphia Story* and set to make a screen test at MGM. Rather superior at first, Heflin allowed Miss Burns to help him piece together material from *The World We Make*, a play that MGM had acquired for Susan Peters and then abandoned. Miss Burns was inspired to pair the experienced actor with Donna in a test to be directed by George Sidney.

The scene was set up and dramatically lighted. Heflin carried most of the dialogue while Donna was seen as an invalid confined to her bed. The result was successful for Donna no less than for Van; her large dark eyes dominated the shots, communicating sincerity and vulnerability. When advised of the test results, Louis B. Mayer said, "Sign them both." Just like that.

Donna Mullenger received a four-year MGM contract with six-month options, beginning at seventy-five dollars a week. "And maybe you think I can't use that money!" she wrote to Joyce Anderson. Because she was only twenty, she went to court in early April 1941 to obtain a judge's approval. Accompanying her was another new contractee, a sixteen-year-old singer named Anne Rooney, who would play a few bits in musicals and drop from sight.

Two years and seven months after she left the farm in Iowa, Donna called home with astounding news. Bill and Hazel Mullenger drove the Dodge into town to tell reporters at the weekly *Denison Bulletin* about Donna's movie contract, but the paper would not print a word until verification came from MGM.

Donna was hardly less incredulous. "Honestly, honey, I have to pinch myself every five minutes to believe it's true," she said in a letter to Joyce that couldn't quite manage restraint. "I guess I'm just about the luckiest person alive!"

CHAPTER THREE

Learning with Leo

From practically threadbare student and servant to movie starlet in two months. The change left Donna reeling. But there was little time to be scared that spring. Unlike some new girls at MGM who spent their days posing for magazines instead of acting, Donna was cast in a movie immediately. She was set to play the Jean Arthur role in a remake of the 1935 *Public Hero No. 1*, now retitled *The Enemy Within*. In a hasty scrawl, she wrote to Joyce Anderson: "It's all like a fairy story—people designing clothes for me, hair dressers, publicity pictures galore."

The makeover was underway. Donna was sent to Palm Springs to reduce the cornfed look that a movie camera would exaggerate. Her hair was swept off her forehead in a more sophisticated Tallulah style. She tried on clothes to determine the most flattering. She was taught how to walk gracefully and use her voice effectively. She was shown subtle cosmetic tricks by Jack Dawn, the head of the makeup department. And her name was changed.

Donna Mullenger might keep her real name today, as Mary Steenburgen did, but euphony and billboard brevity were required in the studio era. The coiners of identity at MGM considered Donna Drake, which was already taken. Then they thought up and threw away the perfect Donna Denison. "They're having an awful time finding a name for me," Donna told Joyce in April 1941. At the end of the month her hometown newspaper in Iowa announced that she would be known as Donna Adams. Hardly suggestive of stardust.

Some film books list her as Donna Adams for her fleeting appearance as a secretary in the Rooney-Garland musical *Babes on Broadway*. However, when she worked on it for two days in July 1941, speaking one line and earning $35, her name had been changed again. Coincidentally, in

Babes she is secretary to a theatrical agent named Reed, whose name appears in bold letters on the frosted office door behind Donna.

One morning in early June 1941 she read in the trade papers that she was Donna Reed. No one had consulted her or even bothered to phone her about the choice. She didn't think that was quite fair. Worse, she didn't care for her newest name, although it reverberated more than Adams. It stuck. Her overwhelming good luck hadn't left much room for objecting to it or anything else. Furthermore, publicity was already in place for *The Enemy Within*, which had been retitled *The Get-Away*. The decades-long cost of feeling uncomfortable with the name Donna Reed can never be known. "It has a cold, forbidding sound," she said after becoming famous. "I hear 'Donna Reed' and think of a tall, cool, austere blonde who is not me."

The Get-Away was a black-steel and white-lead program picture of no distinction aside from introducing Donna Reed and Dan Dailey. He plays her criminal brother, the ringleader of a gang terrorizing defense plants and the target of an undercover FBI agent. Predictably, the G-man, Robert Sterling, falls in love with Donna before having to kill her brother. *The Get-Away* was made quickly in May 1941.

On a modest scale, the magic of moviemaking was demonstrated to Donna during her first time on the set: Day was turned into night and she was soaked by overhead sprinklers simulating pouring rain. That first scene of a long career showed her seeking cover inside a car, talking in the rapid, edgy, flirty manner of a young Bette Davis.

In late May *The Get-Away* had its sneak preview at a theater in suburban Inglewood. This was an industry ritual that tested the response of a random audience (including the usual wisenheimers) to an unannounced film yet to be released. Donna, tipped off by a studio worker, camouflaged herself in a bandanna and casual clothes and drove to Inglewood with her old college standby, Lou Hurwitz. Mainly, she wanted to avoid the notice of the producer and director.

When Donna and Lou slipped into the theater *Penny Serenade* was half over. It was followed by a nerve-stretching cavalcade of shorts—March of Time newsreel, Bank Nite, the hyperkinetic Donald Duck. Finally, Leo the MGM Lion brought on the harshly lit, telegraphic credits for *The Get-Away*. A few days later, Donna described the experience of seeing herself on the screen: "Lou and I hung on to each other, we were so excited. I started to laugh and cry at the same time. It was the biggest thrill of my life!"

The preview audience liked Donna and said so on sheets handed out in the lobby. "Miss Reed a comer," read one. Donna thought *The Get-Away* was "a fair B" and her work satisfactory for a beginner. "I have so very much to learn," she wrote to her confidante in Iowa. The reviews that accompanied the film's release in mid-June briefly complimented her attractiveness. The most encouragement came from Edwin Schallert of the *Los Angeles Times*: "Donna Reed arrives in spectacular fashion as an ingenue heroine with potentialities of a Janet Gaynor, as one remembers from her debut." That fatherly critic overstated the impact she could make in a low-budget second feature.

During the summer of 1941 Donna's fame was chiefly limited to her hometown. In Denison the manager of the Ritz Theater declared Donna Mullenger Days and "premiered" *The Get-Away* on a bill with *The Great American Broadcast*, starring Alice Faye.

On June 15, a Sunday, the Mullengers filled a front row at the Ritz. Hazel was so nervous she could hardly sit through the long program. In the evening she wrote to Donnabelle that she was "still in a daze." Her chatty letter, saved through all the years, refers to plans made by family members to see the movie again, this time free of charge. They were "thrilled to pieces" and so many townspeople and neighbors had come around to offer congratulations, including several who had never been friendly before. There was disagreement on whether Donnabelle looked like Hazel or Bill. At the same time Grandmother Mullenger claimed a resemblance to Donnabelle and people agreed out of politeness.

Humor helped to steady Hazel. Referring to a dark and watery scene in the movie, she wrote, "I didn't know you were in the car when it fell thru the bridge or I would have yelled. Mama could see your knees. Suppose you had a rubber suit on. Anyway, your knees looked pretty shiny when he [Robert Sterling] pulled you out of the car." Only a mother would notice that Donna was wearing Jack Nau's ring on screen—

and perhaps Jack would. Understating her pride, Hazel told Donna: "It seemed to me you acted equally as good as the girl in the other picture." Lavone added a note: "You made Alice Faye look so old and dry."

The times in Tinseltown favored youngsters. Marquee stars were scarcer, and they were making fewer pictures because of higher taxes. Studios were frantically searching for new faces to bolster box-office receipts. Twentieth-Century-Fox catapulted unknowns like Gene Tierney and Linda Darnell into starring roles overnight. Some learned to act later. MGM, comparatively conservative, groomed its contractees for more gradual, perhaps more lasting, success. At all the studios an alarming number never got beyond the rank of featured player.

Knowing that the options of many attractive neophytes were dropped after six months or a year, Donna felt anything but secure. Always in the back of her mind was the question: Next year will I be using my shorthand to learn scripts quickly, or using it to earn my pay in a business office? Seeing herself on the screen wasn't entirely reassuring: she thought her posture was bad, her walk too hurried, her voice too midwestern. "Most of all I was shocked by how sad I looked," she said years later.

Out of her first paycheck Donna bought a silk dress for her mother, a suit for her father, and a white coat for herself. "I was so happy getting my contract because now I can help Lavone buy some nice clothes for the end of her school year. Gosh, there are so many things I want to do like that," she wrote to Joyce Anderson. Keith was bound for the University of Iowa, with her financial aid. Donna's generosity toward her family never wavered; it was well directed, not frivolous. Her experience of the Great Depression was very recent. "I've seen too many summers without rain and with crops spoiled ever to be extravagant," she told a Hollywood reporter.

Lodging at the Studio Club allowed Donna to save about half of her earnings, or thirty to forty dollars a week. That stucco Mediterranean-style establishment on Lodi Place was a magnet for secretaries, models, extras, stand-ins. Earlier, the struggling writer Ayn Rand had stayed there, so behind in her rent that a charitable movie executive's wife had given her money, which Miss Rand used not to pay her bill but to buy black lace underwear.

Donna lived at the club at the same time as another young actress, Marie Windsor, who remembered her as "sort of introverted." Later, Marilyn Monroe would hang her stockings in the bathroom and wait in line to use the telephone. Donna's third-floor bedroom, which had been endowed by Gloria Swanson, was tiny and meagerly furnished. Rules were strictly enforced by the housemother: No men were permitted above the first floor, and any girl coming in after one in the morning had to ring a bell. Inside those walls was a good deal of backbiting, commiserating, sisterly borrowing, and practice auditioning. It is said that the old Ginger Rogers movie *Stage Door* was based on life at the Studio Club. In the dining room or library the usual question was, "What luck did you have today?"

For Donna, the Studio Club was a sort of halfway house, a cross between the social sorority she hadn't known in college and the time-honored guild of nascent professionals. To hopefuls with practiced smiles and tired gams, Donna was a reminder of what *could* happen. To Donna, *they* were, just as surely, a reminder of ineffable and unreliable luck.

From that Dormitory of Disappointments on Lodi Place, Donna rode buses to Culver City, catching the first one in early morning darkness. At the studio, with no time for coffee to chase the bleakness, she was made up and sent to the set. After a long day of shooting or waiting around, she ran to meet the homebound bus. Back at the Studio Club she ate a plain but nourishing dinner, studied or rehearsed, and retired at nine in order to rise at five. Donna's only "extravagance" during those first days in Hollywood was buying records (before owning a phonograph). The recent release of *Fantasia* had introduced her to classical music.

It was not the glamorous life that her former schoolmates in Iowa imagined. But beyond the bus stop, beyond the MGM gates bearing the motto *Ars Gratia Artis*, Donna felt that anything could be made to happen. Her enthusiasm at this time was apparent to a visitor, the publisher of Denison's newspaper. She invited him to lunch in the studio commissary. A dozen diners congratulated Donna on her first picture, among them a married producer who was warming up for a serious pursuit. Then Donna took her guest around to some barnlike sound stages where movies were in production. She was as fascinated as he was by the framing of illusions. The set of *Honky Tonk* showed Clark Gable lolling in a frontier barbershop, his anachronistic rubber heels barely out of camera range. Nearby, the boxing crowd for *Ringside Maisie* was revealed as a painted backdrop. Farther on, where a Conrad Veidt mystery was being filmed, a man was making cobwebs by blowing rubber cement through a fan.

"Right now I'm the happiest I've ever been," Donna wrote to Joyce Anderson. If she had been otherwise, hardly anyone would have known. The girl who had taken Dale Carnegie's book to heart, and whose letters minimized the most impressive turns of fortune, was reluctant to talk about herself. As the summer of 1941 wore on, she posed for hundreds of publicity stills. In August she reported for a small role in *Shadow of the Thin Man*. The popularity of the Thin Man series ensured her a bigger audience.

So far, everything was copacetic. But the anxiety that Donna felt during a long trial period was clear to at least one close friend from college days, Virginia Ricks. As if striving to maintain some sense of reality, Donna often spent Sundays with the Rickses, attending the Unity Church with them and staying for a home-cooked meal. Virginia felt that Donna was unusually insecure, doubtful of her talent, somewhat disillusioned by the Great Glamorous Place. She was very quiet. There was about her "an aura of sadness."

Virginia could only speculate on the reasons for it. Donna was always on display now, constantly having to prove herself and please others. The waitresses on roller skates at Los Angeles drive-ins had more control over their lives. If she went out for an ice cream wearing blue jeans, the studio reprimanded her. Unquestionably, she missed the daily close-by support of her own large family, and she lacked the protection that a serious romantic relationship might provide.

To her Iowa friend who was pursuing a radio career, Donna wrote: "Everyone back in Denison is getting married and having babies! Are we slipping, Joyce?" She still dated guys from college days—Lou Hurwitz, Fletcher Jones, and Bert Todd, who worked for a construction company. Not an Alice-Sit-by-the-Fire, she trekked to Las Vegas with Bert and toured the casinos from dusk to dawn.

But Donna resisted the attentions of actors. Bob Sterling, whom she considered conceited, finally escorted her to Ciro's, where the photographer's flashbulbs startled her. Although she went with Sterling to Judy Garland's birthday party, the Hollywood social scene didn't engage her. Donna's thoughts turned to her high school sweetie, Jack Nau, who was at Jefferson Barracks, Missouri, in the first leg of training to be an army pilot. "I've a premonition he won't live through this war. Maybe I'm just crazy or still like the guy or something," she mused.

Donna was in training too. At the studio she sweated through ballet practice and worked closely with Gertrude Fogler, the voice teacher, and Lillian Burns, the drama coach. Miss Burns became Donna's adviser, protector, and lifelong friend. No one else so completely won the confidence of the budding actress.

Lillian's acting method was a lack of method. If the acting looked and sounded like acting, it was bad acting. Basically, she encouraged Donna to find her own feelings and use them. It was a valuable lesson that Donna explained to a scribe for *The Lion's Roar*: "Emphasis is laid on the fact we must not pretend we are someone else while enacting a role. We must try to be ourselves, merely feeling, believing, and saying the lines of another character." That required a profound, gut-level understanding of the other whose medium was oneself.

Lillian Burns had no delusions about slavish adherence to classical texts. When Maria Ouspenskaya asked her if she used Stanislavski's *An Actor Prepares*, she replied, "No, I do not." The Russian actress was surprised: "Why not?" "Because," Lillian said, "because—I'll take one chapter, for instance, the chapter on body movement. It has one sentence in fourteen pages that means anything. After all, movement is from your mind to your heart to your body, which all expression is." Miss Ouspenskaya responded: "You're the only person in Hollywood I ever heard talk about the heart."

Lillian prepared Donna for her early roles, including the minor one of a soldier's bride in *The Bugle Sounds*, a vehicle for Wallace Beery and Marjorie Main. All but forgotten now, the movie was produced with the cooperation of the War Department. Technical crews and cast members were dispatched to army camps in California, Washington, Kentucky, and

Louisiana to film actual manuevers that showed off Uncle Sam's new tanks. Donna stayed at the studio, doing her scenes on a two-acre backlot that replicated a military post and suffering from heat that reminded her of Iowa. As if foreseeing a future in which other actors tackled sirloin and left her scraps, she expressed doubts about playing the ingenue. The role was "drippy at times," she told Joyce Anderson. "Frankly, I'm afraid of it."

By the end of October *The Bugle Sounds* was in the cutting room and *Shadow of the Thin Man* was awaiting release. Donna's anxiety lifted momentarily when her option was renewed, with a slight increase in salary. This month she was driving her first car, a black Chevrolet club coupe, modest by movie-star standards but dreamy to a girl who had depended on buses.

Cars were not as important to her as books, and the MGM environment was often stimulating. If her career failed to develop, the same could never be said of her mind, by gosh. "As much as I hated to quit college, I wouldn't go back now for anything," she said. "I think I've learned twice as much since. I read more books and get more out of them." Recently she had devoured *Berlin Diary* and *The Road to War*. *Random Harvest* she considered "beautifully written." Her mounting ambition was to act in the film version of James Hilton's novel, but that seemed "a very remote possibility."

Public awareness of Donna Reed increased a jot when *Shadow of the Thin Man* opened across the country during Thanksgiving week. This fourth and far from best entry in the series, about murder at a racetrack, did good business. Photographed in glossy black and white by William Daniels and served up reasonably dry by William Powell and Myrna Loy, it featured Donna as a secretary, tailored and looking pert in a pillbox hat. Late in the picture Stella Adler, the drama coach making a rare appearance as a mobster's moll, stares at Donna and harrumphs, "Isn't she sweet!" Typecast, already.

While others were preparing for the first Christmas with America at war, Donna was in front of the cameras. During the next five months—from early December through April 1942—she made four movies, one after the other: *The Courtship of Andy Hardy, Mokey, Calling Dr. Gillespie*, and *Apache Trail*. She worked every day, including Saturdays, and allowed that even Iowa farmers got more holidays.

One Friday night she drove to Laguna Beach with Moria Turner, who would make a career playing movie bits, television parts, and area playhouse leads. Moria remembered that after they checked into an auto court on the beach Donna received a phone message to report to the studio next morning. Normally self-contained, Donna became hysterical. "She threw herself on the bed and cried buckets," said Moria, who pleaded with her to stay overnight and start out at sunrise. But they headed back to Los Angeles in the night traffic.

Despite the workaday tension, it was a happy time, or would have been without the war. Donna had a recurrent dream that the Japanese were coming. "I fought a number of defensive battles in the Land of Counterpane," she would recall. Six months before the Normandy Invasion, she dreamed of it, even discerning the shadowy date June 6. Less attuned to signs than Aunt Mildred, she later dismissed the dream as coincidence.

Pearl Harbor was bombed just as Donna began the Andy Hardy picture. She was cast as Mickey Rooney's girl, a drab little mouse who is transformed into a glamour puss.

When *The Courtship of Andy Hardy* was released the following Easter, Donna was widely noticed for the first time. Although critics thought the Hardy family of Carvel, Idaho, was wearing thin, they praised Donna. Dorothy Manners noted her "rare camera poise." Wanda Hale wrote: "This Donna Reed is going places. Not a cut and dried beauty, as you know if you've seen her, she is sensitively pretty with a beautifully responsive face and voice." John McManus was no less ecstatic: "Donna seems destined to stick around, so better get acquainted with her now before she pops up on you unawares one day as Juliet or Joan of Arc."

The public lined up at the box office, and friends took Donna to Grauman's Chinese Theater, where her name was in lights eight feet high. "Oh boy, what a thrill," she told the Iowa chum who a few years before had spent evenings with her at the library because neither of them could afford a movie ticket.

Before reaping those plaudits, Donna made a small picture with the odd title of *Mokey Delano*, shortened to *Mokey*. For one of the few times in her career she was outcharmed—by young Bobby Blake, playing her wayward stepson, Mokey. Blake, who in 1993 revealed the terrible physical abuse meted out by his real parents, remembered that Donna Reed was the first adult who ever hugged him.

Mokey, featuring Buckwheat Thomas, seemed a carryover from the Our Gang comedies (in which Blake had acted as Mickey Gubitosi). Although mildly entertaining, the movie is seldom shown on television, possibly because of its blatant black stereotypes with names like Begonia Cumby and Aunt Deedy. Donna, wearing summer dresses, striding down sunlit streets, her long hair flowing, is the image of healthy womanhood.

Without pause, she went into *Calling Dr. Gillespie*, another series film calculated to train and show off new talent. Donna is betrothed to a young man who signals his disturbance by breaking the neck of a puppy. He develops into a full-blown homicidal maniac. In March 1942 Lew Ayres, in the role of Dr. Kildare, was taken off this film because he had declared himself a conscientious objector in the war effort.

The way Ayres was treated infuriated Donna, who had befriended him. "He is a very intelligent, deep-thinking, kindly, generous person, and I admire him tremendously as a person who has the courage of his convictions," she wrote. "And then they send him away to a camp! I could go out and shoot a few people every time I think of it. It's a disgrace to democracy!"

Donna had no time to brood before going off to Arizona for *Apache Trail*, her first Western. It was a low-budget *Stagecoach*, based on a story by Ernest Haycox. During the three weeks of filming, hundreds of real Indians were employed to attack an isolated stage station. Donna, made up as a Spanish girl, liked playing a flashy character for a change. She spoke in a different rhythm and pitch, but one unkind critic observed that she was impeded by her accent. William Lundigan and Lloyd Nolan were among those holed up in the desert. (The obscure *Apache Trail* is not listed in recent television guides to twenty thousand oldies.)

By the time *The Courtship of Andy Hardy* came out in the spring of 1942, Donna's publicity was building to a peak. From the beginning she had been promoted as the wholesome farmer's daughter. *Photoplay* sounded the refrain: "She can bake a cherry pie, she can preserve berries, cook for thrashers, milk a cow, plant a field, and melt any number of male hearts on the side." All true enough. It was announced that a MGM crew would go to the Mullenger farm to film a trailer for *The Courtship of Andy Hardy*, but the plan was abandoned, perhaps because of logistics and Iowa winter weather. No matter. A slew of articles described Donna Reed as cornfed, as an advertisement for the good that milk could do a body.

Which brings up a legendary story. Donna bet Lionel Barrymore that she could milk a cow and won fifty dollars in cash or defense stamps (the details vary). If publicity releases can be trusted, Donna and the avuncular Barrymore went to a dairy in the San Fernando Valley, where she did indeed milk a cow. In a typical photo layout, she is holding a straw hat and wearing shiny cowboy boots and a fetching abbreviated costume that Hollywood thought proper for milkmaids and farmerettes.

Her looks inspired hyperbole. The columnist Herb Howe wrote: "Donna's hair and eyes are autumn brown. When laughing her eyes fizz with golden bubbles like fresh churned cider; her nose tilts and lips part wide for a dazzle you seldom get from beauties not of African ancestry."

Now her name appeared regularly in the newspapers. William Randolph Hearst was said to be an admirer. Columnists found her an enigma because she made no gestures toward Hollywood glamour. They had her signed up for important roles. Although Donna still hadn't starred in a grade-A picture, she was viewed as the likely choice to play opposite Clark Gable in *The Sun Is My Undoing*. The sun never rose on that.

Starting with *The Courtship of Andy Hardy*, she did rate a stand-in, whose name was Frances Haldorn. An attractive brunette of Donna's size, Frances had appeared as a child on the stage with Lionel Barrymore and Ruth Chatterton. After attending Hollywood High School, she nearly died in a car accident. Her long period of therapy was ending when, at the Studio Club, she met Donna, who got her into MGM as a double. Though Frances eventually turned self-destructive, she was connected with Donna for many years.

Donna's star might have risen faster at another studio, but she fitted well into the family-type pictures that Louis B. Mayer favored. Called "a sentimental tyrant" by one long-time associate, Mayer thought of *all* the MGM girls as his daughters unless they crossed him. Esther Williams, who beat out Donna for a bathing-beauty role in *Andy Hardy's Double Trouble* in 1942, remembered that she "never had an aging moment at MGM." Donna, her good friend, also got along with Mayer, but it is clear in retrospect that he imagined her as little more than a marketable junior-sized version of Greer Garson and Myrna Loy, who were "real stars."

In all fairness, Donna was still developing and at a delicate juncture when her young career could wither from mismanagement or leap forward. Donna herself was increasingly torn between her desire for more provocative roles and her desire to please the lonely soldiers who wrote to her: "Always stay just as sweet as you are." So it was with mixed feelings that she allowed a producer to talk her into playing a truly nasty role.

Eyes in the Night, which began shooting in June 1942, was tautly directed by Fred Zinnemann, recently arrived from Austria. Its McGuffin was a weapon blueprint hidden in Ann Harding's house, attracting Nazi spies with nothing to fear but a blind detective and his seeing-eye dog. Friday, the malamute, reportedly had the IQ of a bright ten-year-old human. Donna, ranked third in the cast, is Harding's hateful stepdaughter. Her eyes gleam and narrow with scorn, her well-modulated voice half-spews barely contained and bottomless spite, her body moves with subtle menace and threat in scenes with Harding, whom she loathes for her own reasons. And she photographs strikingly.

When the movie was released later in the year, Donna was considered its chief asset. At his zenith Zinnemann dismissed *Eyes in the Night*, but it was the surprise hit of the 1986 Berlin Film Festival honoring him.

A wholly different Donna Reed could be seen on the streets of Denison, Iowa, in August. The scheming creature of *Eyes in the Night* was in broad daylight the gentle Donna Mullenger. She had boarded the Challenger train in Los Angeles and come home for the first time in two years.

At the Denison depot Hazel was holding a new member of the family, two-month-old Karen Ann. Twenty-one years separated Donna from her baby sister. Nothing had changed; yet everything had. The farm was the same (Donna was photographed with Daisy, the hostile pony of old); yet activity in the house was organized around a new bassinet. Everyone said Donna was the same, better turned out; yet she was a celebrity now.

Reporters and photographers from Omaha, Des Moines, and Sioux City were on hand as she attended a Chamber of Commerce luncheon, and old friends lined up to watch her ride at the head of a parade. She was the main attraction of the Crawford County 4-H Fair. In any accounting of Donna Reed's life, the image of her selling war bonds on the streets of Denison in 1942 is memorable. Candid snapshots show her looking pleased and pensive, every inch the All-American Girl of a fearful time, modestly reenacting a timeless ritual: the triumphant return of one's own.

On a night train back to Los Angeles, Donna was surrounded by several hundred young men on their way to Marine boot camp. Anxious and lonely, cocky and shy, they enlisted her in their singing and card playing. It might have been a scene out of *The Human Comedy*, the film she would begin in October.

During the war Donna was popular with the GIs, who attached her autographed photo to foxholes, torpedo shacks, and bomber noses. They named her Bombardier Queen, Goldbrick Queen, Sweetheart of the Motor Corps. One homesick battalion in North Africa designated her as "the girl we would most like to come home to." She toured Fort MacArthur and other stateside posts, doing her bit to keep up morale.

At the newly opened, barnlike Hollywood Canteen Donna danced with soldiers every week. The pace never let up. In little more than a year she had done eight movies and made an extraordinary impression. Theater exhibitors in the United States and Canada named her a Star of Tomorrow. She placed eighth in the 1942 poll, behind Jane Wyman and Alan Ladd and ahead of Betty Hutton and Teresa Wright. All indications were that Donna would become the big star that Mr. Mayer had underestimated. But exhibitors do not write scripts. Fate does. Now, at twenty-one, she stood on the threshold of a new kind of role.

William Tuttle had made up Donna for all her early movie roles. So in a professional way he knew intimately that fresh face which was easy to prepare for the camera. He was attracted to her complete naturalness.

On Christmas Eve 1941 she was feeling lonely for her family and still somewhat overcome by her good luck. Tuttle was measuring cosmetics when she asked, "By the way, what happens around here on Christmas

Eve?" It seemed so strange to be at the studio that day. Tuttle mentioned the free lunch in the commissary and added that he was going to hang mistletoe in his makeup room. Later she returned for a kiss, and their courtship began.

Like Donna, Bill Tuttle had come west and fortuitously landed at MGM. He was born in 1912 in Jacksonville, Florida, to Ann and Julian Tuttle. His father worked for the railroad, and his mother encouraged him to be an artist. But it was through music that he planned to transcend the ordinary; at age eight he was studying the violin. Bill's parents divorced when he was fourteen, and he became the sole support of his mother and younger brother, Tom. Forced to leave school a year later, he played his violin at nightspots. His little family suffered from the Depression more than Donna's did. They lived in one room and rented the rest of the house.

In 1930, eight years before Donna took a train west, Bill and a friend started out in a Model-T Ford for California, without prospects or connections or enough money; Bill's mother and brother would be sent for later. The boys drove as far as El Paso, where the car collapsed. Amazingly, they sold it for ten dollars and used the money for bus fare to Los Angeles. There they found a cheap room at the Aida Apartment Hotel. As it happened, the landlady's niece was a dancer in pictures, and the good woman got young Bill an interview at William Fox Studios. He held various menial jobs there, on the sly making a talented drawing of the boss, Winfield Sheehan. It brought him to the attention of Sheehan's friend, Jack Dawn, then head of makeup at Twentieth Century Pictures.

Bill almost rejected Dawn's offer of an apprenticeship because the art of makeup seemed a doubtful way to earn bread. But things worked out famously, and when Dawn moved to MGM in 1934 Bill went along as his assistant. By 1942 he was second in command of an expanding makeup department and earning more money than Donna.

Their courtship lasted a year. Bill had curly brown hair and wore glasses that made him look professorial. He was cultivated, soft-spoken, and uncommonly courteous. Like most of the men of Donna's past and future, he was older, by nine years. Strong as Donna was, she needed a protector, and he was responsible and hard-working.

She was tired of dodging married suitors. The producer of three of her early movies, J. Walter Rubin, the husband of a well-known actress, had pursued her persistently—and almost irresistibly because he was a charmer, a hunk. She felt like Little Red Riding Hood among the wolves—until saved by good old Bill. He was not a long-lashed Lothario and (thank God) not an actor. But, being in the business, he could understand the demands on her.

They were on the verge of being engaged in the fall of 1942 when he made her up for the small but showcased role of Mickey Rooney's sister in *The Human Comedy*. It was Donna's first big A picture, and would gross nearly three million dollars in the season of its release. As Bess, she was a nice girl again, with the grace that kept her from seeming saccharine. In one scene she stands in line outside a small-town theater that must have reminded her of the Ritz in Denison.

Immediately after *The Human Comedy* wrapped up, Bill prepared her for *Dr. Gillespie's Criminal Case*, a reprise of her role as a chilly socialite who had certainly never been close to a cow. Although newcomers Van Johnson and Margaret O'Brien showed up to good advantage, Donna was wasted. It was becoming clear that MGM did not know what to do with her.

Before these two movies came out, Donna and Bill were married. On January 30, 1943, they slipped quietly into the Community Methodist Church in Beverly Hills for the ceremony. Their wedding was a surprise to friends and associates alike because their courtship had become more secretive as it deepened. One weekend they'd holed up in a hotel room in San Diego after learning the woman in the adjoining suite was a gossipy secretary at MGM—romance, especially with an older and un-showy man, was not what the studio would have ordered for Donna.

Before the wedding, they had secretly selected and furnished their apartment—four rooms and a bath—at the corner of Beverly Glen and Tennessee avenues. The small space was dominated by a fireplace and filled with books and phonograph records. The studio was only five minutes away, a good thing in this time of gasoline rationing.

The next day Donna reported for *The Man from Down Under*. She was excited to be working with Charles Laughton, who invited the newlyweds to his house for dinner. He was playing an Aussie boxer who at the end of service in World War I takes home two Belgian orphans. They grow up

to look like Richard Carlson and Donna Reed, and feel miserable in realizing their mutual attraction because they are brother and sister, or so
they think. And so it went. Recently a movie archivist seized on the last
name of the coproducer, Orville O. Dull, to describe *The Man from Down
Under*. A contemporary reviewer suggested that Donna, "a capable and
attractive actress," was helpless against such material and deserving of
better.

Although her option was renewed and salary boosted at this time,
Donna was increasingly worried about her career. More new talent was
coming into MGM, and that meant more competition. To her astonishment, she was cast in the role of her dreams, the second feminine lead in
Random Harvest, only to see it snatched away by Susan Peters. She tested
well for the role of Van Johnson's wife in *Thirty Seconds over Tokyo* but
was considered "too pretty" and lost out to Phyllis Thaxter. A plum in
Cry Havoc fell to another actress instead.

Donna's diffidence showed up in small ways. Bill remembered that she
habitually pushed her jaw out as if to compensate for an imagined weak
chin. Partly because upsweep hairdos were in fashion, she had her slightly
protruding ears pinned back by the plastic surgeon who would later op-
erate on Marilyn Monroe.

Bill understood Donna's worry about money, having been poor himself. She told him about farming—how wet crops were often planted in
dry years, and vice versa. She recalled her dear father gathering up seed
corn annually, sitting at the kitchen table making plans. "Now, *next
year . . .*," he would begin.

Whatever insecurity she felt was wholly human, and exacerbated by
the war. Her husband and a brother were 4-F because of medical conditions that concerned her, and the soldiers at the canteen had an aura of
imminent death that touched her heart.

The Tuttles were quietly happy. "Billy is a swell guy and we get along perfectly," Donna wrote to Joyce Anderson in March. She was particularly
proud of his artistic talent—he painted in water colors and sculpted. She
had no such bent and could never rid herself of the feeling that she was a
bit of a plodder, one to whom success came only gradually and after hard

work. The couple went to concerts and lectures (one by the actor Keye Luke on Chinese art), and occasionally could be seen at Ciro's or the Palladium or the Brown Derby.

Under Bill's influence, Donna was stretching intellectually and politically. The Republican conservatism of her Iowa upbringing was giving way to a decided liberalism. Like Bill, she admired and supported Roosevelt and Henry Wallace. After reading *World's End* by Upton Sinclair, she couldn't sleep. "It paints a clear, and probably very authentic, picture of prewar and postwar days of World War I," she reported to Joyce Anderson. "Sinclair tells about the things that happened and were kept out of the newspapers and away from the populace. He spends a great deal of time on Wilson and the peace, and why it didn't work. Honestly, I can see the same things happening now as happened then, and it frightens me to death. Try to find time to read it. (He's pinko, or maybe even red, but that doesn't matter.)"

For two weeks in October 1943, Donna toured camps. Her troupe included a magician and his wife, a black-face comic, a blues singer, and an acrobatic act. With Fay Bainter she did a "silly little skit" in front of five thousand Marines. The experience of a live audience—and it was lively—thrilled her. Thoroughly "scared" before every performance, she tasted the sweetness of vaudeville. One night she forgot her lines and, in a disguised manner, asked Bainter for a cue. After that, she memorized long speeches to sharpen up.

Before her tour, Donna had completed two movies. *Thousands Cheer* filmed the kind of entertainment for troops that she was doing in person, and marked her first appearance in Technicolor. It hardly counted because her cameo role, as a patron at Red Skelton's soda fountain, lasted only a minute. But *See Here, Private Hargrove* brought her closer to stardom, as Robert Walker's girlfriend. As a couple they were cute (no other word will do), equally innocent and cuddly. Based on a best-selling novel about boot camp, the movie packed in audiences when it was released in February 1944. Today it seems dated and stale, but Walker is still attractively boyish and Donna, photographed in a clever way that conveys his idealization of her, is hardly less pleasing.

The Tuttles celebrated their first wedding anniversary in late January, and Donna wrote that they were "very, very happy." But 1944 was to be their last year together. Later, Bill looked back on an early incident as a bad omen. Before doing a scene in *The Man from Down Under*, Donna had removed her wedding ring. Preoccupied, she forgot where she'd placed it. That night the carpenters, who adored her, nearly dismantled the set in searching. The ring was never found.

Both Donna and Bill were still trying to establish their careers and, like thousands of other young couples, they planned to wait until after the war to begin a family. Contributing to that decision was the fear that the studio, benevolent but powerful in its control over private lives, would not renew her option if she did become pregnant. But biology is more powerful, and when Donna conceived she had to decide between childbirth and career. She and Bill agreed that their bad timing made an abortion necessary. There was the usual regret and emotional pain but no argument about this course, Bill recalled. Still, things would never be quite the same between them. The beneficiary, in a sense, was the studio that had invested heavily and expected no interference with its plans.

A happier turn of events was Donna's casting in *The Picture of Dorian Gray*. It was the first attempt to film Oscar Wilde's classic story of soul destruction and remains one of the oddest productions ever to come out of Hollywood. Lacking big stars, very literary and elegant in black and white, the movie appealed to the masses by promising to show, at different stages, a color portrait of Dorian, changing hideously with his moral decay.

At first Donna was considered for the role of the romantic and vulnerable dance-hall singer Sibyl Vane, so she practiced singing "Little Yellow Bird," though she had no ear for music. Then the British actress Angela Lansbury was brought in to play Sibyl and Donna was given the more suitable role of Gladys Hallward, which was invented for the movie. Miss Lansbury remembered Donna: "She was like a Dresden doll, so tiny and perfect. Beside her, I felt like an overgrown puppy!"

Donna, wearing her hair in an unsweep and fitted in period gowns, makes Gladys the image of grace, the one reasonably normal person in Dorian Gray's social circle. She loves the perpetually youthful Dorian without realizing that he is as old as sin. For her alone, he might have reformed once. There is a touching close-up of Donna weeping quietly at the piano. Critics, however, judged her role flat. Their attention was captured by the Cockney girl played by Lansbury.

Straining the patience of everyone in the movie was the scholarly director, Albert Lewin. He required 102 takes of one scene. At his insistence, the deep-focus camera lingered on symbolic and subtly erotic detail in the setting, including depictions of an Egyptian cat goddess. Viewing the rushes, the producer Pandro Berman complained in a memo to Lewin: "This is one of the slowest-paced pictures I've ever seen in my life." Some cast and crew members made fun of Lewin, "the professor," but Donna was always proud of her association. After a half-century, *The Picture of Dorian Gray* looks solid, the evident care in its making lending a credible eeriness to the mood. Unlike the violent horror movies of today, it shows how frightening the suggestion of evil can be.

About this time, in June 1944, *Variety* reported that MGM, in connection with its twentieth anniversary, had officially advanced ten contract players to the "star" category. Donna was not one of them, although a few who were named—Esther Williams, Van Johnson, and Margaret O'Brien—had arrived at the studio after her. She was still on the much larger roster of "featured players."

Donna's agent now at Feldman was an excessively charming, persuasive fellow named Tony Owen. He began telling her that she had to leave ingenues behind and graduate to bigger pictures. Donna herself seems to have been more or less satisfied with her progress, at least at first. The Tuttles began seeing more of Tony. When he joined them for dinner at a restaurant his energy transformed the scene. Occasionally Tony, ever restless in his networking, would invite the couple to the beachside house of Townsend Netcher, a wealthy friend from his Chicago days.

Bill seldom interfered with Donna's work, but he did discourage her from doing *Son of Lassie* because he thought the color process to be used was inferior. She had been tapped to play the grown-up version of the Elizabeth Taylor role from *Lassie Come Home*. Another experience she missed, because *The Picture of Dorian Gray* took so long to film, was impersonating a bass fiddle player in *Music for the Millions*. June Allyson filled in.

The last movie Donna made in 1944 was a good little Western with a bad title, *Gentle Annie*. It was an adaptation of McKinley Kantor's novel about two likable brothers who rob trains with the help of their mother, endearingly acted by Marjorie Main. They plan to stash enough money to move out of Oklahoma, where "the wind blows all day and coyotes howl all night." Confederate sympathizers, they feel justified in stealing northern gold. Donna is a sort of homeless orphan taken in by the outlaws. She calls them "the most generous people I've ever met."

Donna fought hard to make her character (a saloon waitress in the early scenes) outspoken and independent-minded. Supported by the director, Andrew Marton, she won the fight before the camera but mainly lost it in the cutting room. Predictably, the censors objected to the waitress getting pinched on the rear while serving the rough cowboys. Neither was she allowed to spill two trays of soup on them. So in the editing Donna's waitress lost some sass and strong reason for quitting in a huff.

Gentle Annie was unusual because the characters were somewhere between black and white. Reviewers were troubled by the "moral tone" of a movie with semi-sympathetic lawbreakers. Out of place in a grade-B Western! A few recognized its superiority to most oaters coming off the assembly line, but that was no help to Donna Reed. Maybe she really did need a hard-hitting agent like Tony Owen.

When Donna wrote to Joyce Anderson on October 10, she never hinted of any trouble with Bill. In a chatty letter she mentioned that her mother and baby sister had visited them for a month. She had enjoyed doing a radio show called "Too Many Husbands" with Frank Sinatra. Bill had sculpted a bust of the crooner. "He can do anything he tries in the artistic field," she boasted. "Take me, I have to work like mad to get what little I've got, but c'est la vie! Shore am proud of him." That was less than two months before they separated.

Early in December, Donna returned from a publicity tour—but not to the apartment on Beverly Glen. She went to her sister's place instead. Bill was shocked because tensions had not built to a blowup. Later he remembered her saying that she didn't feel secure with him, but he gathered that she felt not so much financially insecure as professionally. He also remembered Tony's seductiveness and a lavish bouquet sent to Donna with the message: "To BA [Best Actress] from BA [Best Agent]."

Friends seemed as surprised by the breakup as they had been by the wedding. Donna's thoughts were entirely private as she flew to Juarez on January 8, 1945. Next day she obtained a divorce from Bill Tuttle on grounds of incompatibility. "This has been coming for a long time," she told reporters, and that is all she would say.

The evening of January 9, Donna boarded a plane across the border in El Paso, but a moment before takeoff she was bumped from the flight to make room for a military officer. Early the next morning, approaching Burbank in heavy fog, the airliner crashed into a mountainside. Everyone on board was killed.

One part of Donna was in mourning over the divorce. The news of the crash jolted her numbness, and she came to that Spanish sense of the nearness of death. She was filled with wonder. Why had she been spared, and for what? The intersection of fate and circumstance had never seemed more piercing.

CHAPTER FOUR

A Wonderful Life

E arly 1945 found Donna, like other Americans, restless, impatient with restrictions, tired of war's imprint on everything from cereal boxes to pop songs. Letters might still bring grief, but newspaper headlines were looking more hopeful. In January, Churchill warned Germany of imminent defeat, and the following month saw the Stars and Stripes finally raised on Iwo Jima.

In fact, Donna's four years in Hollywood had been war-crossed. The constraints of that time, and her native frugality, had called for cramped apartments and make-do cars. She had never traveled to New York or even to San Francisco. Her career had also been constricted. Though a creditable sweetheart, she lacked the singing voice and dancing legs for MGM's biggest productions, the musicals that diverted war-weary audiences.

Free again, Donna, like the nation itself, sensed larger possibilities. For her they were more and more linked to Tony Owen, her agent and suitor. She was deeply attracted to his vitality and dark good looks. In background, temperament, and interests, they could not have been more different.

When Donna was a toddler on the Iowa farm, Tony was a teenager in New Orleans. He was Irving Ohnstein then, the son of a socially prominent couple who lived at 25 Newcomb Boulevard. Samuel Ohnstein was president of Union Paper Products and through his wife, Naomi Kahn, connected to the F. Hollander Liquor Company. In 1924, when Irving was seventeen and his sister Sarah fifteen, the Ohnsteins moved to Chicago. There, Samuel headed the Crescent Engraving Company, which employed artists to illustrate the Sears Roebuck and Montgomery Ward catalogs.

Like most of the Jewish aristocracy in Chicago, the Ohnsteins lived on the south side, in a large apartment on Drexel Boulevard. Young Irving was an extrovert, manic about sports. He briefly attended the University of Chicago, playing on the tennis team; but the city was his classroom. Ann Straus, who became a fashion publicist for MGM, remembered Irving Ohnstein as an office boy in her father's firm, S. W. Straus & Company, Bonds and Mortgages. His main duty was to drive a car to the Straus building, one of Chicago's earliest skyscrapers, and wait for Mr. Straus to collect it. Irving, with his southern drawl and sleek appearance, was a charmer. He was, Ann observed, "quite the patent leather kid."

Irving Ohnstein entered Chicago society through the Standard Club, which had been organized by well-to-do German Jews in 1869. He made a hit performing in the club's annual revue on George Washington's birthday. In the 1929 production he sang and danced in front of the chorus, drawing praise as "the Standard Club's John Barrymore and Harry Richman combined." Two years later he produced and directed the show, also playing a gigolo and singing "Walking My Baby Back Home." According to Ann Straus, then a club member, Irving got in with a fast crowd from the fashionable north side. "They made a big fuss over him, and it turned his head."

Performing was not Irving's ticket to anywhere. He fell ill while trying out on Broadway for *Grand Hotel* and returned home feeling like a flop. About this time Hollywood called. Paramount was interested in Irving because he resembled Rudolph Valentino, but nothing came of his screen test. Samuel Ohnstein, who looked down on the movies as a career, practically ordered the young man back to Chicago and business.

The patriarch died in 1932 at the age of fifty-seven, ruined by the Great Depression. And Irving, the adored son, was soon broke. "I started this world wrong—with a gold spoon in my mouth. Then I worked steadily down to the bottom," he said years later.

When Irving was hired as a police reporter on the *Chicago Herald-Examiner* he changed his name to Tony Owen, ostensibly to shorten his by-line, but probably to ward off anti-Semitism. That job brought him into contact with the roughest elements of Chicago, and by the time he was signed as amusements editor of the *Daily News* he knew his way around the underworld. The city after dark was his beat, the famous Chez Paree on the near north side his haunt. It was the perfect position for a playboy, a coarsened Chicago version of a bon vivant. Before he was fired in 1939 for vaguely political reasons, Tony Owen nodded toward convention by marrying a dancer named Lee Belmont, one of the Chez Paree Adorables.

Family legend says that Tony bought the Detroit Lions football team after leaving the *Chicago Daily News*. In fact, he formed a partnership with Freddy Mandel of department store renown, becoming vice president and business manager of the Lions. He was thus occupied until America entered World War II. The day after the attack on Pearl Harbor, Tony, along with most of his players, joined the army. At thirty-four, he was old enough to be called Pop Owen by other privates in the horse cavalry at Fort Riley, Kansas.

A bad knee put Tony out of the service in September 1942. The same year brought the death of his devoted mother and the breakup of the Ohnstein family home in Chicago. During that low period, he looked westward to California, as Donnabelle Mullenger and William Tuttle had done. Unlike them, he had prior connections. The upshot was a job paying fifty dollars a week at Charles Feldman's talent agency in Los Angeles. His marriage to Lee lasted another year.

Friends and relatives always had trouble pairing such complete opposites as Tony Owen and Donna Reed. He was genuinely a glad-hander, gamester, gourmet—spiritually a mixture of genteel New Orleans and hat-grabbing Chicago, of Montaigne and Al Capone, of the smoothest scotch and the greenest beer. Donna was reserved and refined. She loved the fine arts that bored him, and was soon bored with the sports that he loved. If he was a "character," she was an enigma. The overdrive that was apparent in his case was quieter but perhaps stronger in hers.

"I'm going to marry that girl," Tony said when he first met Donna at the Feldman agency, forgetting the existence of Bill Tuttle. He was impressed because she was the only person in Hollywood who called him Mr. Owen. That was the story he used to tell reporters.

Donna was irresistibly resistant to his charm, and after he became her agent they "fought like cats and dogs" over scripts, career moves. Who can say exactly when she fell passionately, helplessly in love for the first time? "I was longing for excitement," Donna once disclosed. Certainly Tony was attractive, fourteen years older than she, possessing black hair and eyes, "hide the tan of saddle leather," and an athletic horsiness that "looked right in tobacco tweed." Donna confided to a family member that she would no doubt be unhappy if she married Tony—but miserable if she didn't.

The wedding was set for mid-June. It was already April when Donna reported to MGM for *They Were Expendable*. For several months John Ford had been directing battle scenes in Key Biscayne, Florida, which was made to replicate the Philippines in every detail except insect life. No expense was being spared in filming William L. White's story about the Americans who fought hopelessly in patrol torpedo (PT) boats while the Philippines fell to the Japanese early in World War II. Donna's scenes as an army nurse, Lt. Sandy Davyss, were mostly interior ones that could be shot on the lot in Culver City.

Her assignment required fortitude. In a 1980 interview with Lindsay Anderson, Robert Montgomery, who played the commander of a PT squadron, revealed what Donna endured on the set. When she was due to face the cameras, some wardrobe people brought her before John Ford for costume approval. He ignored her as she stood around for half an hour. Finally the people attending her dared to ask Ford to see her. He snarled and told them to take her away because no one cared about costumes in a picture like this. "She was intruding into the men's game, you see," Montgomery said. "She was very intelligent. She didn't let Ford upset her: she used his attitude—played off it. It gave her strength." In a few weeks Donna won the respect of the crusty Ford. Her portrayal of the nurse reminded him of the dedicated servicewomen he had seen during combat duty in the South Pacific. She was authentic, he said, "as typical as a Liberty-head dime."

Donna Reed has more *gravitas* than most women in war films. In *They Were Expendable* she stands among the men, silently heroic, too involved with coping to have time for illusions or sentimentality or even wisecracks. As the bombs fall outside the underground hospital on Corregidor, she assists the surgeon, her face in the makeshift light reflecting pain and fatigue. Not a word is necessary, just the natural nobility of that face held in close-up.

At a dance where she hooks up with PT skipper John Wayne, Donna is briefly the All-American Girl from Iowa, but their attention turns toward the sound of war coming closer. The same muted sense of doom hangs over the meager dinner Donna takes with the men before reporting to a field hospital on Bataan. Delighted to have her at their mess, they offer homemade biscuits and a serenade.

Just before the dinner scene was shot, Ford pulled from his pocket a string of pearls and presented it to Donna. The gesture demonstrated his mastery in establishing the right emotional pitch. In effect, the director was honoring the nurses taken prisoner at Corregidor. Deeply moved, Donna faced the camera thinking, as she would for years afterward, about their fate.

Finished before the atomic bomb fell on Hiroshima, *They Were Expendable* was released early in 1946. Donna traveled to Washington, D.C., for the premiere, arriving too late to ride a PT boat down the Potomac. From Admiral Chester Nimitz she received an autograph, and from General Leslie Graves a small box containing pale green crusted sand from the site of the atom bomb test in New Mexico. Forty years later, after her death, that box of sand was found in her personal effects.

Expendable was only moderately successful at the box office because audiences wanted to forget the war. Critics recognized its quality, however. The exacting James Agee wrote, "Visually, and in detail, and in nearly everything he does with people, I think it is John Ford's finest movie." It was certainly the turning point in Donna Reed's career; full stardom now seemed assured. The *New York Times* called Donna's acting "extraordinarily touching."

A woman in Missouri was *not* favorably impressed. Claiming that Donna's role (Peggy in White's book) was based on her tenure as an army nurse in the Philippines—that she was humiliated to be shown in a love affair with the Wayne character—she sued MGM and eventually collected $290,000.

Louella O. Parsons reported that John Ford "put the whole troupe through their paces, trying to finish Donna's scenes" in *Expendable* by June 15, 1945. On that day she married Tony Owen. The ceremony at the Community Presbyterian Church in Beverly Hills was attended by a dozen people, including Lillian Burns and Louis B. Mayer. Lavone Mullenger was maid of honor. The bride was conservatively dressed in a navy blue gabardine suit and white hat. An hour later Mayer saw Judy Garland and Vincente Minelli married in the same church by the same minister.

Then both couples boarded the same train, their compartments adjoining. Before the Super Chief departed, Tony Owen hosted a reception in the observation car, urging drinks and hors d'oeuvres on the crowd, enjoying the pops of the photographers (doubled for the Minellis, who did not show). That was pure Tony.

En route to Chicago and New York, Donna and her groom stopped off in Iowa. The farm was green, offering luxuries like butter and bacon. Tony hadn't seen thick cream since—before the war. A Hollywood agent used to backbiting and oneupmanship, he marveled at the Mullengers' attitude of all for one, one for all.

From Iowa the honeymooners entrained (a stylish word of the day) for the East. Donna's first good view of New York was from the thirty-eighth floor of the Waldorf Towers. In four days she and Tony saw five shows, ate at 21 and El Morocco and the Automat, rode the subway and ascended the Empire State Building, visited all the big stores, and walked blocks and blocks. Donna's favorite show was *The Glass Menagerie*. "Laurette Taylor is positively perfection in acting—I never hope to see a more complete character on the stage or screen," she wrote to her old school chum, Joyce Anderson. Soon they sped toward Tony's Chicago. In a few weeks the couple crowded in a lot (despite their bouts with strep throat). A man in the know had opened up two great cities to the new Mrs. Owen.

Home. Seeing the sun on the water when they woke up in their tiny beach house at Santa Monica made Donna and Tony feel that life was a long vacation. Their Early American furniture and barrels of Ohnstein family silver, arrived from New Orleans, practically put them outside the walls; but plans to build were in the air. They often joined their good friends and neighbors, Pat and Randolph Scott, for dinner and swimming. The studio was ten miles away.

By January 1946 Donna was driving there to make *Faithful in My Fashion*, an unpretentious romantic comedy. For the first time she was billed above her leading man, Tom Drake, a new heartthrob. Old reliables like Spring Byington, Harry Davenport, Margaret Hamilton, and Edward Everett Horton aid Donna in an elaborate masquerade: When soldier Drake returns on a furlough, she continues their romance to spare his feelings, though her heart now belongs to another. To prepare for her role as a sales clerk, Donna spent a day in the shoe department of a Los Angeles department store. Her talent for "comedy indecision" was noted by one reviewer, but the only thing about the movie remembered today is a love song, "I Don't Know Why."

Meanwhile, *They Were Expendable* hit the theaters. The director Frank Capra saw the picture and immediately wanted Donna Reed to play Mary Bailey in *It's a Wonderful Life*. Jean Arthur and Ginger Rogers had already spurned the role because it was "colorless" and "bland." But Capra saw in Donna a flowering of womanhood that departed from the brassiness of his earlier screen heroines. "She looked like she'd fall in love with a man and love him forever," he said. "It was a mother quality, almost. That honest, clear, clean face of hers—and she had an attitude about her that made her looks real."

After dickering, MGM agreed to loan Donna to RKO, where shooting began in April. *It's a Wonderful Life* proved to be the hardest work she had ever done. Capra was extremely demanding, exploiting Donna's own perfectionism to the point of exhaustion. She was twenty-five in 1946, and the role of Mary Bailey required her to age from eighteen to forty. It required her to sing, dance, and swim—skills not in her repertoire. The reassurance that Donna needed from Capra and her costar, James Stewart, was not forthcoming. Just back from the war, feeling their way in a new Hollywood, both men were wracked by anxiety. Years later Donna recalled the tenseness on the set. "Everybody was looking for approval but nobody was in a position to give it," she said. "I was terrified most of the time."

Nevertheless, she gave a performance of great poise. Much has been written about *It's a Wonderful Life* since its rediscovery on television, but not much about Donna Reed's part. Mary Bailey is more central to the story than she appears to be. She is not merely the childhood sweetheart turned wife who keeps George Bailey home when he wants to be exploring Tanganyika and building skyscrapers. She is as much a spiritual agent as Clarence Oddbody, for she leads the prayer that brings the second-class angel to earth. And it is really Mary, not Clarence, who reunites George with humanity. When the mislaying of public funds brings his crisis of fear and despair, she rallies the support of the townspeople. As they arrive at the Bailey house bearing hard-earned gifts, she cries, "It's a miracle! It's a miracle!" But the miracle has been based on her faith.

At the end of the movie, as a roomful of old character actors sing "Auld Lang Syne," Mary snuggles up to George by the Christmas tree, seemingly a bystander in the supernatural drama and unaware of how much has been her doing. Only an actress of Donna Reed's genuine sweetness of spirit and arresting physical presence could have brought things to this end while maintaining dramatic credibility. Almost any other actress in the role would have produced an entirely different movie.

Some first-rate writers who worked on the script would have changed Mary Bailey. As late as January 1946, Michael Wilson felt that Mary tended to be "a negative character, with little to do but burst into tears and become periodically pregnant." He drafted a scene showing George walking Mary home. She is excited because they are going away to college together next day. George says, "Why, it was just last year you were seventeen," and Mary replies, "I'm catching up with you, George. Remember—we're going to be in the same class at Cornell."

Wilson felt that the relationship between husband and wife needed to be "sharpened and enriched." He wanted to give Mary more edge. When George is called to take a physical exam for military service, he has Mary say, sarcastically, "Well, you got your wish. You always did want to get out of Bedford Falls." She wastes no time in asking Sam Wainwright (Hee Haw) for a job in his factory. "I'll be a welder, anything."

The scene revealing Mary's fate (because George wasn't alive to marry her) went through several versions. In one, Mary is the embittered wife of Wainwright, temporarily putting up in Potter's old house. "I've been living in New York the past twelve years, and to tell the truth there isn't much about Bedford Falls I wanted to remember," she says coldly to a visiting stranger (the unborn George), who frantically seeks her recognition.

(The version that was filmed, showing the spinster Mary Hatch locking up the library and fleeing in terror from the husbandly advances of the stranger George, has been criticized for its implausible stereotyping. When Frank Capra received the Lifetime Achievement Award from the American Film Institute in 1982, he confided to Donna that he wished this scene had presented Mary Hatch less hysterically, as strong and competent, unmarried or not. It was the only change he would have made in the movie.)

Preproduction revisions eliminated an interesting detail in the famous telephone scene that sealed George and Mary's engagement. In the original script, she offers him cake (rich in suggestions of domesticity and religious communion) at her house. Over the phone he rejects Sam Wainwright's offer of a job in plastics. He can't believe that Mary doesn't seem to care. "That's funny," he says, "most girls would think that I should settle down, knuckle down, feather the nest, make my pile." To which Mary replies, "If you want to spend the rest of your life building a bridge to the moon, that's your business." Then, smiling: "Sure you don't want some cake?" He's a goner. Incidentally, Reed and Stewart did their complex telephone scene, erotic without cake, in a single take.

Perennial viewers who have learned the dialogue of *It's a Wonderful Life* know that the proposed changes above didn't get filmed. Mary Bailey wasn't turned into a wry Jean Arthur or a chilly Constance Bennett or an independent Barbara Stanwyck—or even Rosie the Riveter. The last script took form in March, just as Donna Reed was being considered, and it is likely that her casting influenced the final conception of Mary Bailey. Capra (as well as Jo Swerling) was rewriting some of the scenes while directing Donna. She seems to have come close to his original image of Eternal Wife and Mother.

Like Jimmy Stewart, Donna got reams of advance publicity. In June she sat down in a wheat field for her first *Life* magazine cover. The home folks in Denison, Iowa, were proud but miffed because the magazine article referred to their town as "tiny." That month brought another bonus—named Penny Jane.

Coming from a large, happy family, Donna craved one of her own. So disappointment was acute when a doctor told the Owens they could not produce babies. Donna felt that she had a "knack" for mothering. And whatever her doubts about the high-stepping Tony as a husband, Donna wanted his fighting spirit passed on to her future children. Through him, she had come to appreciate the toughness needed to survive and succeed, especially in a place like Hollywood. Some years later, when her brood had grown to four (two of them proving that doctor wrong), Donna said in a remarkable interview: "I'm rather shy and gentle. Now what would have happened if I had mated with a man of the same disposition? Would all our children have turned out mice instead of men, timid little thumb-suckers instead of healthy, lively girls? The probability is strong. Wouldn't we have had real problems adjusting to the rough and tumble outer world? If I'd married a man of similar temperament, somewhat steady and cheerful, practical and quiet?"

Now, in June 1946, Donna asked Frank Capra for time off from *Wonderful Life*. A copper-haired baby girl was waiting for the Owens at The Cradle in Chicago. They flew to Iowa to pick up the Mullengers and then on to Illinois. Four-year-old Karen thought it "was the most exciting way to get a baby." Donna had brought her sister "a really cute rag doll with yellow overalls and she said the doll's name was Penny." The real Penny went back to California sharing Hazel's middle name, Jane.

It was a wonderful time for the Mullenger family. Lavone had signed with the Conover modeling agency in New York after her face appeared on the cover of *Coronet* magazine. She adopted the professional name of Heidi because her fresh looks reminded the Conovers of the Swiss heroine. Keith was a high-powered engineer with General Electric. Bill, at twenty, was still on the farm, garnering agricultural honors and winning friends with his ebullient personality. Donna was an established movie star with the release of *It's a Wonderful Life*.

The hoopla that attended the premiere of *Wonderful Life* in December petered out as box office returns fell early in 1947. Capra and Stewart, but for some reason not Reed, went on the road to drum up interest. Ads for the movie began to highlight the ordinary and surefire: a romantic triangle between "good girl" Donna, Jimmy, and Gloria Grahame, who was considered "bad" because she flirted and wiggled in her tight summer dress.

If *Wonderful Life* was out of joint with the more cynical postwar era, it was also a casualty of the general decline in movie attendance. The loss of foreign markets, higher cost of living, and tendency of reunited families to stay home at night made 1947 one of the worst business years in Hollywood history.

Critics had been impressed by Donna's gracious and self-possessed Mary Bailey. But the important roles she expected didn't materialize. Incredible as it seems now, she was blamed for the financial failure of *It's a Wonderful Life*. In the forties' world of Hollywood, run by and for men, she was an easy target.

In 1948 Donna was scheduled to appear opposite Van Johnson in *The Stratton Story*, but he was judged wrong for the ballplayer and replaced by James Stewart. Stung by the public rejection of *Wonderful Life*, Stewart rejected Donna as leading lady; and she was replaced by the ubiquitous June Allyson. Donna, who had already been costumed for the role, heard that Stewart was simply "thinking of his professional life." Believing they had acted together well, she was very hurt. "It was a hurt that lasted for years," said one who was close to her. Whenever Donna was asked to participate in a function honoring Jimmy Stewart, she would inquire, "Have you asked Miss Allyson?"

In the late forties no one would have predicted a wonderful afterlife for Frank Capra's movie. The medium of its eventual rebirth was being stifled: in 1947, Paramount was the only major studio interested in television. Most big-screen stars refused to appear on TV, partly because of the low pay. MGM decreed that its features and shorts could not be televised.

Although *It's a Wonderful Life* was broadcast on radio three times between 1947 and 1951 (with Donna and Jimmy, and Victor Moore as Clarence), the movie was more or less forgotten. In the early fifties, when

Donna Reed was asked by the *Saturday Evening Post* to write about her favorite role, she chose that of Marguerite Patourel in *Green Dolphin Street*.

Donna liked playing Marguerite, the daughter of a nineteenth-century shipowner in the Channel Islands, because her character changed and grew. The plot took some kind of prize. Marguerite's beau goes to New Zealand and in a drunken stupor writes a letter, mistakenly addressing it to *Marianne*, Marguerite's sister, and proposing marriage. Marianne, who also loves him, accepts his offer—leaving her sister to the nunnery. "Marguerite reacted to disappointment in love not by sitting around and sighing but by building a new spiritual life for herself," wrote Donna. Before taking the veil, though, she got a chance to wear such period costumes as a silk gown with a gauze collar and leg-of-mutton sleeves.

Donna can be excused for embracing a role that gave her something to do. At first she doubted that the hero would ever choose her over Marianne, who was Lana Turner. "Who's going to believe that? Lana's gorgeous," she said. "If I play that part, it'll ruin the picture." But she did lose the man, to her moral and dramatic advantage. When *Green Dolphin Street* was released on videocasette in the late eighties, the critic Rex Reed asserted that Donna had the best scene, one showing her in a cave, torturously climbing up and through to reach a convent.

In black and white, oddly enough, *Green Dolphin Street* was a big splashy production with thrills: an earthquake, a tidal wave, a shipwreck, a Maori uprising. The reviewers, suffering from surfeit, made sounds like urping. But the movie grossed a lot of money, five million dollars on first run. It was Donna's last for MGM under a long-term contract.

The Mullengers from Iowa visited Donna on the set of *Green Dolphin Street*. Little Karen shyly sang "Fuzzy Wuzzy Was a Bear" to crew and cast members. There is a memorable photograph of her and Bill and Hazel and Aunt Mildred watching Donna, who is wearing what appears to be a wedding gown. Bill looks as if he'd rather be on the farm.

The year 1947 was filled with moves affecting Donna's family. In June the Owens flew to Chicago to sign adoption papers for a three-month-old boy. Tony Junior was described a year later as "very quiet, observing, and sensitive." Big Tony said his son would probably end up playing the violin or flute. A bit later the family moved to a colonial-style home in

Beverly Hills. Donna was delighted, after two years of "living in dreary houses with bad furniture, no closet space, and two-by-four baths."

In a curious way Donna's Iowa past and Hollywood present overlapped. Her high school chemistry teacher in Denison, Edward Tompkins, the one who had advised her to read *How to Win Friends and Influence People*, later worked on the atom bomb at Oak Ridge, Tennessee. Seeing his name on the list of scientists, Donna wrote to him. He replied, wondering if a movie could be made about the bomb's implications for civilization. Tony Owen went directly to Louis B. Mayer, who enlisted producer Sam Marx in the project. Ultimately, Tony and Sam went all the way to Washington for President Truman's approval. The result was a movie released in 1947 titled *The Beginning or the End*, with a big cast headed by Robert Montgomery. Although Donna didn't play "the only woman who knew the secret of the bomb," she was linked with the making of the movie in newspaper articles. The headlines mixed sex and Donna Reed and the most serious topic of the time.

Dr. Tompkins was a technical adviser for *The Beginning or the End*. Tony Owen received acknowledgment in the titles and forty thousand dollars. The money was needed at home because Donna's salary was far from astronomical. She was the financial mainstay of a growing family. When Tony didn't receive what was owed him, she marched into Louis B. Mayer's silver-gilded office. Tony was paid. At MGM, she said much later, "you learned to plant your feet and fight." One who knew that very well, Mickey Rooney, wrote in *Life Is Too Short*: "Donna was sweet and demure. Inside, she was a tough dame."

In fact, Donna struggled long and hard for self-assurance. If she quickly gained a kind of sophistication, she still didn't feel at ease with Hollywood executives and luminaries. Her conversation didn't center on self—a disadvantage in the marathon of talkers who never centered on anything else. She hadn't completely emerged from her shy reticence when she married the gregarious Tony. For several years she was under his sexual spell.

"I *want* to do the things Tony wants me to do," Donna told a reporter. "If he wants to go to a movie, we go to a movie. If he wants to picnic on the beach, we picnic on the beach. If he wants to sit home by the fire, we sit home by the fire. I take pleasure in doing what he wants to do." At parties she would open her mouth to speak only to find Tony had the floor. Finally she was fed up. One night she shouted at him, she was so angry. She had a very un-Donna-Reed–like fit. He was amazed. "I can't believe it," he said. "You mean I talked over you? I didn't hear what you said?" Gradually she was granted a voice.

In the fall of 1947 Donna was set to do *The Long Grey Line* with Alan Ladd. She was ordered to West Point for a scene. Tony couldn't go with her, and she objected to being out there alone because the director had a reputation as a womanizer. "She didn't want to be put in that position," said the publicist Ann Straus, "so she called me up one Sunday and asked me to go along." Ann needed permission from Howard Stricklin, a tough boss. "I guess it's all right, if you have nothing else to do," he grumbled. Scared off, Ann went to Donna's house on Alpine Drive that evening. She took with her a Victorian English policeman's billy. "Donna, you'll have to take this club to protect yourself because I can't go," she said.

But Donna was determined not to go alone. That very night she called the producer to protest. Besides, her part at West Point was so small she could practically telephone it in! The next day Ann Straus was appointed chaperone and told to get packed. "Evidently the powers-that-be at Paramount called the powers at MGM and said that if Donna Reed didn't get to West Point happily the film deal was off. She got her way. She was becoming a strong person." On the train, she thoughtfully washed out Ann's stockings and insisted that her friend take the lower berth in the sleeping car.

Donna was on loanout to Paramount for *The Long Grey Line*, which was released in 1948 as *Beyond Glory*. She replaced Joan Caulfield as the widow of an officer whose death on a Tunisian battlefield was supposedly due to the negligence of soldier Alan Ladd. Cadet Ladd, now a plebe at West Point, faces a board of inquiry. Donna is an unexpected comfort to him. In one scene she dances with a new actor named Audie Murphy.

Beyond Glory was reasonably well done, containing more psychologizing than most other war movies and many flashbacks. One theater exhibitor in Georgia complained, "My patrons hate pictures to backtrack!" But business was good. Although reviewers liked Donna as the forgiving widow, she didn't think much of her role or the picture. It was all "pretty silly," she told Joyce Anderson. However, Alan Ladd was number two at the box office and costarring with him couldn't hurt.

Responding to a slump in the industry, all the studios cut budgets and payrolls in 1948. Donna Reed survived Metro's purge, but Lucille Ball and 123 other contract players did not. Since MGM had no parts for Donna, Paramount put her with Alan Ladd again. This pairing was even more profitable.

Chicago Deadline reflected the trend of postwar moviemaking. It emphasized story instead of expensive production values. The mood was "realistic," not Wonderful-Lifeish. Most of the characters were venal, some respectably so. Exteriors were shot, economically and authentically, on location in Chicago. (Movietone cameras, recording sound and image on the same filmstrip, were hidden in city streets; a special process ensured professional quality.)

Donna and Alan Ladd never acted together in the same scene. She is dead when he finds her in a cheap rooming house. A reporter, he reconstructs her life (through flashbacks) by running down the assorted characters named in her diary. He is intrigued by her mystery and becomes protective of her memory. "The spectator is made to feel that extreme danger hangs constantly over Ladd's head," said one reviewer when *Chicago Deadline* was released in 1949.

Donna had liked Warren Duff's screenplay and the original title, *One Woman*, meaning her. But the final result? She hoped friends would "carefully avoid me in my latest cinema adventure." To Joyce Anderson, now Joyce Fisk, she confided, "It really is pretty bad, and I don't do much to improve the situation."

Less critical than Donna, audiences loved *Chicago Deadline*. In 1949 it earned more than two million dollars, surpassing Ladd's highly touted *Great Gatsby* of the same year. Still not available on videocassette, it is widely considered an interesting example of film noir, the name later given to a class of moody, dark movies that mainly explored the urban underbelly.

Eight years under contract to MGM left Donna crying for a change.

Chicago Deadline had offered an offbeat sinner-saint role; but at the end, as at the beginning, she was a corpse while *Alan Ladd* acted. In 1949 she told a journalist, "With the exception of *Green Dolphin Street*, everything I have done has run along these lines: in scene one the hero says, 'Now honey, you stand here and wait while I go out and defeat the enemy, save thousands of lives, discover who has stolen my secret formula, find the murderer, or save my pal from the clutches of the law,' and then he comes back just in time to enfold me in his arms for a final clinch."

Well, she was tired of being a passive agent. "The next part I play must have at least one vital and dramatic scene, and it must be at the climax of the picture," she said. "To play colorless roles and try to add color to them is one of the most exacting duties that I know. But I've had all that training I want."

Still, Donna was grateful to MGM. Obtaining a contract while still in school, graduating from obscurity and financial need—what that had meant to her personally "could hardly be imagined." The studio had offered her the equivalent of a university education. She had learned about history, art, drama, and literature; learned foreign languages, photography, as well as styles in furniture, textiles, and clothing. "In a few years," said Ann Straus, "a little girl from Denison, Iowa, could hold her own with the best of them—in manners, knowing what to say, do, and wear."

She had a following. Adoring fans would attend her occasional radio broadcasts and present flowers. Her doings were described in a paper called *Donna's Reeder*.

That was nice. But no stargazer was needed to predict her future at MGM. When the studio cast her in the innocuous *Bride Goes Wild* she rebelled and June Allyson had to take the part. The end of a long association was sealed when she left *Scene of the Crime* for the best of all possible reasons.

CHAPTER FIVE

To *Eternity*

As if defying the doctors who had pronounced Donna and Tony barren, Timothy Grant Owen arrived squalling on July 19, 1949. A home movie shows a car pulling up to 704 Crescent Drive. The parents, looking very young and happy, are bringing their blanketed bundle from the hospital.

Four months later Donna was describing Timmy as "a very husky healthy guy." With dark eyes and hair, he looked like his daddy, except when he smiled. Then he looked like her.

This was November, and Donna was still incapacitated. A virus had settled in both her knees soon after Timmy's birth. She had been flat on her back in bed for weeks and now hobbled painfully on crutches. The worst had passed, after bad reactions from sedatives and procaine injections. "Ray Milland's experiences in *Lost Weekend* were mild compared to mine with Nimbutal," she wrote to Joyce Fisk. "Not only did I see things crawling on the ceiling, I rode up and down a fast elevator, went into tailspins, looped the loops, and found myself clinging to the bed in order to *stay* in bed. For two hours I had a real bender!"

Close friends were worried that Donna might never walk again without crutches. Lillian Burns went to her bedside almost every night. About that time, early in 1950, Lillian's husband, George Sidney, was directing *Annie Get Your Gun*. One evening the Sidneys invited Donna and Tony over to listen to Judy Garland's recording of the score. The men made a sling with their arms and carried Donna upstairs. Judy's rendition was rousing, but the group heard it with regret, knowing that personal problems had taken her off the film. When the music ended, Donna said that she was going—to—walk—down—those—stairs—without—any—help. "And she did," recalled Lillian, "and she did."

In 1950 Donna was eager to return to moviemaking. Her prime years were slipping away, and with them her chance for important roles. While convalescing, she read enough scripts to realize the rarity of good ones. Under contract to Columbia Pictures by July, she "got pushed into do-ing" *The Hero* with John Derek.

Pushed by Tony, she might have added. For several years he had been associated with Columbia, beginning as an assistant to the president, Harry Cohn.

Tony seems to have liked the much-hated Cohn, who once boasted of paving Gower Street with the bones of people he crushed. Cohn was drawn to the chutzpah of the former Chicago newspaperman. He spent four years wooing Tony away from the Feldman-Blum agency, finally hooking him by guaranteeing a yearly salary of fifty grand and an office next to his own. As it turned out, there was no office for Tony when he ar-rived at the studio, and his first paycheck was for a measly $350. When he complained, Cohn said, "Well, the boys in New York weren't happy with the deal I made with you."

Now in 1950 Tony's career was moving modestly. He had just produced a Joan Davis vehicle, *The Traveling Saleswoman.* Costing only $200,000, it was turning a profit for Columbia.

Tony would remain a minor producer, but Columbia was not a bad place to be in the fifties, when the studio brought in such independent filmmakers as Sam Spiegel, Jerry Wald, and Stanley Kramer. Lillian Burns Sidney, sometimes called Donna's alter ego, arrived as Harry Cohn's ex-ecutive assistant. For a few years Donna would feel as secure as an actress ever can. She had no illusions about Cohn, but got along with him. In fact, the Owens and Cohns became social friends, going out to dinner and visiting back and forth. "Harry had the greatest respect for Donna," said Lillian, who never heard him say anything stronger than *goddamn.* "He had one saying: He knew a lady from a tramp, and I think he acted accordingly."

Cohn wanted Donna to play the upper-crust Melissa in *The Hero,* soon retitled *Saturday's Hero.* She passed the arduous test, a three-page scene that took two and a half days to shoot. The director, David Miller, sensed the passion behind Donna's self-containment. "She had something inside her—like a pacemaker that pumps the heart," he said. This quality of tightly controlled combustion was right for the role of Melissa, a socialite involved with a football player whose college scholarship offers escape from the poverty of his Polish immigrant parents.

Donna subtly combined her own warmth and sincerity with the coolness and cynicism of the character in Millard Lampell's novel and screenplay. The result was a performance that some reviewers found neurotic and strangely disturbing—as if ambiguity belonged to a novel but not to a film.

Early on, the script ran afoul of the moral arbiters in the Breen Office, who thought that Melissa's close relationship with her possessive uncle suggested incest. Miller satisfied the censors by coaching Donna and Sidney Blackmer in the use of posture, movement, and eye contact to convey their nonsexual struggle for dominance and release. He was an old-fashioned craftsman who believed that movies, like children, should be seen more often than heard.

Other difficulties loomed in the making of *Saturday's Hero*. Because it exposed the corruption in collegiate sports, no Ivy League university would permit location shooting. Finally, the backgrounds were pieced together from various campuses. Twenty UCLA and USC football players appeared in action sequences, but a firm agreement blocked screen credit and publicity. Undeterred, Donna, John Derek, and other members of the cast and crew felt a special obligation not to dilute the message of the movie, David Miller recalled.

Saturday's Hero was widely noticed in 1951. And no wonder. An advertisement read: "Here is the real story of the kept men of big-time college sports. You'll listen to the boys' own mocking laughter at what used to be—and is still called—the honor system. You'll see the injuries bought and paid for. You'll meet coaches who have to win, or lose their five-figure salaries. You'll watch boys accept passing marks for exams they never took. You'll get to know the touchdown-hungry alumni."

In spite of reviews praising its honesty, the movie was not commercially successful. No wonder. Angry sportswriters broke into unaccustomed eloquence. At the moment of its booking into theaters, the producer, Sidney Buchman, testified before the House of Un-American

Activities Committee, admitting to his former membership in the Communist Party without implicating others or invoking the Fifth Amendment. Theaters showing the movie were picketed by groups not easily identifiable—and not knowing who to sue was a frustration to Harry Cohn, according to Alexander Knox, one of the players. A reporter for *Look* magazine wrote, "As a sidetent of Americana, *Saturday's Hero* will please more Communist propagandists than college presidents." All this hurt.

"To all intents and purposes it is a top production," Donna told Joyce Fisk. But she thought that her romantic pairing with the baby-faced John Derek, five years her junior, was "preposterous." If that comment seems irrelevant now, the topic of *Saturday's Hero* is more relevant than ever. It is the most neglected good movie she made.

Donna was too busy living to play the star. Unlike many professional beauties who smiled only with their mouths to avoid crinkling about the eyes, Donna seems never to have pampered her looks, beyond the usual rituals. Her letters during the early fifties are filled with homey news—childhood illnesses, visits from the family in Iowa, gardening. She was keenly interested in the careers of her siblings, stayed connected to old friends, indulged interests like photography, collected antiques, yearned to travel, and read and read. Boredom wasn't in her vocabulary.

She loved being mother to the "self-sufficient, aggressive" Penny; the "sweet, affectionate" Tony Junior; and pretty Timmy, who would slip into her bed to cuddle. By late 1950 the Owens had moved to a house in Coldwater Canyon. A Georgian colonial, modeled on Mount Vernon, it was "too large in some respects" and boasted a flagstone terrace built around huge oaks—but no swimming pool. "Got room for at least three more kids!" she told Joyce.

Tony set up office at home after leaving his position at Columbia. He had been an all-purpose man, even a chauffeur, for Harry Cohn, arriving early before the secretaries and leaving late, often missing dinner with Donna and the children. Finally, she spoke out: "You'd better decide which you'd rather be, my husband or Harry Cohn's stooge." That stung. For all his wheeling, Tony could be naive. When he beat out other studios for a Hugo Haas picture (probably *Pickup*, starring Cleo Moore), Cohn was so happy that he promised him twenty-five percent of the gross. Costing only $110,000 to make, it earned over a million in one year. But Tony never got a percentage. "I didn't have it on paper," he explained to Bob Thomas later. Instead, he got a Christmas bonus in 1950—a blue Cadillac convertible.

The Owens had increasing responsibilities. With Tony's career in abeyance, Donna had to make more money, not more babies. Tony, for his part, was always full of ideas and projects. He might do a series of semi-documentary science films for youngsters or, less nobly, produce a musical exploiting beefcake instead of cheesecake. In January 1951 Tony, accompanied by Donna, attended a meeting of the Professional Football League in New York. According to the *Los Angeles Examiner*, one of the teams had offered him the job of manager. It didn't develop, and another fantasy bit the dust.

Professionally, the year wasn't a distinguished one for either Owen. Donna costarred with John Derek again, and this time her name was billed above his. *Scandal Sheet* was based on a Samuel Fuller novel with a better title, *The Dark Page*. Broderick Crawford played the sleaze-mongering, murdering editor who finally becomes the quarry of his two ace reporters. William Holden had rejected Derek's role, perhaps knowing of the studio's intention to produce the movie as cheaply as possible. However, Burnett Guffey's black and gray and pearly white photography is not cheap, and Donna looks somberly attractive. *Scandal Sheet* got no respect when released, but today it has a considerable following among film noir buffs.

"Busy, busy, rush, rush!" was how Donna described her life in the fall of 1951. While on a tour to promote *Saturday's Hero*, she stopped in Detroit to see Joyce Fisk, now a radio broadcaster. At the local station the engineer cut off an interview before Donna could talk about her old school chum. After returning to California, she reflected sadly on the subordination of friendship to nearly everything else. "I found myself being weepy over not seeing more of you in this all too short life," she wrote to Joyce. "I have many acquaintances, but the fact suddenly struck me: I don't know anyone here for whom I have great regard or feeling, and certainly there doesn't exist a sympatico that did and does with us."

Denison, Iowa, seemed farther away than thirteen years. Excitement now depended less on the world of movies and more on the world away from them. In January 1952 Donna and Tony boarded a Boeing Stratocruiser for South America. As part of the American delegation to a film festival in Uruguay, they were given every "courteous attention" and greeted by crowds. Although the screening fest at Punta del Este was "a joke," the gorgeous sea and shore opened up one's senses. Some of the countryside looked "just like Iowa with a little California foliage thrown in." Routine was a crazy jumble, with morning sleep-ins and all-night dancing. During this twenty-thousand-mile trip, Donna caught "the tourista bug" for life. From the air she photographed the "frightening" Andes and the "visionary beauty" of Rio de Janeiro. Her favorite city was Buenos Aires, in spite of the omnipresent signs of Evita and Juan Peron.

Donna wanted to stay a month, visiting the friendly Argentines in their estancias. But not even a movie star could afford such luxurious laziness. Back home, she reported to a studio that had no roles for her. In the early fifties a movie career was harder to sustain because the studios were earning and producing less, partly due to the encroachment of television. In 1946 an average of ninety million people had gone to the movies every week; by 1950 the number was down to sixty million a week and falling rapidly. "The swimming pools are drying up all over Hollywood," one wag said.

Tony finally asked old friend Randolph Scott to use Donna as a leading lady. In April 1952 she joined Scott on the set of *Hangman's Knot*. This color Western was solidly made in eighteen days at Lone Pine and a North Hollywood backlot. Claude Jarman Jr., who had appeared memorably as Jody in *The Yearling* and was reduced here to soldiering, remembered Donna's refined prettiness but was more fascinated by newcomer Lee Marvin. In the screen universe of the stiff-lipped Scott there was no place for Donna (or for Jeanette Nolan, a former Lady Macbeth) except as nurse or chattel. When *Hangman's Knot* opened on a double bill in Los Angeles, one reviewer counted only fifty-four corpses in it. Hollywood shot too many pictures and not enough actors, he said, quoting Bob Hope.

That spring Donna got a stab at comedy, but on radio. She and John Lund taped "The Mating of Millie" for airing on *Screen Guild Theater*,

Easter Sunday. Playing for laughs was "fun," and she probably "needed a little more practice." It was in the nature of a dare, like making an untried souffle for dinner guests. Although Donna wanted to try summer stock—*The Moon Is Blue* would be delicious—she was still terrified of television. Tony, however, was filming some half-hour TV programs. And Heidi had beaten her big sister to the home screen. When the New York model appeared live on *Blind Date*, Donna was "so scared" for her she could hardly watch.

It was a strange year, 1952. Donna's letters reveal frenetic activity in her career and yet a sense of stasis. Even in droughttime, she was leading lady in three pictures and flew around on promotional tours, but clearly often felt that she was "merely collecting a weekly paycheck" while "nothing, absolutely nothing" was happening at the studio. She yearned for more challenging assignments and yet seemed comfortable with tub-roilers like *Raiders of the Seven Seas*. She guarded her time with the children, and wanted more "after I get a few more pics under my belt," but of course her options were limited by the three she already had. Timmy, in particular, was upset by leavetakings. So many things seem to be pulling at her in these hasty, newsy, somewhat unfocused letters!

Summer found Donna on a Movietime USA tour through Montana, arriving at town squares as bands played. At a huge buffalo reserve near St. Ignatius she was officially adopted into the Flathead Indian tribe and named Princess Eagle Feather.

In the fall she was a countess—behind cameras. Romanced by the pirate Barbarossa, or John Payne, Donna was splendidly costumed in *Raiders of the Seven Seas*, which was filmed nowhere near the water. It was a B picture, the kind associated in memory with rainy Saturday matinees at Rialtos and Bijous reeking of hot popcorn and peanuts.

Before winter came she shot *Trouble Along the Way* for Warner Brothers—not a B, because John Wayne costarred and Michael Curtiz directed. And not very good, either. Playing college football for chuckles and sentiment, *Trouble* made money with hokum, whereas *Saturday's Hero* had lost with honesty.

Donna appears as a social worker whose frigidity is cured by Wayne's first rough embrace. Away from the camera, she took shorthand and transcribed Duke's letters, according to the Warner publicists. They made a brainy woman with wide-ranging interests sound as bland as the public Pat Nixon. But Donna *was* a fifties' female, telling the reporters, "Stenographers make the best wives. As a secretary you get to know the likes and dislikes of men, how they think, and how to handle them." For *Trouble*, Donna earned considerably more than a stenographer— $30,000, or enough to keep the household in Coldwater Canyon going. The movie has no standing, but latter-day devotees of James Dean, who supposedly was an extra, still look for his phantom.

The year ended with few aware of Donna's protracted fight for the most extraordinary role of her career. It was a humbling, if not humiliating, experience.

Donna knew the odds against her in campaigning for a role that countered her wholesome image. In Hollywood, as elsewhere, creative and business decisions were based on rigid notions about the scope of any talent. In the past Donna had auditioned extremely well for different roles— and lost because someone just couldn't "see" her in them. So without much hope she tested for the prostitute Alma in *From Here to Eternity*.

At least fifty chesty, curvy actresses vied for the star-making role. Shelley Winters and Gloria Grahame were serious contenders. Fred Zinnemann, preparing to direct, wanted Julie Harris. No one wanted Donna Reed—certainly not Zinnemann or the producer, Buddy Adler, or the actors already cast. No one but Harry Cohn, who was afraid of losing artistic control if a Columbia player wasn't among the principals.

Donna tested twice with Aldo Ray, Cohn's choice for the part of Private Prewitt. The camera held on his face and showed only the back of her head or partial profile. Zinnemann took her no more seriously than a prop, a feeder of lines. "Then came a dreadful silence," said Donna later. "No one at Columbia even called to thank me." She had dyed her hair black and now had to bleach it because Michael Curtiz wanted a blonde for *Trouble Along the Way*.

A few months later Cohn ordered Donna to test with Aldo Ray again, with her hair colored black. "Don't ask any questions, just do it," he said. More silence followed.

A third test paired her with Montgomery Clift, Zinnemann's choice for Prewitt. This time she was shown full-face. It was the scene in which Alma expresses her desire to be "proper." But Donna faltered, and not simply because she had a virus that day and a temperature of 101.

Cohn ran the test for Lillian Sidney and asked, "What's wrong?" Lillian answered, "It's clear they didn't want her, and she knew it. She doubted. She doesn't know at the moment what she's doing with that girl because there's been no discussion."

At Cohn's request, Lillian telephoned Donna. For an hour they talked intensely about early days in Iowa, when Donna had witnessed hardship, worn second-hand clothes, felt snubbed by the town girls—and about early days in California, when she had cooked and laundered and scrubbed floors for her room and board. They talked about what it meant to work so hard for everything, about the legacy of a father's roving mind and a mother's discontent. "Donna wanted that farm in Iowa to be the best," said Lillian. "She wanted her family to have the best." Alma in James Jones's novel was also fiercely determined: She wanted to own a house on the right side of the train tracks and belong to the country club and the Book-of-the-Month Club. Such ambition the "dog soljer" Prewitt could never understand. Just as some close to Donna never understood what drove her.

According to Lillian, Donna got "the essence" of Alma's character from that phone call; really, from herself. Testing continued. Now she was competing with a dark-haired actress named Roberta Haynes. For months in 1952 she was "diddled with," to use the language of her daughter's generation. Then on a Friday in late February 1953, almost at midnight, Cohn called to offer Donna the role of Alma. She was to report for rehearsal on Monday morning.

"One could not forever say no to Cohn," wrote Fred Zinnemann in his autobiography. He conceded that Donna fit the description of "princess," as Alma was called by the other women at the New Congress Club. Paradoxically, she also brought to the role the "bourgeois quality" that James Jones had intended.

The first scenes of *Eternity* to be filmed were those in the club. The

Breen Office, worried about immorality, insisted that Alma and the other prostitutes be portrayed as hostesses in a legitimate business. During scenes with Montgomery Clift, Donna realized that no close-ups were being shot of her. Years later she told the Hollywood biographer Bob Thomas that she dared not complain to Cohn. When she approached Zinnemann, he said, "That's the trouble, you worry about things like that." But Donna, who had learned a lot about lighting and camera angles, made a list of the missing shots. Then she conferred with the editor, William Lyon, who went to Cohn. The requisite close-ups of Donna were ordered—and filmed, not without difficulty.

Family members say that Donna experienced alienation on the set of *Eternity*. She was present, everyone knew, because of Harry Cohn's power. For other reasons, she didn't quite fit in. Though hardly a prig after more than a decade of picture-making, she seems to have felt out of place among some fast-livers and hard drinkers. Hanging out with the company was James Jones, who later boasted of his sexual success with the women. There was an aura of European sophistication and a soup-çon of snobbishness—Monty Clift, with his boyish intensity and Broadway background, was the pet. Despite Monty's professional helpfulness, Donna couldn't have felt at home on that set.

Donna's favorite scene—the final one on shipboard with Deborah Kerr—was also the most fearful. During rehearsal her impulse was to say "excuse me" and reenter, because for the first time in her career she was sharing the spotlight with a leading actress of serious repute. Overcoming her diffidence, Donna looked on the scene as an acting duel with Kerr, one in which there could be no tie. "She was relieved when the scene was over, and came away feeling that she had won," said a confidant of later days.

Deborah Kerr, who praised Donna's playing, was unaware of her sense of being outside. "We seldom met during the production," Miss Kerr wrote, "and it is true that the cast tended to concentrate on their relationships—mine with Burt Lancaster and Monty Clift and Frank Sinatra—and probably Donna *did* feel separated from the whole." An April flight to Hawaii for location filming was emblematic. Donna wasn't on board with her costars and took another plane. Cohn was irate because she couldn't pose with them for the paparazzi.

Harry Cohn inserted himself into the production whenever possible, once threatening cancellation if Clift did not play "Taps" for the Sinatra character, Maggio. Cohn was especially interested in how Donna fared. In late May, with the shooting completed, he issued sheets of cutting or editing suggestions. "You forgot to sell the character of Lorene [Alma]," he wrote, referring to her meeting with Prewitt. Cohn thought the first scene between them was "badly out of balance and should be recut." In the margin, someone, possibly Zinnemann, responded, "I like you just the same but should *not* be her CU." Cohn fussed about other details involving Donna: Wouldn't it be wiser to keep some of her footage in this scene or that? Did she look "too brittle" when Prew saw her at the New Congress a second time? Was there enough passion in her speech about wanting to be proper?

Zinnemann has always asserted that Montgomery Clift's acting drew Donna beyond the limits of her talent. So it is ironic that Donna, during the making of *Eternity*, considered Clift "no great shakes as an actor." He was, she told Joyce Fisk, "extremely intelligent and sensitive: quite good to work with, aside from the talent aspect." But when she saw the movie several years later it was Monty who moved her to tears. Her own role she didn't think much of, at first—or Deborah Kerr's, either. She told Hedda Hopper, "The women were completely overshadowed by the men." As usual.

And yet, and yet. While the prostitute provided a dramatic leap, she was "the easiest thing I ever did," Donna reflected ten years before her death. How much harder to play a reasonably normal woman and make her credible and interesting, and how little anyone noticed! The juicy women's roles were exaggerated or stylized. What was subtle about Joan Crawford of the wide shoulders suffering under mink? Or Bette Davis of the poached eyes having a hissy? Or Rosalind Russell of the vivid presence cracking wise?

Alma wasn't exaggerated as Donna played her, but she was a character. For the role Donna dyed her hair almost black, flattened her voice and adopted a speech pattern unlike her own, even changed her walk. She wore no makeup. "This was to make me look not so good, but I'm wondering if that Iowa look didn't come through instead!" she wrote to Joyce Fisk just before the movie was released.

Cohn wanted the publicity to emphasize Donna. In August she appeared on her second *Life* cover—"as James Jones's Alma." *From Here to Eternity* was released that month to fanfare that lasted the rest of 1953 and much of 1954. Donna attended the opening at the Capitol Theater in New York; her name was ranked with Burt Lancaster's on the front of the marquee. Seating nearly five thousand, the Capitol was filled and emptied and refilled around the clock. The theater set a box-office record for a premiere run.

A lot of ink was spilled over "the new Donna Reed." She told one interviewer: "Pish and tosh! Nothing cooks with a *new* me. It's just that I've been able to crawl out from under all those nicey nice parts that have been smothering me for twelve years."

Some Hollywoodians criticized Donna for not looking or acting like a whore. But to her that was the whole point of Alma, whom James Jones described as having a "Madonna face." Her impersonation confounded those who expected the stereotyped girl-next-door to play the stereotyped prostitute. It was a polished performance, subtle where it might have been broad, and upstaged by male bravura—much as Claire Trevor's carefully nuanced prostitute in *Stagecoach* had been outgunned and john-wayned.

Alton Cook of the *New York World Telegram* wrote, "This is a man's picture, and the poetic playing of Deborah Kerr and Donna Reed becomes undeservedly incidental." But foreshadowing latter-day opinion, Manny Farber of the *Nation* thought Donna and Frank Sinatra were the best things about the movie. Clift is intent on giving a "big" performance, said Farber. Lancaster "does everything with a glib, showy Tarzanism." Kerr "is a fluent actress who never lets you forget she is acting." But Farber would award a "laurel wreath" to the "unknown person who first decided to [cast] Frank Sinatra and Donna Reed in [their] unsweetened roles." Miss Reed, he said, "is an interesting actress whenever cameraman Burnett Guffey uses a hard light on her somewhat bitter features."

On the evening of March 25, 1954, Donna was assured a place in motion picture history. She and Tony and Esther Williams and her husband, Ben Gage, arrived at the Pantages Theater in Los Angeles for one of the industry's first televised blowouts. Donna won an Academy Award for her portrayal of Alma in *From Here to Eternity*, and no camera ignored her. When Walter Brennan announced her name, she ran all the way from the rear of the theater to the stage. After her acceptance speech, she turned to leave and sharp pain shot from her neck to the top of her head. "I've been beside myself with excitement," she would write to Joyce Fisk a few days later. "That old Oscar is darned hard to catch—and he's mighty pretty to look at too."

Sinatra was a shoo-in for his award. Although billed as stars, Donna and Frank were nominated as supporting players. Today the winners in that category may be obscure to the general public, but in the sunset of the studio era they were often names evoking memories. So, in a sense, Donna was attended in her victory by the sweetheart of Andy Hardy, the moral preceptor of Dorian Gray, the doomed nurse on Bataan, the gracious wife of George Bailey—as well as by the determined prostitute who, Donna felt sure, would never find social acceptance.

Back in Iowa the Mullengers, watching television in the farmhouse parlor where Donna had once sewed and played piano, laughed as she sprinted down the aisle at the Pantages. Hazel, noting the decolletage of Donna's blue-gray lace gown, remarked, "Well, I don't think that's a very nice dress for her to be wearing." Then, overcome with happiness, she cried.

It was a late hour, too, for the Owen children. At the house in Coldwater Canyon they were in pajamas and lounging in front of the TV set. That evening four-year-old Timmy became aware that his mother had a public face.

CHAPTER SIX

From *Eternity*

It's a Wonderful Life had promised major stardom without delivering. Now, seven years later, Donna seemed to have a second chance. The studio was "hysterically happy" about her performance in *From Here to Eternity*, she told Joyce Fisk in April 1953. But she was apprehensive, as if viewing a replay of her trained self picking up speed on a sharply curved Olympian track.

A month later she was knocked for a loop: Harry Cohn cast her in a fifteen-day B. It was to follow her highly visible role in the year's most important movie! No way, said Donna. Cohn answered in effect: no pay. Then he relegated her to routine Westerns.

For all the excitement over *Eternity*, the period stretching from May 1953, when it was completed, to February 1954, when Donna was nominated for the Oscar, was an unhappy one for her, personally and professionally.

Later she referred to the "agony" of those months. Marriage to Tony was increasingly difficult, and moguls like Cohn—who was "a little dictator"—didn't allow her to forget their power. The career of Donna Reed illustrates how little use Hollywood had for a leading lady who was beautiful without being dumb, intelligent without being abrasive, strong without being unfeminine, sexy without being sirenish, and interesting without being neurotic.

The first of three "dogs" (Donna's word) in a row was *Gun Fury*, filmed in June with a likable newcomer named Rock Hudson. Donna could read the signs: The studios customarily paired actresses past their peak with young actors on a rapid climb. Nominally directed by Raoul Walsh, *Gun Fury* was typical except for the gorgeous color of the Arizona background. Audiences were thrilled by fists and rattlesnakes striking out at them, but the 3-D process had already lost its novelty. There was "not a single peaceful moment" in the movie, wrote one reviewer. Another, surprised to find the star of *Eternity* mixed up in it, politely nodded her way: "Miss Reed's artistry shows through as she makes her role more than the usual oater heroine."

For months Tony had planned a picture to be photographed in Africa and England. The footage for *Duel in the Jungle*, starring Dana Andrews and Jeanne Crain, would prove costly because the quality was disappointing and the assistant director drowned in the Zambesi River. But the commercial project began as an adventure to please the Walter Mitty side of Tony. In August 1953, after making myriad arrangements, he flew with the cast and crew to Johannesburg for six or seven weeks of rigorous location shooting in South Africa and Rhodesia. Donna wrote to him every day.

Her long letters to "Dearest T.O." that fall were signed "Bug" or "Donnabug." Alternating between affection and anger, they reveal the strain in their relationship. "Tony, it isn't impossible to love you, you are making it impossible!" she wrote in early September. "You have charm, charm, charm for everyone, especially the women, and *nothing* for me. Dutiful devotion, criticism, and childish ideas about what a woman should be! For the hundredth time, a little more charm and sweetness for *me* and you won't find me as difficult as you think I am."

Even at long distance, there was quite a bit of "grinding" between them. Tony, evidently jealous of male attentions to her, hammered away. She had had enough: "It really is ridiculous, and I am adamant. No more talk about the above-mentioned persons or I shall have to stop or alter drastically my correspondence with you."

Donna could give as good as she got. Hardly blind to Tony's womanizing, she wrote: "Oh boy, wait until you hear the details of the Kinsey Report. It has caused some hullabaloo. Won't go into detail, but he seems to have found that women enjoy sex to a much riper old age than men. They reach their peak ten years later than men (about 28) and from there on things stay fine until about 60, and other interesting things have come out too." A December letter was half-teasing: "Tell——not to hold her breath until you return, in case you do come home for Xmas—she might expire! (I couldn't miss seeing the note from her which you kept in your files!)"

Always closing with "love and kisses," these letters show how hard Donna was trying to hold everything together. A traditional woman committed to motherhood, she was taking the children shopping, nursing their illnesses, preparing meals when Jessie was off, sewing and altering clothes with a frugality taught by her own Depression childhood. Typing in capital letters, she related "cute" stories about handsome Timmy, gentle Tony, and bright Penny to "Daddy Wise Eyes" across the seas.

Committed to her marriage, Donna forwarded Tony's mail and advised him not to leave London (where interiors were being filmed) until the movie was finished, even if that meant missing Christmas at home. "Don't run out because of your restlessness," she wrote. "Remember what has happened before in similar circumstances. *You* are the loser, and a few extra weeks of not being with your family or having better food are unimportant compared with the loss you generally suffer careerwise and financially, so don't louse it up!"

Donna fed her husband news headlines that he might miss in remote Africa: Adenauer had won a big victory in West Germany, Florence Chadwick was swimming the English Channel, Lana and Lex and Rita and Dick were marrying ("Oh dear! Poor souls!"). She warned him to watch out for the snakes and wanted to hear more about the Zulus. She handled his complicated business affairs, shifting money from her bank account to his to prevent checks from bouncing. Because she wasn't drawing a full salary and his was slow in reaching her, money was short. Obligations were long. "It seems we're always in a financial mess for some reason or another," she wrote. "*Something* must be done to put us on a better basis. This stinks."

Donna's wide-ranging letters say little about Columbia's treatment of her since *Eternity*, apparently because Tony had forbidden the subject. But her displeasure with the studio is manifest in a September letter. Sick with a bad cold, she called a Columbia executive to beg off going to Portland for the opening of *Eternity*. He sent a doctor to the house to check her. Although Donna felt miserable, the doctor ignored her symptoms until she demanded three days of bed rest. Finally the doctor used the telephone to describe her condition to the studio executive, who relented. "How I hate that mean nasty man—he's as bad as Cohn!" she told Tony. "*Everything* is a Dreyfus case."

That fall another low-budget Western was thrown at Donna. *They Rode West* put her with Robert Francis, who was assuming leads in minor films after scoring in *The Caine Mutiny*. (Several years later he would die in the crash of a private plane.) Like *Gun Fury*, the film used to groom Rock Hudson, *They Rode West* is competently made but entirely undistinguished. Donna, a flirtatious belle visiting a cavalry post in the 1870s, is shown singing (the voice was dubbed) at a campfire: "Kiss me quick and go my honey, and bring me back some Irish whiskey, I'm feeling mighty low."

Before this assignment, Donna sent a letter to Tony containing rows of XXXXX's. She explained: "The preceding two lines which have just been scratched out were comments on my career, which in a moment of forgetfulness slipped out, and since you so vehemently asked me to avoid such I shall do my best to do so, except when it concerns my whereabouts."

Some of the tension between them was dissipated in humorous chiding. She thanked Tony for a newspaper photo: "The clipping in which you are featured wearing a California sports shirt at luncheon in dear old England—now really, aren't you working overtime being a character? You look well, but hardly appropriate. (I think you photograph better in foreign lands.)"

Donna was emotionally and economically joined to this impossible man, and she missed terribly his vital presence. So did the children. As the holidays approached, they thought every plane that flew over was bringing him home and wanted her to drive quickly to the airport. He was shipping English bicycles for the kids, but when they didn't arrive on December 21 Donna scurried to buy and wrap presents in his name.

Tony was expected by Christmas Day. Then a cable from him on December 22 read: "Sorry I can't make it after all." On Christmas Eve a friend called from New York to say that he had just talked with Tony in London and could connect Donna with his transatlantic line. She was resigned to his absence when, that evening, the doorbell rang—and there stood Tony.

He had been phoning from New York, faking the faraway sound. That Tee-Ooo! From his coat jumped a black French poodle puppy, a breed that would turn silver in maturity and was still rare in America. Choufleur soon accepted the Owen family and answered to Chou Chou.

Donna was playing in all the theaters as 1953 ended. *From Here to Eternity* was the top-grossing picture; *The Caddy*, which Donna had made just before *Eternity*, was the runner-up when released. If *Eternity* is the apex of her movie career, the Martin and Lewis *Caddy* is close to the nadir. She is required only to look bunny-soft and in the pink as Dean Martin sings "That's Amoré." A journalist who admired Donna in *Eternity* wondered why she was concurrently in something like *The Caddy*. "What Miss Reed is doing in such giddy company is at least open to conjecture," he wrote.

Similar puzzlement was expressed by reviewers of *Three Hours to Kill* in the fall of 1954, after Donna had won an Oscar. Reminiscent of *High Noon* in some respects, *Three Hours to Kill* features Donna as an unmarried mother whose lover, Dana Andrews, is charged with the murder of her brother. Little in this situation is developed from the woman's point of view. Socially and dramatically she is marginalized while her wrathful lover faces down the town. Tense and spare, *Three Hours to Kill* is the best of the trio of Westerns that Donna was assigned on the heels of *Eternity*. But it was barely promoted—not even her children have heard of it.

Donna's billing below the title of *Three Hours to Kill* was a sign of her fallen estate at Columbia. She couldn't account for Harry Cohn's cavalier treatment of her after *Eternity* was wrapped up. She had thanked him for the role of Alma, proved she could act, and never wasted time on temper tantrums, however strongly she felt. It made no sense that her future at Columbia was being devalued, no more sense than her fate at MGM after *It's a Wonderful Life*. Perplexed, and demoralized after a string of Westerns that she never bothered to see, Donna asked for—and was granted— release from her contract in early February.

Four days later she was nominated for the Academy Award. That thrill was accompanied by a sense of irony. Being under contract to Columbia had bestowed *Eternity*, but for contractual reasons she was nominated for support while Deborah Kerr, whose role was no larger, was nominated for best actress. (In the sixties Patricia Neal would win the top acting award for a role—in *Hud*—smaller than Donna's Alma.) If Hollywood life wasn't always fair, it could be good, and away from Columbia might get better.

At thirty-three Donna craved more important romantic leads and another child, and the clock was ticking away. Tony, more interested in producing than parenting, worked to acquire screen properties for her. She wanted to costar with Kirk Douglas in *Heaven Knows, Mr. Allison*, the story of a nun stranded with a marine on an island. Tony was within minutes of buying the screenplay when the owner exercised his option; the part eventually went to Deborah Kerr. Donna longed to play the Eurasian doctor in *Love Is a Many-Splendored Thing*, and didn't (the title song would be sung at her funeral many years later). By March 1954, when Donna hurried down the aisle at the Pantages Theater to receive her Oscar, two roles were lined up for her: that of an American expatriate in *The Last Time I Saw Paris* and that of Mrs. Sigmund Romberg in *Deep in My Heart*. Her schedule couldn't be arranged for the composer's wife.

Donna's first outing as a freelancer was *The Last Time I Saw Paris*, a big MGM production with color-drenched bistros and boulevards. A cherry bombe drowned in raspberry and lemon sauce. Partly shot in Paris and on the Riviera, it offered Donna a stretch, if not a trip abroad. She is the nastiest kind of American Puritan, living with her cowed husband in Paris. They are guardians of the daughter of her late sister (Elizabeth Taylor), who died through the negligence of her husband (Van Johnson), an alcoholic writer. After some time in America, a successful and sober Johnson returns to Paris to beg the unforgiving Donna for custody of his little girl. That situation is taken from F. Scott Fitzgerald's "Babylon Revisited." But all that made the short story haunting and nostalgic is lost when the movie invents the Taylor-Johnson scenes in flashback and moves the time period from the reckless twenties to post–World War II.

The embittered sister-in-law played by Donna is the strongest throwback to Fitzgerald's story. Disapproval of Johnson's character is evident in her set face and flickering dark eyes. But the movie blames unrequited love for some of her bad feeling and gives her trite dialogue. *The Last Time*

I Saw Paris shows how hard it was for Donna to act the bitch, even the self-righteous kind described by Fitzgerald. Not because of limitation in talent but because she had brought to every role, including Alma, an essential gentleness and sympathy that was now expected by industry colleagues and fans alike. Firmer direction might have saved her from the criticism of being "vapid." But being "not nice" was risky. One of Donna's most fervent admirers, the novelist John O'Hara, was sorry to see her "unique" personal attractiveness camouflaged in *The Last Time I Saw Paris*.

Wardrobe for *Paris* wasn't finished in late March 1954, so Donna stayed home when Tony returned to England. During the fifties he was often abroad, producing low-budget movies with titles like *The Atomic Man*, *Case of the Red Monkey*, and *Postmark for Danger*. Tony would engage American leads—Richard Conte, Gene Nelson, Mona Freeman, Terry Moore—who agreed to a salary cut and percentage of the profits. Filling out the casts were British actors. However implausible, these thrillers about Communist agents, diamond smugglers, and abnormal scientists boasted foreign backgrounds.

Tony, always interested in dramatizing topical and off-beat subjects (cornea transplants, for example), sought to capitalize on the current trend toward independent filmmaking. There might be money in overseas production because of tax breaks and reduced overhead. The signs seemed favorable as he and Donna formed their own company, called Todon.

Today it is hard to determine Tony's hand in the half-dozen or so movies that took him out of the country, hard even to list all of them with certainty. He apparently acted as an executive producer whose main job was to recruit American talent. But he also had the workaday producer's skill at arranging details and calculating costs, as his family could testify.

Tony was sharp, said Gene Nelson, who starred in *The Atomic Man*. And warm-hearted. He was fondly protective of Nelson's mother, Lenore Berg, escorting her around London. The dancer-turned-actor was paid $15,000 for *The Atomic Man* and 15 percent of net, "which there was never any of." But he enjoyed making this movie in England, as well as *The Way Out*, a tale of murderous truckers produced by Todon in 1956. Mornings a chauffered car would take Nelson from the Dorcester Hotel to the studio in Wimbledon. Some evenings he and Tony went to the White Elephant, a dinner and gambling club in the West End. Tony knew how to play. "He was a swinging kind of guy," said Nelson.

Tired of being separated, the Owens hoped to work together in their company. But Donna would star in only one, rather disastrous, movie under the banner of Todon. Though frustrated by lack of good roles, she was never consumed by career. Unlike a Davis or Crawford, Donna had a real life centered on husband and children, however rationed her time with them. When Tony was away, she tried to be home in Coldwater Canyon.

"Donna took her parenting seriously," said Karen Moreland. "She always had an instinctive maternal way, and she always wanted to read up on the latest things, on how to bring up children the right way. I watched her carefully."

Karen, Donna's baby sister, was born in the same decade as three of the Owen youngsters and used to play with them. With mother Hazel she would ride the Pullman out from Iowa, "a great adventure." Karen remembered doing the alphabet while sitting next to the attentive Tony. He was altogether charming, but even as a child Karen sensed "a lot of tension in the house."

If family life in Coldwater Canyon wasn't exactly like that in *The Donna Reed Show*, it was fairly normal by Hollywood standards. Donna's midwestern values of honesty, courtesy, and responsibility were strictly enforced. When the children misbehaved, she often revoked privileges: no television for a week, no guests for a month. Saturdays they all piled into a station wagon and went grocery shopping at Ralph's. Donna, lightly disguised in dark glasses and a head scarf, still enjoyed some privacy. Sundays she might take the kids to the beach at Santa Monica or the zoo at Griffith Park. Ocasionally she ushered them to the neighborhood theater to see *The African Lion*, *Peter Pan*, and the like. She adored them, guarding and often photographing their times of togetherness.

They adored her, without being immune from the traumas of childhood. Penny is a poised and attractive woman today, but she was not the petite and pretty little princess that people expected a daughter of Donna Reed to be. Highly intelligent and not particularly docile, she was caught between trying to be and trying *not* to be Miss Perfect. She liked school, graduating with honors, but the other children did not, and that was beyond the comprehension of a Depression-era believer in education like Donna. Later, Penny earned a degree in English from Mills College. Now, managing a home and a branch office of *Sunset Magazine*, she recognizes in herself much of Donna's carefulness.

Tony Junior, perhaps the most sensitive of the three, never ran with the offspring of celebrities in his Beverly Hills school. Because of difficulties with reading and math there, he was put into the less demanding Los Angeles system. After much testing, he was diagnosed as dyslexic, but the condition wasn't well understood in the fifties and little could be done. Donna couldn't save the boy from increasing introversion. In his teens he sought self-assurance by joining a fundamentalist religious group. (When he was thirty-two, Tony Junior mentioned to his mother "how letters, numbers, words, changed around, disappeared, then reappeared when sentences didn't make sense," and she then informed him of his dyslexia. "This knowledge cleared my mind of any thoughts of being a 'slow learner' who wouldn't amount to much, which is what the majority of my teachers and 'professional' experts had told my parents—which of course trickled down to me," said Tony.)

Not athletically inclined, Tony Junior felt the emotional distance between him and his father. All the children were required to take tennis lessons, and Tony Junior recalled a father-son game at the Palm Springs Racquet Club in 1962 that didn't end well. "You're not going to get anywhere in this world if you're not competitive," his father told him. Winning, overpowering the opponent, was equated with manliness. "This quality of competitiveness was the *touchstone* of who was successful, who was not; who was the 'real' man, who was not," said Tony Junior. "I wanted his affection and attention and respect because of who I was as a person." But the boy couldn't have a dialogue with his dad, and he drew closer to Donna. "Mom to me was always a mother."

Later Tony Junior withstood the pressure to attend college, preferring a top trade school. In 1970 he earned his pilot's license and today teaches aircraft mechanics at a junior college in California, the only one of the children to stick to an early interest, aviation, and parlay it into a career. A gratifying victory for a former "underachiever."

Timothy inherited his parents' looks and irresistible charm. He conquered chronic bronchitis and celiac disease in his earliest years and grew robustly, though he would lack the size to compete in high school football. Little Timothy craved hugs from his mother. If in trouble with her, he'd go to Jessie, "a big black beautiful woman" who cooked for the family. Sometimes Jessie read the Bible to him, or they'd listen to Vince Scully announce for the Los Angeles Dodgers. "She was full of it, old Jessie was."

In time Tim demonstrated ability at a rigorous military academy in the Valley, but he hated the system of demerits and the absence of girls. He successfully resisted his father's efforts to make a lawyer of him. Tim, who presently works for a newspaper company in order to support his songwriting, realizes that he was "a privileged character." The backyard of the colonial mansion in Coldwater Canyon was a "magical, dreamy place for kids." There were waterfalls and fishing ponds and jungle plants. From the yard a fire trail ran briefly up a mountain. Coyotes, raccoons, and deer lived nearby.

In preschool years Tim missed his dad and often his mom, who left regularly for long hours at the studio. "I was brought up by a zillion nannies—that's why I'm nutty," he said, laughing. "I want to do this horror movie called *The Nanny from Hell*. No, seriously, if I had a kid, no nannies would be allowed during the first four years, which are formative." Then, reflecting on his lost parents: "But, hey, they were doing the best they could, and they were excellent providers."

Donna's stand-in, Frances Haldorn Lomas, came to the Coldwater Canyon house early one summer morning in 1954. She packed the children off on a plane headed toward Jackson Hole, Wyoming, where their mother was filming *The Far Horizons*. Tony Junior remembered seeing her on the set, looking so altered in her full makeup and Indian garb that he cried and ran away. Told that Mom's feelings were hurt, he picked a bouquet of wildflowers for her. Penny got into trouble when she accidentally started a car and cruised a hundred yards. Timmy talked with Charlton Heston, who had not yet risen to the majesty of Moses.

Donna was serious about playing Sacajawea, the Indian woman who helped Meriwether Lewis and William Clark on their historic expedition to the Pacific Ocean. She knew from Penny that Sacajawea was an inspiration to the Girl Scouts, and the script led her to read everything available about the Shoshone guide. Deeply impressed by this example of womanly courage and service, Donna campaigned to get Sacajawea into the Hall of Fame.

Because Donna honored history, it is hard to believe she was happy with the movie's fictional romance between Sacajawea and William Clark. But she was able to persuade herself that the Indian woman felt warmly toward the white explorer, and vice versa. In his 1804 journal Clark praised her work and called her Janey. Lewis, evidently unmoved by Janey, wrote that his partner protected her from the abuse of her French husband, Charboneau. It is a shame that *The Far Horizons* wasted scenes on a made-up jealous quarrel between Lewis and Clark when the great subject of the expedition is in itself dramatic beyond drama. The real Sacajawea carried a newborn baby on her back all the way from present-day North Dakota to the mouth of the Columbia River, but that proof of her perseverance is missing from the movie. It certainly would have impeded romance.

Yet Donna's belief in the nobility of Sacajawea is conveyed in her eyes and movements and voice. Even the tritest dialogue and most questionable action cannot cancel the beauty of her performance. The critics were sarcastic, slamming Heston and Fred MacMurray and the kind of hokum that showed President Jefferson greeting Sacajawea in the White House. While admiring the color photography, they agreed that Donna Reed was "the best thing about the picture."

It has become a sort of camp classic, without ever intending to be one. James P. Ronda, author of a book about the expedition, reported that *The Far Horizons* was shown to members of the Lewis and Clark Trail Foundation meeting in Montana in 1987. The younger historians had a whoop over it, but the more august ones stalked out.

Donna hoped to make a movie of the entire life of Sacajawea. It would have used clips from *The Far Horizons* showing her as the young guide and new footage showing her as the aging woman. This is a sad footnote because Donna didn't live to tackle the project. Her research revealed two schools of thought, one pointing to Sacajawea's demise in her twenties, the other to a long life in Wyoming. The Indian woman's fate was still undetermined when Donna planned her vision, but scholars are now reasonably certain that she died young in South Dakota.

Donna photographed the scenery around Jackson Hole and was herself photographed with hundreds of visitors to the set, including Della Gould Emmons, whose novel *Sacajawea of the Shoshones* was adapted for the movie. A medical emergency spoiled some of the pleasure of that summer shooting. Donna was flown out of Wyoming to a hospital in Salt Lake City, where a painful abscess on her back was excised. So plans for a vacation trip to Iowa and beyond were nixed.

Greater health problems faced the folks on the farm, and Donna was worried. Hazel Mullenger was suffering from Parkinson's disease. Bill Mullenger was entering a rough passage too. He had invested heavily in sheep, which lambed in the coldest weather and caused endless trouble. His energy undermined by a lung condition, he spent most of 1955 in an Omaha hospital. From there he wrote Donna a touching letter: "I have lots of time to think down here and naturally thoughts of our family are dominant in my mind, and one thing that always looms up is the remarkable fact that every one of our five kids is a standout. Many many people have mentioned this to me and to say the least I am very proud. And Donna I truly believe that because of your early and continued success, and your all-around helpfulness and behavior, you have been an inspiration to the whole family and because of you we have all done better."

Though momentarily slowed down by back surgery, Donna seemed to be disproving the fifties' gospel that one could *not* be a devoted wife, mother, and daughter and *also* be a career woman, active citizen, and well-nourished private self. More like the later Hillary Rodham Clinton than the current Mamie Eisenhower, Donna was trying to have it all.

In the mid-fifties the word Donna would have used to describe her life was *busy*. The columnist Sidney Skolsky observed, "She appears to be calm and serene but there's a motor speeding within her which manufactures a determination hard to defeat. She can cram more activities into a day than the average three people, though she rarely appears to hurry." Interviewers like Skolsky were claiming more of Donna's time. The hard-headed Dorothy Kilgallen called her "my idea of a beautiful woman." The hat-headed Hedda Hopper called her "a dame men kill for."

Picking up a new Ford Thunderbird in Chicago, remodeling the big house in Coldwater Canyon, promoting U.S. savings bonds on the radio—thus 1954 dwindled down for Donna. That year color television sets were introduced, and in November she appeared on *Ford Theater* in "Portrait of Lydia." It was her acting debut on TV, concerning an art student in Paris who falls in love with Robert Horton. "A silly darned thing," Donna confided to Joyce Fisk. Now she knew what doing television was like: "It's hard work and the quality isn't good—so! If I can, I hope to keep busy in motion pictures."

Donna read with an eye on cinematic possibilities. *The Bad Seed* offered a great role, that of a mother who gradually realizes her little girl is a murderer. None of the studios would touch William March's novel until it was successfully adapted for Broadway. Donna wanted to buy the property for herself—so desperately that she toyed with the idea of selling the house in Coldwater Canyon to raise the money. Having children to consider, she dared not take the financial risk. *The Bad Seed* moved quickly to the stage with Nancy Kelly, who would reprise the mother's role for the screen. Donna was sick with disappointment.

In the old days at MGM, Donna had seen her career charted in a gradually ascending arc. But as a freelancer, she saw how its contours were determined by chance and capital—and by personal decisions. She was offered *Around the World in Eighty Days* and declined because another ethnic role, coming so soon after Sacajawea, didn't seem a smart career move. Shirley MacLaine stepped in as the Indian princess and captured everyone's attention in the biggest picture of 1956. Meanwhile, Donna could be found in *Backlash*.

A mystery-western in color, *Backlash* was reasonably holding. Donna comes riding in on a horse, dressed not as a lady would be in 1870. She is, in sexist language, quite a tomato, delectably filling out her expensive white shirt and jodhpurs. Her skin and hair gleam as if she'd been living on filet mignon and cottage cheese at a tourist ranch and soaking in the springs. She is pursuing the truth about what happened to her dead husband—and some stolen money. Richard Widmark's search (for his father) interconnects with her own.

Donna was interested in the widow because she pitted her wits against the ruthlessness of some gunmen. Her best scene, hardly more than a shot, is wordless: she exits a station cracking a whip and slips into a coach. From its interior can be seen only her dark eyes, in a side-long and then backward glare as she rides out of the frame. This quick scene, emphatic and smoldering, is often missing when the movie is televised today.

In character, Donna wore a proper dust-catching crinoline on the streets of Old Tucson. *Backlash* was filmed there and at the huge Vaca Ranch, not far from Nogales. Several hundred Papago Indians were hired as extras, and they gifted the leading lady with amulets cut from semiprecious stones. Donna, who still wanted another child, was told that the charms could invoke the benign spirits of fertility. At the moment, she yearned more for a cool breeze—the temperature on the set stayed above a hundred degrees for days.

If *Backlash* added little to Donna's prestige, it showed how much the Oscar had boosted her earning power. She received $8,000 a week, more than twice her salary for *Trouble Along the Way*, made shortly before *Eternity*. Since her assignment lasted only five weeks, she didn't clean up, as Widmark eventually did. He made the movie for no salary but fifty percent of the profits and was still collecting checks thirty years later. "It paid off like a slot machine," he crowed. That sort of financial arrangement, introduced by Jimmy Stewart in the fifties, was more or less closed to women. By this time, Donna was sharply aware of the advantages enjoyed by men in Hollywood.

Ten pounds lighter after working in the Arizona heat, Donna reported to Universal for *The Benny Goodman Story* in early July 1955. A few weeks later sad news came from Iowa: Grandmother Mullenger was dead at the age of ninety-one. Donna had visited Denison in January, and her birthday tribute to the pioneer woman had been published in the local newspaper. Unable to return to Iowa because of filming, she had to cope with her sense of loss at long distance. Mary Mullenger had mailed homemade jellies and doughnuts to Donna during her first lean years in California, and always had sent delightful newsy letters. Two decades had flown since Donnabelle stayed with her grandmother in Denison. "I might never have got to high school without her," she wrote Joyce Fisk.

The Benny Goodman Story reunited Donna and William Daniels, who had photographed her as a beginner in *Shadow of the Thin Man*. The great cinematographer of Garbo and the silent *Greed* sent roses to Donna before the cameras rolled. Benny Goodman and some of his musicians jammed especially for Miss Reed outside her dressing room, according to studio publicity. But Steve Allen said that Goodman, who assembled his old band members to pre-record the standards for the movie soundtrack, was never seen at Universal during the filming.

Making his big-screen debut, Steve Allen benefited from Donna's help during rehearsals. Their first scene together is in a Chicago speakeasy, circa 1920. Alice Hammond (Donna) is dragged there to meet an obscure clarinetist named Benny Goodman (Allen). They will eventually marry, but for now she is unfavorably impressed—with him and the surroundings. "We saw some men coming in. They looked like gangsters," she says. Benny replies nonchalantly, "They are. They own the place." The upper-crust Alice is aghast.

That scene would be repeated in Donna's own life when she was starring on television. After being honored at a Mother's Day function in New York, Donna flew with Tony to Chicago, where they attended a party. After Tony introduced her around, Donna whispered to him, "Almost everyone here looks like a gangster." Tony replied, "Everyone is." If the former Chicago night-life reporter knew some of the big boys, the nation's model of suburban motherhood preferred not to. She steered toward the door.

Donna and Steve somewhat resembled Alice and Benny Goodman physically, but neither was overconcerned about being faithful to personality. They essentially played themselves—the comedian sans his humor—because the public didn't know Alice or the private Benny anyhow. Just as well. The real Benny was too "negative" and unlikable to make the audience care much about what happened to him. "Goodman was un-doubtedly the best jazz clarinetist of all time, but as a human being he left considerable to be desired," said Allen.

The famous music was expected—and was delivered with technical perfection. The stars had to compete with it while making up for the flat script and direction. Their professionalism saved them; the critics praised Allen's and shorted Donna's. But who can say that her great beauty, high-lighted by William Daniels, is any less a pleasure than the music-making?

Goodman's biographers have sneered at the movie, which brought a revival of the King of Swing. It was among the top thirty money-makers of its year, though not as profitable as the earlier *Glenn Miller Story.* (At the *Goodman Story* preview, a member of the audience, enchanted by the close-ups of Donna, wrote: "Finally someone's life without June Allyson.")

In the fall of 1955 Donna was looking forward to her long-delayed first trip to Europe. "What a provincial soul I am. Everybody in Hollywood is flying around and I've been sitting at home raising babies," she told a re-porter. She couldn't pack until another big-budget production was under her belt.

That was *Ransom*, originally an hour-long television drama titled "Fearful Decision." Padded out to movie length, the story lost edge but provided a good role for Glenn Ford, the father who refuses to pay ran-som when his little boy is kidnapped. Donna, as the distraught mother who opposes his decision, takes to her bed. She seemed at odds with the role, possibly because it confirmed her feeling that strong women weren't being allowed on the screen. This basic tension in her playing—between expected passive victimhood and her own intelligence—was sensed by re-viewers but not approved. In their eyes she was either overneurotic or overstoic.

Filmed at an executive's mansion in the Stone Canyon area of Los Angeles, *Ransom* shows the family under siege. The atmosphere is pent-up, partly because the camera never cuts to the kidnappers. But in a lim-ited space the camera can be bold, once completely circling Donna as she sits trembling on the brink of tears.

Ransom was touted as an MGM blockbuster. Ads focused on a huge telephone, behind which hovered a strained Donna and Glenn Ford. The hype died out soon after the movie was released in January 1956. Public attention was revived forty years later, when the popular remake with Mel Gibson invited comparison. As Molly Haskell recently noted, there is more contrast than comparison between the "cozy suburban" fifties world of Ford and Reed and the nineties' one of Gibson and Rene Russo, isolated in their "penthouse eyrie."

Donna and Tony and the children, with Jessie the cook in tow, flew to England in December 1955. Badly needing this change of scene, the hardworking actress cheerfully accepted accommodations at Bryanston Court on George Street in West London. Tony had asked his friend Doris Cole Abrahams to ready a flat for them in her building, which had a romantic history. Mrs. Wallis Simpson had lived there when courted by the Duke of Windsor, and Tony wanted Donna to arrive like royalty.

Doris found the only available apartment in disrepair—dirty, faded, and "full of horrible overstuffed reproduction furniture." Frantic because the arrival of Tony's queen was nigh, she joined a crew of cleaners and painters and finally resorted to covering the place with banks of roses and exotic flowers. Gerald Abrahams, amazed by such futile industry, predicted that Doris and Miss Donna Reed would loathe each other on sight. "Instead, it was love at first sight," said Doris, who later made her mark as a Broadway producer. "Donna was a fabulous sport. She was exceedingly warm, natural, and enthusiastic from the beginning."

Penny, Timmy, and Tony Junior stayed in London while their parents filmed *Beyond Mombasa* in Africa. Nearly forty years later Tim remembered shivering in the fog, grinning for the photographers at Heathrow, and trying to make the Buckingham Palace guards laugh. "All I wanted to do was play baseball, and it was hard to find over there. I hated England. It was wasted on a little punk." The children were enrolled at the American School in Grosvenor Square.

For some weeks that winter, before embarking for Kenya, Donna traveled across London to the Elstree Studio, bundled up in wool slacks, two wool sweaters, a full-length fur coat, a wool scarf, and fur-lined high boots. Although verging on influenza much of the time, she loved

London—the endless sightseeing, the atmospheric pubs and restaurants, the cozy theaters where patrons ate and drank between acts and applauded almost everything on the boards. But during that first visit she had reservations about the English people. "Their stubbornness is shocking, and their manners a coverup for getting their own way about things!" she wrote to a friend. "In other words, rather than argue or disagree, they look you right in the eye, smile, give their most charming assent, turn their backs and do just as they please or had intended! I positively hated working there!"

At London Airport in late January, just before enplaning for Africa, Donna met with Greta Garbo, who was traveling under the name of Gustafson to New York. Garbo, an early admirer of Donna, had recently obtained a print of *Backlash* for private showings. It was a rare encounter for the recluse and was not reported. Then Donna and Tony flew out of Heathrow. They saw the sun rise on the Nile during the twenty-eight-hour flight to Mombasa.

For nearly a month Donna filmed in Kenya, living at a hotel on the Indian Ocean. It was a dream place, if not perfectly satisfying. The food looked appetizing but made her sick—she would suffer from bouts of amoebic dysentery for years afterward. Animals were nowhere to be seen as she drove into the African jungle. Farther on, "it all looked and felt as one might expect," she wrote. "Hot, humid, dirty, and the natives apathetic, happy looking, with the women all topless, pregnant, and trailed by several young." She observed that the only unhappy natives were the ones exposed to big-city life in Nairobi. "As for the others, it's a shame anyone has ever bothered them, particularly the missionary."

Beyond Mombasa is something of a *film maudit*. Shooting on location in Africa was a snap compared to what it had been for the pioneering *Trader Horn*. Todon could simply use the facilities of the MGM office in Nairobi. Nevertheless, there was enough physical discomfort and sickness to put everyone on edge. Tempers flared. The veteran director George Marshall, of the macho John Ford school without Pappy's inspiration, drank Pernod all the time and doctored the script. According to a reliable source, Marshall "treated Donna like a novice and showed no respect for her as a person." She was humiliated in front of the company.

When Marshall telephoned her in the states, she refused to speak with him. And later the director was prohibited, contractually, from any association with *The Donna Reed Show*.

Although Tony engaged Cornel Wilde as leading man and Frederick Young as photographer, *Mombasa* was beyond saving. It is a clichéd African adventure with uranium mines, leopard men, plunderers dressed by a forerunner of Banana Republic, and a "lady anthropologist" who looks like Donna Reed. "The cast is smoothly professional and entirely wasted," said the *Los Angeles Times*. This first junket for producer husband and star wife was a failure. "Donna put me out of business!" said Tony later, when success in television made such joking possible.

Donna was anxious to return to London after twenty-five days in the jungle, her longest separation from the children. In England the family resumed sightseeing, with varying degrees of interest. "Not another goddam castle!" said seven-year-old Timmy. Then Donna and Tony toured the continent, spending early April in Paris down with the flu at the Raphael, a "pure French" hotel undiscovered by Americans. Donna was depressed by the still-bombed-out Munich, where amputees dined alone, but delighted by Vienna, where she was surprised to see sister Lavone, and by all of Italy, her favorite country.

Back in Hollywood, the future looked bootless. "Been reading some dreadful scripts, even worse than any of the pictures I've ever done, and so here I sit!" Donna told Joyce Fisk in the fall of 1956. "Suppose we'll all end up in TV within a few years anyway, well, those of us who care to end up acting at all—and I'm not sure I do." Soon she faced the television cameras, impersonating a war-torn Eurasian in "Flight from Tormendero," and cringing in embarrassment when it was shown on *General Electric Theater* the following February.

Thankfully, real life was intervening. Donna gave birth to Mary Anne on May 7, 1957. Having wanted this baby for so long, she now feared, unnecessarily, that she had nothing left to give a fourth. Tony, who had not wanted another child, fell helplessly in love with Mary Anne.

Six weeks after she was born, the Owens moved out of Coldwater Canyon. But not before a legal imbroglio. Jack Benny's daughter and her husband backed out of a deal to buy the house for $95,000. The Owens, who later sold for less, after incurring expenses, sued. Upset, Donna told her old college friend Virginia Ricks Hill: "I suppose I should have a nervous breakdown, but farm girls from Iowa don't have breakdowns!"

They moved to a house on North Alpine Drive, a one-story affair with a lanai and small swimming pool. Though a tiny tropical garden couldn't satisfy Donna's yearning for country, the closeness to schools and services was a blessing for a busy mother.

The houses had gotten better over the years, but Hollywood still seemed strange to Donna. She revealed to a reporter: "When we lived in Coldwater Canyon, I used to go for walks and hang over the back fences when I wasn't working in a picture. I always wanted to start some neighborhood social activity. Oh, people were polite enough, but nobody ever said, 'Why don't you and your husband come over tomorrow night?'"

If movie stardom worked against a sense of belonging anywhere, it afforded entry to a larger world for one who loved to travel. In the fall of 1957, Donna returned to England for filming. The entire family went along; a planeside photo shows her holding baby Mary Anne. "The effort expended to get there with four children, and then setting up housekeeping, is not quite to be believed," wrote Donna. "But they were fine voyagers, all; even Mary was contented and good."

Adjusting to the time change in London took two weeks, and until December Donna rode in the dark to and from the studio, as she had done during those first years in Hollywood. *The Whole Truth*, made at Walton-on-Thames, was to be her last movie. It is a jigsaw with corpses real and phony. Donna plays the loyal wife of producer Stewart Granger, who is accused of murdering a temperamental actress. This writer recalls seeing *The Whole Truth* in Times Square and overhearing comments about its unexpected quality. After nearly four decades, a scene sticks in the mind: a long-held medium shot of the prettiest profile that ever was.

At thirty-seven, Donna's beauty was refulgent yet. But a long phase of her career was ending. "Time is a terrible enemy in this business, and I don't want to be fighting it too much longer," she confided to Joyce Fisk. "I'll leave that to Dietrich and Rogers and Crawford; I haven't the energy to worry about every light and lens on the camera to ensure that dewy look."

While in London Donna taped for television a mystery called "The Other Side of the Curtain," which was shown on the *Suspicion* series late in the year. The filming was followed by a ten-day family jaunt on the Continent (only a weekend in Paris because the city irritated Tony).

Home again in January 1958, Donna hinted at plans for a family television show. "The money involved, especially if one can stay on for two years, is too good to turn down. It's the kind of setup which allows a lot of tax-free money, legitimately of course, and frankly I'm tired by now. I'd like to get my hands on a hunk and then work only if I get an urge, and I suspect it would be rare."

That spring Donna was tagged for television's "nostalgoria" called *This Is Your Life*, hosted by Ralph Edwards. For the first time since 1942, when the starlet Donna sold war bonds on the streets of Denison, the entire Mullenger family was reunited. Hazel, holding her trembling hands inside a coat, was gray-haired and dignified. Bill, equally handsome, remembered how hard Donna had worked on the farm.

The past was present on camera in the form of teachers and friends— Marian Drake, who had taught Donna in the one-room country schoolhouse; Edward Tompkins, who had advised her to read *How to Win Friends and Influence People*; George and Annie Johnson, whose home she had worked in while attending college; Bill Smith, the Feldman agent who had spotted her photograph in the *Los Angeles Times*. And, not least, Joyce Anderson Fisk, her high-school chum and lifelong correspondent. Aunt Mildred, who had brought Donna to California, did not appear, evidently because Tony neglected to invite her. Hurt, Mildred blamed the elder Mullengers and never again spoke to them.

It was a misty-eyed closing of a chapter. And the opening of a new one, for as the show ended Ralph Edwards announced the enterprise that would make Donna Reed truly a household name.

Hazel Shives and William Mullenger before
their marriage in 1920. Courtesy of Mary Owen.

Left: Baby Donnabelle in 1921. Courtesy of Mary Owen.

Below: The Mullenger farm-house. Courtesy of Lavone Flynn.

Right: Donnabelle as a high school graduate in 1938. Courtesy of Joyce Fisk.

Left: Donnabelle, Keith, and Lavone in Iowa in the 1920s.

Below: Lavone, Keith, and Donna at the Stork Club in New York in the early 1950s. Courtesy of Lavone Flynn.

Right: Donna on a visit to Denison in the summer of 1942. A new celebrity, she sold war bonds on the streets there. Courtesy of Mearl Luvaas.

Above: At the Palladium in the early 1940s. Left to right: Jack and Kelly Quinn, Donna and William Tuttle. Courtesy of Kelly Quinn.

Left: Anthony Ohnstein, at about the time he became Tony Owen. He was given a screen test because he looked like Valentino. Courtesy of Mary Owen.

Donna and Tony Owen on their
wedding day in June 1945, with Louis
B. Mayer. Courtesy of Mary Owen.

Donna Reed and Jimmy Stewart in the celebrated
telephone scene from *It's a Wonderful Life*, 1946.
Courtesy of the Academy of Motion Picture Arts and
Sciences and Wesleyan University Cinema Archives.

Right: Donna's family visits the set of *Green Dolphin Street* in 1947. Seated: sister Karen, Hazel Mullenger. Standing, left to right: William Mullenger, Aunt Mildred Van Kampen, and Donna in costume. Courtesy of Karen Moreland.

Below: Donna and a friend from school days, Joyce Fisk, in 1950. They maintained a correspondence for almost fifty years. Courtesy of Joyce Fisk.

Left: The Owen family at home in the early 1950s. Donna and Tony with, left to right, Tony Jr., Timmy, and Penny. Courtesy of Mary Owen.

Below: The Owen family at home in the 1960s. Left to right: Tony, Timmy, Donna, Mary Anne, Tony Jr., and Penny. Courtesy of Mary Owen.

Above: Donna with
Montgomery Clift in
From Here to Eternity,
1953. Courtesy of
Academy of Motion
Picture Arts and
Sciences.

Left: Donna's sister,
Lavone, became a top
Conover model known
as Heidi. Courtesy of
Lavone Flynn.

Most Beautiful Co-ed Named at Los Angeles City College

Students Vote Award During Queen's Ball Held at Biltmore With Accompanying Ring Ceremonies

Top left: Donna visits her grandmother, Mary Mullenger, in Denison early in 1955. During her high school years Donna stayed in town with her paternal grandmother.

Bottom left: Donna visits her Aunt Mabel Yankey in a rest home in Denison in the early 1980s. After Hazel Mullenger died in 1975, Aunt Mabel was like a second mother to Donna. Courtesy of Mary Owen.

Right: The photo that launched a movie career. When Donna's picture appeared in the *Los Angeles Times* on December 2, 1940, the studios called. Courtesy of Mary Owen.

The photo that launched a television career. It inspired her
casting in *The Donna Reed Show*. The photo originally appeared
in the *Omaha World-Herald Sunday Magazine* in 1952.

Paul Petersen was a young boy when *The Donna Reed Show* began in 1958. Shown with Donna, Carl Betz, and Shelley Fabares. Courtesy of Columbia TriStar Television.

Above: Paul, center, was a young man when the show ended in 1966. At that time the cast and crew posed for this picture. Paul's sister, Patty (in front, by Donna), joined the show in 1963. To Paul's left is Candy Moore. Courtesy of William Graf.

Below: An antiwar activist in the 1970s, Donna co-chaired Another Mother for Peace. At right is Dorothy B. Jones. Courtesy of Mary Owen.

Above, left to right: Kitty Bradley, General of the Army Omar N. Bradley, Donna, and Col. Grover W. Asmus. This photo was taken in January 1972, before Donna and Grover married. The Bradleys stand in front of an oil painting of them. Courtesy of Grover W. Asmus.

Right: A photo portrait of Donna made in the summer of 1985 by her son Tony Jr. Courtesy of Tony Owen Jr.

CHAPTER SEVEN

The Donna Reed Show

Donna Reed came to series television at the end of a golden age. Lucy, Uncle Milty, Coco and Caesar, Alice and Ralph Kramden had milked the medium for laughs. The warm ethnic situation comedies *Mama* and *The Goldbergs* had started on the small screen as early as 1949. That year brought two other transplants from radio, *The Aldrich Family* and *The Life of Riley*. A swarm of sitcoms followed in the early and middle fifties: *Father Knows Best*, the placid Ozzie and Harriet, the mugging Joan Davis, the wisecracking Miss Brooks, the fluttery December Bride, the haunted Cosmo Topper, *My Little Margie*, *Private Secretary*, Bob Cummings, Danny Thomas. Making little noise in 1957 was *Leave It to Beaver*.

By 1958 viewers were tiring of situation comedies. Only about fifteen were scheduled that fall, half the number of so-called adult Westerns. Donna and Tony had not even considered a sitcom at first. "All the family shows truly bore me," she confessed. "I had *never* looked at *one* until this year, when I felt I must!"

The Owens spent months angling for ideas. How about a series starring Donna as a bullfighter (a *lady* bullfighter)? As a racetrack tout? As an elevator operator in the Empire State Building, stopping at different stories every week? As secretary to the secretary of state, moving between pratfall and intrigue around the globe? Tony toyed with "The Secretary's Secretary" for weeks without getting a satisfying script.

Then one day John Mitchell, a Columbia vice president in New York, noticed a framed photo in Tony's office. A smiling, breeze-blown Donna was shown on the Iowa farm. She was surrounded by her children and young sister Karen, who were petting a lamb. One glance at the 1952 photo and Mitchell knew that television should present Donna as she actually was: a wife and mother.

He had to persuade the star and producer. The public was used to seeing grandmotherly types like Molly Goldberg in mother roles. Loretta Young could swirl before the cameras in glamorous gowns, but Donna would be condemned to drab housedresses and confined to the kitchen. She considered Mitchell's proposal a joke before realizing the simple rightness of it. So for the second time in her life, a photograph launched a career.

A series was like a parfait, layered to suit different tastes but consistently flavored in the spooning. In the preparation, cute titles like "Aw Gee, Mom!" and derivative ones like "Mother Knows Better" were tossed aside. The obvious "Donna Reed Show" was daring because few women in television had successfully traded on their names.

William Roberts, a veteran screenwriter at MGM, was called in to create the characters. Diane West, later changed to Donna Stone, was inspired by Virginia Molony, the sympathetic wife of a Los Angeles pediatrician, Dr. Clement Molony. Mrs. Molony knew from experience that doctors, on call at all hours, saw other people's children more often than their own. That situation, adapted to television, allowed Donna the domestic forefront without sacrificing the authority of Dr. Alex Stone, whose office was in a back room at home.

Roberts, in his typewritten treatment, or bible, suggested the scope of Donna Stone. She was "wife, mother, companion, booster, nurse, housekeeper, cook, laundress, gardener, bookkeeper, clubwoman, choir singer, PTA officer, Scout leader, and at the same time effervescent, immaculate, and pretty." He insisted on a typical American family, living in the small midwestern city of Appleton (ultimately Hilldale, though Donna disliked the made-up sound). There were two children: teenage Andra, changed to Mary, who was "mercurial, romantic"; and prepubescent Jeff, described as "serious, intense," and to be more rambunctious in the acting. Familiar enough—but with crisis at their doorstep the doctor and his wife had "more than ordinary acquaintanceship with joy and sorrow, life and death."

In July, while a script was being drafted, Donna and Tony and the Owen children vacationed at Hotel Del Coronado, on the Pacific near San

Diego. Donna dashed off a postcard to Joyce Fisk: "Heading back to begin filming our TV show, so all I have left is one more week of freedom."

The future had forked. Earlier in the year Frank Capra had offered Donna the feminine lead in *A Hole in the Head*. She almost accepted because "the last time Frank Sinatra and I appeared together in a movie we both won Oscars." Tony vetoed. "They don't take Oscars at supermarkets," he argued. "Security they do."

Andrew McCullough remembered the casting of *The Donna Reed Show*. Hundreds tested for it and for other shows at Screen Gems, the TV subsidiary of Columbia Pictures. It was "a cheap lot" where actors were herded around, said McCullough, who directed Donna's pilot and many subsequent segments. A graduate of live television shows like *Studio One* and a Peabody Award winner for *Omnibus*, McCullough had directed Katherine Cornell in her TV debut, and Helen Hayes and Orson Welles on the New York stage.

When he met Donna Reed during the testing for her show, she said, "I'm nervous—I can't do comedy." McCullough reassured her, "Don't be nervous because I'm *brilliant*. I'll make you look good." She seemed startled by that so he told some funny stories. McCullough didn't care whether she could do comedy or not because the script was more sentimental than funny—what the trade called a warmedy. But it was soon clear to him that Donna had an instinct, a knack, for comedy.

With the star firmly set, various groups were put together in support. Fourteen-year-old Shelley Fabares was tested as daughter Mary. McCullough thought that Shelley conveyed an old-fashioned quality which made the other girls seem ordinary. She finally beat out an actress who had been poised to sign. In Shelley's corner was twelve-year-old Paul Petersen, formerly a Disney Mouseketeer, now chosen as Jeff Stone. The year before, they had been paired as brother and sister in tryouts for a show featuring the puppeteer Shari Lewis. "Clearly, Paul and I were destined," mused Shelley much later.

The hardest role to cast was that of Dr. Alex Stone. From the beginning Donna insisted on a male figure commanding respect, not the idiotic husband and father endemic to sitcoms. (She hated the very phrase *sit-*

uation comedy because of the stereotypes it conjured up.) Dr. Stone had to be a strong presence while playing second toledo. Carl Betz, originating from the eastern theater circuit, projected sharp intelligence and gentle humor, a combination not so common. Tall and sturdy and open-faced, he was an appealing match for the petite Donna.

Filming began on the soundstage that had been used for the New Congress Club, the pseudo-bordello in *From Here to Eternity*. Millions of viewers who became familiar with the interior of the Stone house may have recognized pieces of it from other sitcoms. Screen Gems productions shared basically the same layout, and changes—a window here, a door there—had to be negotiated. Some things never changed, though. Donna had worked since the early fifties with part of the crew, including the makeup man, Clay Campbell, who commuted every day from his retirement home in Corona Del Mar.

Deeply experienced as she was, Donna was worried. She had never before assumed the major responsibility for carrying a show. Had never played any comedy to speak of. Had never worked on a regular basis with juvenile actors. Had never been burdened with so many details (like Lucille Ball, she was co-owner of the producing company). And had never felt so torn between family and career. She tried to make up for time lost by organizing special moments with her children. But she still felt guilty about "deserting" Mary Anne, who was eighteen months old when the series began.

The Donna Reed Show premiered at nine o'clock on Wednesday evening, September 24, 1958. The Stone family was shown trying to get out of town for a weekend. "Right off the bat, Carl and I had to play a delicate romantic scene. I don't know which of us was more nervous," recalled Donna. The small story of conflicting commitments was suited to the intimate medium, and the fadeout demonstrated that no one was better than Donna Reed in a conjugal clinch. Andrew McCullough's old college roommate, Jack Lemmon, had seen the pilot and predicted a hit. But the pilot that Harry Ackerman, the new head of Screen Gems, had sold to the sponsor was too long, and when cuts were made for commercials it was less impressive.

Critics who saw the premiere were harsh. "Probably a nice family to live with, but you wouldn't want to visit them for laughs," said one. A hash of *Father Knows Best* and *Leave It to Beaver*, sniffed another, who found it "mixed not very well." Some thought this sitcom had arrived ten years too late to make an impact. Most predicted a short run. Friendlier reviewers employed modifiers like "mild" and "potentially pleasant." They had nothing against Donna Reed, who was still "lovely to look at." Indeed, she was "the best thing to come from Iowa since Herbert Hoover."

That first autumn a treasured letter came from an ungushy, if not unprejudiced, observer. "I always forget to tell you how nice you look," wrote Hazel Mullenger. "The back of your hair looks so nice and bouncy when you turn and run for the door [in the opening credits]." Later, Donna reflected, "My mother loved having me on television because she could see me every week. That was very important to her. She identified. She should have. I was playing *her*. Not me."

Family pride aside, the first reports were painful to see in print. Pitted against *The Millionaire* on CBS, *The Donna Reed Show* drew a Nielsen of 8. (The mark of success for new shows was 20 and above.) The puny rating and poor reviews depressed the cast and crew. Donna tried to reassure them—the public will like us, you wait and see—but privately thought of going home for good. She and Tony were frustrated by circumstances: the late hour for family viewing, the scheduling snarl that resulted in even later showings in eastern and southern cities, the lack of promotion by the network. They expected to be completely flattened in October by the most formidable of all possible competitors.

And they were. Milton Berle's new variety show on NBC steamrolled over *The Donna Reed Show*. The make-or-break Nielsen sank to 6. Panicky junior executives at ABC wanted to rush in a replacement. Rumors of cancellation reached the set, but the disciplined Donna acted as if the show had been renewed. One evening she attended a charity affair that seemed like a funeral. "People would say hello and walk away. It wasn't unfriendliness. They were just embarrassed to death because they thought the show was folding," she recalled later.

At this low point, after the fourth show, the sponsor called—or rather, a representative of Campbell's Soup. Bill Roberts and the writer Nate Monaster were gloomed-out in Tony's office when the phone rang. "I guess you saw the Nielsen," answered Tony with a sickly smile. "What's that?" said the nice Campbell's voice. "We don't care about the ratings. Keep working, don't collapse."

In an era when single sponsors had more clout, Campbell's kept Donna Reed from drowning in the soup, so to speak. At home in the Hollywood Hills, Shelley Fabares could go to sleep with the assurance that the bountiful Mrs. Campbell loved *The Donna Reed Show* as well as *Lassie*. Mrs. Campbell aside, Donna and Tony feared that ABC would not pick up the first option. ABC did, quietly and partly because Leonard Goldenson, the network founder, thought the show "had legs." But in today's more punishing climate, when new television programs are canceled after six weeks or less if they don't click, *The Donna Reed Show* would not get a chance.

What happened in the fall and winter of 1958–59 was akin to a miracle. By late November, after eight segments, *Donna Reed* began to rally a bit. Its Nielsen rating in January was 19, still below Berle's but strong enough to help doom *his* show, surely one of the ironies of television history.

With better ratings came better reviews. The most eloquent appeared when most needed, during that first winter. "In an era when wisecracking, brash and brassy blondes infest the air like locusts, Miss Reed, corn-fed and wholesome, is as welcome as a late summer breeze through an Indiana hayfield," said the critic for *TV Guide*. "And she actually acts like a mother, an impersonation that hasn't been successfully perpetuated on television since Peggy Wood left."

At the same time, another writer compared Donna's show to "antiseptic oatmeal." A disdainful New Yawker thought it was "a bleary bit of blancmange." The metaphor of choice for reviewers was mommy food.

Signs of public acceptance surprised the trade, especially since no changes were made in the format, no gimmicks were introduced. Donna wouldn't allow them, in spite of pressure from network and studio. She wanted the show to be true, in its details, to ordinary family life—the kind she might have had by staying in Iowa.

As the 1958 holidays approached, Joyce Fisk saw improvements in the show, and said so in a letter. Donna replied: "Everyone says, as you do, that our stories are getting better. I say, not much, maybe a little, and you're only *liking* the people in them more. Could be? Actually, if you'll think about it, Father Knows Best, Danny Thomas, et al, barely have plots or stories—they're just friendly faces reacting to situations." Shrewdly, Donna had pinpointed the secret of sitcom success: ensemble acting. She also knew, but didn't say, how much depended on the public's liking of the star.

The show conveyed the feeling of a real family, not overnight but early on. Shelley Fabares recalled the rapport among the four actors, apparent on the screen after a few months. No script could have supplied the bonding that developed. She and Paul Petersen found in Donna (and to some extent in Carl Betz) a surrogate parent. They called her Miss Reed throughout the years of the show. The girl whose childhood was hardly typical, the boy whose home life was unstable—they came together with Donna and Carl.

Donna and Paul Petersen had Iowa in common. His mother had been born near Denison a month after Donna, and his grandfather had known Bill Mullenger in the twenties and thirties. Paul spent his infancy, after World War II, with his parents and uncle and aunt on a farm in Cherokee County, Iowa. Wilma Petersen shepherded him to endless lessons and recitals (in his first amateur show he performed as a glowworm). The reward for all this agony came at age eight in 1954, when he was hired for the Mickey Mouse Club. Paul played hide and seek on the soundstages and took no guff from the other Mouseketeers. A casting man persisted in calling him the hated name of Mouse. One day Paul punched the man in his ample stomach, shouting, "Don't call me that, Fatso!" Walt Disney saw what happened and promptly fired the boy.

"I was incorrigible, with broken teeth and a funny little smile," said Paul. As Jeff, he livened up *The Donna Reed Show*. Donna found him undisciplined but "an absolute joy to play a scene with." Years later she confided to a friend, "I say, immodestly, that *our* scenes were from the beginning, until he was too old to mother, the whole crux and mainstay of the show."

Mary Stone had to stand the onslaught of the wild child who was her brother. Shelley Fabares thought of Mary as being a nice, sweet girl until she saw reruns years later. "I was really snippy toward Jeff, and there was a good deal of 'Oh, Mo-ther-r!' Mary could be sort of a pain in the ass." But she was also idealistic, compassionate—she wouldn't go to a prom because her girl friend, who had pimples, hadn't been asked.

A painfully shy Elsa Fabares had determined that her daughters would not be so. Shelley and sister Smokey pirouetted on baby toes in dancing classes. Modeling led, for Shelley, to television shows like *Annie Oakley* and *Captain Midnight*. Shelley was an actress before she was old enough to attend school, but she was never that dreadful creature known as a moppet. She had a grave quietness, perhaps instilled by her Catholic training. When she was nine, Frank Sinatra crooned to her in a TV special. Like Paul Petersen, who had acted with Cary Grant in *Houseboat*, she had been on the big screen—as Rock Hudson's daughter in *Never Say Goodbye*, missing school for the filming. Coming to *The Donna Reed Show*, Shelley was, for all her seasoning, timid and young for her age. "I lived in a sheltered cocoon," she recalled.

From the beginning Shelley worshiped Miss Reed. "I wanted to grow up to be just like her. I thought she was the most beautiful, smartest, kindest, most wonderful woman—and I had a pretty wonderful mother of my own." Donna, aware of Shelley's adoration, responded maturely. She was a role model on a personal level; a mother on a professional one, with lines finely drawn. For reasons that trail off into feminine psychology, Donna had a more complex, though no less caring, relationship with Shelley than with Paul.

Lacking Paul's brash confidence, Shelley doubted her acting ability. To her mind, he was "naturally gifted" and she had to learn. She shared all of Mary Stone's insecurities. "I thought I'd never be asked out on dates; thought everyone else was better looking; my hair wasn't right, my hips too big, my fingernails too short, I weighed too much." The fears of Mary Stone might be touched on in a script, but in the real life of teenage Shelley, in the repressed fifties, those fears were likely to be kept inside, not hauled out and discussed, not even with the most understanding television mother of all.

The father, Carl Betz, contributed to the chemistry that bound the cast. Born the same year as Donna, in Pittsburgh, Pennsylvania, Carl first acted out parts in his grandmother's basement. He studied drama at Duquesne University and Carnegie Tech and in 1941, as Donna was lucking out in Hollywood, he was locked out of the New York theater and living on hamburgers and coffee. After war service in North Africa and Italy, he played in summer stock for sixty-four consecutive weeks, getting tapped by movie scouts while appearing with Veronica Lake in *The Voice of the Turtle*. A contract with Twentieth-Century-Fox came to little, partly because movie executives couldn't decide whether he was a hero or a heavy (he dueled with "Andrew Jackson" in *The President's Lady*). He showed up better on television, acting a handsome dog named Collie Jordan in the soaper *Love of Life* before answering the call for Dr. Alex Stone.

Carl played Dr. Stone like the ordinary, thoroughly American guy next door Donna might have been expected to marry, and never did. Like Don Murray. Though Carl seemed perfect for the role of the conventional (some would say dull) doctor, he was in real life totally different: artistic, cultured. A dedicated Anglophile who lived elegantly, he devoured Shakespeare and drove fancy English cars. According to Paul Petersen, "Carl was a ball to be around because he was not at all what many consider manly (like a growl), not a hunter or a fisher but a thinker and a sensitive man." His wife, Gloria, thought that "Carl would have been a very popular professor of literature and drama at a girls' school." Shelley Fabares agreed: "He loved being an actor but even more than that he loved the English language, great books."

Though Carl and Donna looked right together, he was not really her kind of man. Like many refined women, she was personally attracted to testicular types with the charm of Lucifer. Their television marriage lasted eight seasons because of their professionalism—because Donna was secure enough to share the spotlight and Carl knew that he was not the star. After years of nomadic striving, he welcomed a regular salary (about $500 a week) and a chance to become nationally known.

Donna was fond of Carl, but his physical clumsiness could be exasperating. The Stone set always presented obstacles to him. Later Donna wrote: "As for my husband, TV that is, I may write a book! While he is a man of great integrity, gentleness, humor, wit, and nicely educated, I must say that in front of the camera he was, and is, a clod, the bane of my whole existence. May I just say that he has tripped, staggered, reeled, careened, shuffled, bumbled, and once even hit the door frame, accidentally of course, with such force that he entered the house, cameras rolling, with a three-inch gash in his forehead and blood streaming down one cheek, all in the *mere* course of entering the front door and closing it. Any prop larger than a toothpick became a lethal weapon in his hands; a good morning kiss usually landed in the vicinity of the left nostril on the first take, ad infinitum! Furthermore, if he were asked to do any of the above things in a scene comedically, he would protest that, for example, only an idiot would miss his wife's lips kissing her good morning, and he would be unshakable in that belief."

In fact, the scripts seldom exploited Carl's awkwardness. That viewers were unaware of it is tribute to his mental concentration and perhaps to the film editor. Mainly because of the attractiveness of Donna and Carl and the youngsters, and because of their increasingly skilled ensemble acting, *The Donna Reed Show* survived the initial low ratings and bad reviews. But, for Donna, the first two seasons were a protracted nightmare.

Not since her early days in California had Donna worked so hard. Up at five-thirty in the morning, she was at the studio by seven, prepared for shooting or rehearsing by nine, and often returned home after sunset.

At home the second shift began: taking care of the children, helping them with their schoolwork, memorizing fifteen or twenty pages of script. She gave in to exhaustion while reading the morning newspaper at bedtime. And there was no letup. Her seventeen-hour days continued one after another for thirty-nine straight weeks (television seasons are half as long now).

"This is about as glamorous as working on a chain gang," Donna told a reporter. On weekends she was, blessedly, glued in with the kids, but professional demands—wardrobe maintenance, business dinners, public appearances, interviews, and photo sessions—often intervened.

The pressure caused Donna to lose sleep and shed pounds. She looked drawn during those first months. Her show was taking a hit from every quarter. True, she had Tony behind her, handling money details, talking back to the front office, lending his toughness. Though Donna gave him full credit, she carried the creative load, concerning herself with sets and costumes, writing and directing. "When I should have been thinking about the script, I was worrying about a thousand little production problems," she said later.

Andrew McCullough remembered her total professionalism. "She wasn't overseeing everything. She *knew* everything. She had the best sense of a set of anyone I ever worked with." Her attentiveness could be almost scary. One morning she arrived on the set, said good morning, and asked casually, "Who is that on the catwalk?" No one else had noticed that a man was sleeping there.

Of course, her main energy went into acting Donna Stone. She feared that different scriptwriters every week would make it hard for her to portray a consistent character. Then she realized that, no matter, Mrs. Stone was really an extension of herself. What seemed the easiest assignment in the world was actually the hardest. The ordinary doctor's wife couldn't be dull or saccharine. She couldn't be Pollyanna or Miss Fixit or Mrs. Boob. She had to make things happen without seeming too aggressive. In the Eisenhower era she had to be subtle in making decisions without consulting her husband. She had to be credible on the plane of idealized reality, bright without a barrage of funny lines, affecting without big dramatic scenes, and forever fresh in spite of a pace that would kill a mule.

Always a perfectionist, Donna thought she overacted terribly in the early episodes. Carl, trying to make Dr. Stone more interesting, got into dark, offbeat things that were inappropriate to the character. Overcorrecting, he came off as too flat at first. Paul was too brash; he and Shelley needed stronger direction. During that opening season, Donna felt that she was holding the show together by herself. "There was so much bad film on everyone that they always ended up cutting to me, and that's death for a performer," she told a friend. Exhausted from being in every scene, she finally asked the scriptwriters to plot around her when possible. They had never before heard a star say, "There's too much of me. Let's divide it up."

The stories were simple—little morality plays without loud preaching. Donna teaches Jeff boxing from a book and chaperones (using a caterer) some boys on a camping trip, Jeff feels that his parents prefer Sister, Mary is ashamed of the Stone household when a rich friend visits, Dr. Stone is a real pain as a hospital patient, Donna tries to collect money owed him.

Donna Stone is always matchmaking, raising funds, taking in stray children and animals, bolstering the socially inept, helping the indigent while saving their pride, employing reverse psychology to get others to defend what they had at first rejected. The scriptwriters were instructed to make her "a strong personality who approached situations positively." They dared not suggest the overbearing mother described by Philip Wylie in *A Generation of Vipers*. Donna winced at the title of her show in West Germany—"Mother Always Knows Best."

Not written by a committee, as sitcoms are today, *The Donna Reed Show* permitted some individual stamp on a script. Creativity was limited (or challenged) by a strict moral code. The twin beds were for reading; babies might have sprung from Athena's forehead. According to Nate Monaster, the only writer to have his own office at Screen Gems, "You used maybe three percent of your vocabulary and about two percent of human ideas."

Even so, Monaster wrote more subtle, complex scenarios than most of his colleagues. Donna "loathed" Nate's first effort, which portrayed Alex as threatened by his wife's domestic authority. She fought against that framing of their relationship. But the segment was retained because she and Tony didn't want to lose "one of the best TV writers in the business." He went on to script some of her favorite episodes.

Nate Monaster and Tony Owen shared a Chicago background. The bookish Nate grew up in a Jewish-Italian neighborhood on the West Side. "Four people on my block went to the electric chair," he said. As a police reporter, Tony knew some of the same Chicago characters. "Is the shit-heel in?" Nate would whisper to Tony's secretary. That was the way the boss talked. But Nate curbed the camaraderie that Tony invited. The tension between them was partly political: the producer was a conservative, the writer a liberal and feminist. "I know you're a f—— commie, but I happen to like your family," Tony told Nate.

During the second year Nate complained to Tony that no blacks had appeared on the show. The sixties hadn't happened, and those blacks visible on television were stereotyped: Rochester the valet, Beulah the pancake cook. Tony phoned the casting agency and said, "Nate wants a black face." Making the honchos there jump—that was a way of proving his power. So, in a future segment of *The Donna Reed Show*, a well-dressed black woman and her small daughter were glimpsed shopping in a department store. It was hardly a breakthrough, but Nate "felt like Abraham Lincoln." The color barrier still stood in 1965, when a part for a black neighbor boy was written into a story. Before it could be filmed, Donna was called out of town. She remembered, "When I got back everyone had fallen down on the show—the network, the sponsor. We'd be blacked out in the South, they said." A white actor was substituted.

Nate's participation in the Writers Guild strike of 1961 annoyed Tony and Donna. Tension increased between the high-strung, extroverted producer and the equally high-strung but inward writer. Feeling unhinged, Nate betrayed as much to Tony on the day he announced, "I'm quitting the show." Tony countered, "Don't quit! I'll pay for your therapy!" So Nate went into psychoanalysis, underwritten by the show. After a year of counseling, he returned to face the executive producer. "Tony, I want to tell you something," he said. "I owe you more than I can ever say. Sending me to an analyst was a great idea. Now I have enough courage to tell you that you're the worst SOB I've ever known, and I'd rather die than work for you!" He walked out.

One writer who was afraid to walk *into* the studio was Alfred Levitt. He had been blacklisted by the industry after appearing before the House Un-American Activities Committee in the early fifties. Levitt wrote for *The Donna Reed Show* using the name Tom August, collaborating at first with Jerry Davis.

One day Davis persuaded his invisible partner to come to the studio for a script conference—it was about 1960 and perhaps a bit safer. Levitt entered the studio warily, was recognized by the secretary, and fled in panic, taking refuge in Nate Monaster's office as if it were a foreign embassy. "Tony knows me! He knows me!" Al said to Nate. Al certainly knew that he was known when Tony Owen said to him, rather jokingly, "Donna has been asked to make a speech for John Foster Dulles. Do you think it would be good casting for you to write the speech?" Al replied quietly, "No, I don't think so."

It was a strained situation. Tony's attitude was *"don't* tell me." Although he obviously knew that Al was blacklisted, Tony was protected as long as he could say he did not know. If Al's status had been made known, Al would have been fired, along with those who could *not* say they never knew. Al's wife and usual writing partner, Helen, was also on the blacklist. The Levitts always felt that Donna knew their true identity and that she was the one who let them go on working.

Helen Levitt—or, rather, Helen August—went from her own kitchen into Donna Stone's. She wanted all the nonessentials to be real, so her scripts called for Donna to make toast, scramble eggs, in a kitchen with a functioning stove, refrigerator, and sink. The Stones came together at the breakfast and dinner table. In her political activism and cultural background, Helen Levitt was very different from this television family, but as a mother who had washed dishes and scrubbed floors, she understood and respected Donna Stone. All the scripts she wrote for Donna were inspired by a neighbor in North Hollywood—"a Southern Baptist lady who went to church with Tennessee Ernie Ford."

Like Nate Monaster, the Levitts wanted to stretch the medium. They were friends of the cinematographer James Wong Howe, who had to go outside Los Angeles County to get a license to marry a Caucasian woman. In 1961 they dared to suggest a script about an interracial couple, a Japanese woman married to an American. Phil Sharp, producing at the moment, predicted the higher-ups would never approve the story. Surprisingly, they did; and the Oscar winner, Myoshi Umeki, guest-starred as the wife who is befriended by Donna. Stretching further, capitalizing on the Kennedy physical fitness craze, the Levitts had a notion that excited Tony: bringing real sports figures into the show. Segments were written around Don Drysdale of the Los Angeles Dodgers and Willie Mays of the San Francisco Giants. "No one had ever done that before," said Helen.

Television consumed writers, but a coterie made an impression. Bill Roberts rewrote half the scripts during the first season without claiming screen credit or residuals. John Whedon was another wordsmith who could take a realistic idea and give it a humorous twist. Paul West, who produced for three years, wrote with a warm Capralike sensibility. Phil Sharp, who had written for comedian Phil Silvers, specialized in con scenes—he would have had Donna selling used cars, but his talent was checked. His wife, Barbara Avedon, gave her scripts a feminine, sometimes a feminist, edge.

Donna had a large but gentle say in the stories. She was, said Paul West, "the steel fist in the velvet glove." Andrew McCullough remembered, "In conferences she picked up what was wrong with a script and how to fix it, and at first the writers didn't like it. So she had to play the part of a woman—she had to shift from saying, 'You know, we need a scene outside the house where this can happen,' to saying, 'Well, I don't know anything about writing, but just as a woman it would be difficult for me to do this.' Then the writers would gladly fix it." They learned to listen because "she had a bright, bright story mind," said director Jeffrey Hayden.

She had a clear sense of her character. Today, Donna Stone is often blasted for being selfless, sexless, faultless, blah. She is seen, negatively, as the Perfect Wife and Mother. In a 1992 book, *The Erotic Silence of the American Wife*, Dalma Heyn declared that a woman's personal fulfillment depends upon "the murder of Donna Reed." But in the early nineties, marathon showings of *Donna Reed* revealed a surprising amount of feminism. Surprising, that is, for the period of its production, and for a format not given to slapstick or the trading of insults.

Mrs. Stone is acutely aware of how the culture comes down in every exchange between men and women. Time and again she tells Alex that he is just like a man—"smug" and "ever so faintly patronizing." At the end of one segment, when he reasserts his status with a half-hearted apology for some misdeed, she replies, in a voice full of sugar and acid, "The most unselfish selfishness I've ever heard."

Barbara Avedon, who later helped create the female-buddy series *Cagney and Lacey*, wrote a script in which Alex and a colleague go duck hunting. Beforehand, at the Stone house, the men agree that "modern woman has been pampered by push-button housekeeping." Donna insists, "We can do anything our grandmothers did if we have to." Alex takes a parting shot, "Don't you be mad, Donna. I still think you're pretty cute for one of those new models." Challenged, Donna invades the woods where the men are and finds ways to prove her pioneering grit while waiting. Alex and his friend arrive at the cabin with no ducks bagged. Now Donna has them: "I have a question for modern man: How many ducks did you get?" They mumble zero, and in a close-up she says, mocking their earlier condescension, "Aw-w-w-w-w!" That evening, pampered man dines on imported ham.

Nate Monaster wrote two episodes that showed Donna fighting the labels stuck on women, who might be independent-minded even though they stayed at home and didn't swear off brassieres. Both are classics—in scripting, pacing, and acting as good as anything in the genre. In one, Donna fiercely resists being called "sweet," a word that had always dogged her in real life. Some evening guests compliment her sweetness, and after they leave Donna fumes, "They were trying to say I'm a goody-goody brought up on Pollyanna and Florence Nightingale!" Alex demurs, but she knows. "Women are only nice to other women when they feel sorry for them." Next day, Donna stands firm, saying no, no, no, to everyone. "I have been used, victimized, and exploited by my children and husband," she tells a delivery man who has also taken advantage of her niceness. And she isn't going to be a sap anymore.

In the other, later, segment Donna takes umbrage at the term "housewife" because it diminishes women who play many roles: "nurse, psychologist, diplomat, philosopher." She lists them for an oily radio announcer who corners and interviews "little housewives" at the supermarket. "We're not part of a herd," Donna says to the radio man, who is momentarily stunned by signs of intelligence in the bakery section. The broadcast makes her a heroine among the neighborhood women, but nothing is likely to change. "You start a serious discussion with a boy," remarks Mary, "and he acts as if you should be home baking a cake."

"My TV series certainly aggravated men," Donna asserted two decades later. "Hollywood producers were infuriated that Mom was equal and capable." Resentment occasionally leaked out on the set. "Early during the show she tried nicely to influence some of the crew members only to be rebuffed because she was a woman," said Colonel Grover Asmus, her third husband. "She then became as forceful as necessary to make sure that the show was the show she wanted to be part of. More than once she allowed technicians to embarrass themselves to prove her point."

Outside, *The Donna Reed Show* drew a level of criticism never directed against *Father Knows Best*, although the Andersons were as idealized as the Stones. It had something to do with the fact that for the first time on weekly television a pretty, soft-spoken, intelligent, youngish suburban Mommy was actually the lead (Jane Wyatt and Barbara Billingsley were not the topliners of their respective series, Harriet Nelson was an extension of Ozzie, and Gertrude Berg and Peggy Wood had not been young). Did Donna Reed think she could play in the same position as high-powered males like Robert Young? She was visible game for Jack Paar and for David Susskind, who made a joke (that palatable form of hostility) of "The Madonna Reed Show."

The syrupy image stuck in spite of (or because of) every attempt to make the show recognizably human. Three decades before *Married . . . with Children* and its ilk, Donna thought "many family sitcoms on the air were so far out in their situations, so ludicrous in their presentation of people, that no audience could identify with them." If shrill caricature was taboo, so was the passive Stepford Wife favored by the sponsor. Overcoming Campbell's reluctance, Donna and Tony instructed the writers to include fussing, even blood-in-the-eye sparring. But the colorless Karo image stuck. Carl Betz objected. "I got sick and tired of hearing that word *bland*. In some scripts we had arguments and discussions, even funny pratfalls, but nobody saw those shows."

Virtually everyone who worked with Donna Reed said that she was not temperamental on the set. But her low opinion of many Hollywood directors was well known. Too often they were insensitive to performers and hostile to women. When a staff member asked to direct, Donna insisted that he enroll in acting classes first. Technical skill was important; knowledge of human beings more so.

Oscar Rudolph directed nearly all the episodes during the first year. He was a roly-poly man who treated everyone like family, a competent craftsman who kept one eye on the clock and turned out a formulaic product. Donna grew tired of Rudolph's direction, desired freshness, but many of his segments (recently seen in reruns) are much better than she thought at the time. His greatest success came later with *Batman*.

Several young directors got their footing on *The Donna Reed Show*. Jeffrey Hayden had spent two years at MGM making a movie when he signed on. The husband of Eva Marie Saint and father of two small children, Hayden understood Donna's "informed and caring" point of view. Incidents from his own family life strayed into the stories. While directing the show he was the most popular fellow on his street in Brentwood. Long afterward, Hayden reflected on the mixture of quiet humor and tenderness supplied by Donna and the producer, Paul West. Another talented beginner on the show was Robert Ellis Miller. He directed one of the funniest segments, titled "Mary's Driving Lesson." Shelley Fabares recalled, "The moral of it was—never teach someone you care about how to drive a car, it portends bad things."

Using different directors was a safeguard against acting that lapsed into stock gestures and facial expressions. Starved for the viewpoint of another woman, Donna was pleased when Ida Lupino directed briefly in 1959. In those early years, Norman Tokar, a movie veteran of light comedy, took the Stones in hand. The elegant Fred de Cordova, helmsman for *The Johnny Carson Show*, brought fun to his stints. Gene Nelson, who had danced and acted in *Oklahoma* and *Tea for Two*, carved a new career in directing the show.

Andrew McCullough returned, he felt, to assure the kind of working milieu Donna wanted. "Everyone had to come up to her professional standards," he said. "She was upset with people who didn't keep learning, studying, growing." Such drive might easily have resulted in tenseness on the set, but the head woman established a happy tone. Fun without horseplay, candor without abrasiveness. A director who bullied didn't stay long. Tony Owen's pungent language was restricted to the back area—when he was around. "If I needed him for anything, he was out playing golf, betting at the races, or getting laid," said McCullough, wryly.

Like most shows of the era, *Donna Reed* was photographed by a single camera. After rehearsal the red eye turned on: master and close-up and over-the-shoulder shots were made, rarely in story sequence. The movies had trained Donna in this method. Because dramatic momentum was not possible as in a continuous performance, the actor had to retain the emotional memory of related scenes filmed at different times so that the editor could match them in a final cut. It was a neat trick. Music and canned laughter were added later.

Most sitcoms today are done with three or four cameras whirring. For Shelley Fabares, the experience of making *Coach* was very different from that of *The Donna Reed Show*. Twice on Fridays, *Coach* was performed straight through like a play, with the actors being caught by multiple cameras and timing their lines to accommodate the laughter of the studio audience. What was seen on the home screen was the best of the two performances spliced together on film. In *Coach* Shelley knew the stress of a stage actor who cannot easily stop or start over after the curtain rises (or camera begins). The tension in filming *Donna Reed* came with the repeated takes—a wearisome process. Those retakes partly explain why older shows like Donna's have a more polished look, if not a more spontaneous feel.

Donna believed that her right jaw was too square and wanted to be photographed in profile from the left. Her hair, which was thin and hard to manage, didn't always provide cover, so she asked directors not to shoot her "bad side." Jeffrey Hayden could never convince her that she looked good from any angle. Sometimes, because of the way a comedy situation was constructed, getting the best side of Donna was hard. "She was never bitchy about it," said Gene Nelson. Carl Betz paid little attention to the camera, but Donna always knew exactly where the lens was cutting her. Schooled in the grammar of film, she dreaded the moment when Gert Anderson, the cameraman, shouted "Lower the key lights!" That meant she was looking old and tired.

Off-camera, she wasn't chained to the mirror. Her grooming seemed effortless to intimates who never saw her hair in curlers. Being at MGM, where everyone looked good, and sitting next to Ava Gardner, Lana Turner, and the young Elizabeth Taylor had long since put beauty in perspective. "She could have been a lot more out there with her beauty than she was," said her daughter, Mary Owen.

Donna came to rehearsals wearing hardly any cosmetics, and Andrew

McCullough thought she looked loveliest then. "She had good coloring, great skin—many movie stars have bad skin from all the paint." McCullough pleaded to photograph her with minimal makeup. But Clay Campbell, the professional and conventional makeup man, and Donna herself weren't comfortable with that. Directors didn't always have the final say.

If different directors could give a new dimension, so could guest stars. An early guest was Virginia Christine, later known to Americans as Mrs. Olson, the Folger's Coffee lady. Like Donna, Virginia came from Iowa. The water tower of the Swedish community of Stanton, her birthplace, now resembles a coffeepot, in her honor. After moving to California, Virginia sang at the Iowa picnics in Long Beach; she studied music at Los Angeles City College while Donna was there. Tutored by the German actor Fritz Feld, whom she married, Virginia started in movies about the same time as Donna and by the fall of 1958 she was a seasoned actress in every medium.

For Virginia Christine, *The Donna Reed Show* was an easy, but memorable, assignment. Dr. Stone got roped into judging a baby contest, and Virginia entered her jug-eared darling. One scene called for the infant to be dressed under the hot lights. Virginia and Donna, being mothers, knew the reaction would be loud crying. "Let me worry about that," said the director. "Yes, but it isn't going to work," said the women. "Who's directing this picture?" he asked. So they shut up. What should have been a quiet scene was a disaster. Virginia, Donna, and Carl hovered over the baby, who screamed lustily on being undressed. The director ordered, "Bring me another baby!" The result was the same, but the director, heating up, was adamant about getting the shot. Now the baby was truly furious, and the actors shouted to be heard above the squalling. Suddenly the little one, a male, let out a stream of pee. "All three of us got good and wet right across the kisser," said Virginia. "It must have been a marvelous outtake."

Two other veterans, Kathleen Freeman and Howard McNear, played a riotous neighbor couple, the Wilguses. They made a half-dozen appearances in the spring of 1959 and might have, should have, stayed on. Celia Wilgus was a child-woman, bossy and pouty. Kathleen saw her as an eternal type who let the world know that hubby wasn't quite up to snuff and never spared his feelings, but in a second could turn on him and vow her love, love, love. A comical touch was that Celia wore her hair in a tight, incongruously elegant topknot.

Kathleen and Howard brought fun to the set of *The Donna Reed Show*. The star, burdened by responsibilities, seemed to need their levity. She wanted them to continue in their roles, but some executive, speaking for American taste, took them out. Though Donna wished to avoid over-sweetness, the powers that made her show possible wanted more angel cake. The Wilguses were just a bit off-flavor.

The first Christmas show, which has never been syndicated, was something special. Buster Keaton was the hospital janitor impersonating Santa Claus. The spindly comic suited up during a three-minute silent routine. Bill Roberts remembered that the crowd gathered behind the camera choked back laughter; Donna stuffed a handkerchief in her mouth.

Three other old-timers appeared a few episodes later, in "Miss Lovelace Comes to Tea." Estelle Winwood, the English actress, charmed the Stones into hiring her as a housekeeper. Margaret Dumont, famous as the portly foil for the Marx brothers, took a final call, as did Esther Dale, a snooty clubwoman and poisonous gossip in many a movie. In retrospect, all this classical talent in a single half-hour sitcom seems a coup, but at the time no one noticed.

One evening several years ago, Esther Williams turned on her TV and saw the segment she did with Donna in 1960. She liked it. "We were completely without artifice, talking like girls, both so pretty," she said. "I was playing a clothes designer, and here I am now designing swimsuits." Esther had been approached to do her own series, but dropping in on Donna's show gave her pause. "I observed the producer [Tony Owen] in the office and thought how removed he seemed from the problems and how embroiled she was in them." Another guest from MGM days was Fay Bainter. "Donna worshiped her. She was kind of like a little girl with Bainter around," recalled Andrew McCullough.

Some guests appeared semiregularly, like Jimmy Hawkins, who had been Donna's youngest son in *It's a Wonderful Life* and was now old enough to be Mary Stone's boyfriend. Jimmy alternated between *Donna*

Reed and *Ozzie and Harriet*. There was a cross-pollination of stars from other shows being shot at Screen Gems. Jay North, or Dennis the Menace, visited the Stones, making a mess for Donna. And Lassie, looking more expensive than anyone, glided in.

Harvey Korman, the future sidekick of Carol Burnett, will always remember *The Donna Reed Show* because it provided his first professional acting job in Hollywood. For three days of work, he was paid $125, "which is considerably more than I earn now as an actor." George Hamilton also made his television debut, as Mary Stone's date for a dance. During the filming he suffered from stomach virus and required heavy makeup to cover his most unusual paleness.

Shelley Fabares had a huge crush on the singing idol James Darren, who stopped in Hilldale. "I couldn't breathe when he was on the set and turned every shade of fuchsia when he looked in my direction." Nevertheless, she acted cool in front of the camera, she thought, until called upon to cry. Then she couldn't turn off her tears. Donna divined the reason. "It was lunch time," recalled Shelley, "and Donna spent the entire hour walking me back and forth on the empty stage with her arm around me, holding my hand, talking to me about the kind of feelings I was having and how hard the week must have been for me and how proud of me she was that I had been able to perform my job as an actress—all these wonderful soothing mother noises."

A change to a better hour for family viewing—eight o'clock on Thursday nights—at the beginning of the second season raised ratings. In a few months *The Donna Reed Show* bested its competition in that time slot, *Bat Masterson* and *The Betty Hutton Show*.

Real success came in 1961, when Donna was the only woman to head a weekly television series—Barbara Stanwyck, Loretta Young, June Allyson, and the others had been cancelled. It was harder now for opinion makers to ignore her. Some were snide. *Newsweek* wondered how Donna had stayed afloat in such a pointless vehicle, descending from *Eternity* to *here*.

By 1962, *Donna Reed* was firmly anchored, with an audience exceeding thirty-five million. In one evening Donna was seen by more people than might have seen her in movie theaters during an entire year. The heavy mail was the kind known to every celebrity: requests for personal totems, perhaps a castoff shoe; requests from schoolchildren engaged in class projects. The guardians of rank and fact were also watching. The Michigan Council of Churches protested when a minister was portrayed as a killjoy in one segment. The U.S. Park Service complained because a park attendant in one show wore a forest ranger's uniform with the badge upside down.

Donna received the coveted Golden Globe as the best female star in television in 1962. She didn't expect to win an Emmy, and never did. Though harder to play than straight drama, light comedy looked easier and was less likely to be awarded, she thought.

She was now a major public figure, constantly being asked to kick off this, chair that, say a few words. Typical was a sticky eulogy to mothers (written by Norman Vincent Peale) that she delivered at the Waldorf in New York. The emphasis of the Donna Reed legend was shifting. Once she had famously milked cows on the farm; now she was "doing more for American motherhood than Mother's Day." Increasingly, she was seen, and saw herself, as a counselor to young people. "When you assume you are worthless, or that there's very little you can accomplish, you're assuming that God made you without a purpose," she addressed them in the mid-sixties. "Nothing is going to be required in life that [you] won't be able to handle. Someone wise once said: Do the thing and you shall have the power."

Fans by the carload gawked at the Owen house in Beverly Hills. Some walked to the front door and rang the bell. Privacy was confined to those four walls. The children particularly hated the fuss that went along with eating in restaurants.

During the years of *The Donna Reed Show* the Owen family was often photographed at home on the patio. Mary Anne, the precious baby girl, was on her mother's lap. Touched by sunshine, dressed in sporty California style, they all beamed for the camera. A tall pitcher of lemonade or fruit juice was at hand. The public saw "the wonderful world of Donna Reed." That was the phrase splashed across a magazine advertisement which showed Donna and Tony standing on a Royalweve carpet.

Though less visible, Tony enjoyed the spotlight more than Donna. At Chasen's he claimed a front table; she wanted a back one. "He lived high on the cob, and she was more circumspect," said Karen Moreland. Growing up with money and seeing his father bankrupted, Tony knew that fortune might be temporary even with the best management. Growing up without money and coming early to the prospect of fortune, Donna would manage never to be short again. If she was careful, he was often extravagant. He gave her a turquoise necklace on her thirty-ninth birthday, diamonds and pearls at Christmas, a Rolls-Royce for their fifteenth wedding anniversary.

The silver Rolls was waiting when they arrived at the London airport in April 1960. Donna and Tony, with Barbara Avedon and her husband, drove to Blenheim Palace, Churchill's birthplace, in the $12,500 cloud-on-wheels. A week or so later it entered the States as a used car at reduced duty, a common practice.

Donna never cottoned to the Rolls, preferring to drive a Ford station-wagon. "She didn't like ostentation," said Barbara. Neither did the kids. Timmy would duck down in the seat when the Rolls approached his school; he was afraid of being seen by classmates and teased about his airs. The family cook, though, was mightily impressed. One day while the Owens were gone she got the key to the Rolls and went cruising, and that finished her.

Some close to Donna thought her marriage to Tony was by this time fairly loveless. But, as Tony's sister, Sukie Mergener, said, "No one ever really knew those two." They certainly cared about each other. Published interviews reveal their affectionate sparring. Tony and Donna reminded one reporter of Leo Durocher and Laraine Day: "They can be turtle-dovy one moment and fiercely argumentative the next."

Barbara Avedon would have cast Tony Owen as "a charming Chicago hood" in a movie. He certainly could give a good imitation of a bad guy, said Paul West. When Paul started as a writer-producer, Tony's first words to him were, "I want you to remember somethin'. I can have any guy in this town rubbed out for five hundred bucks." His swarthy appearance and gravelly voice seemed to back up the words. Of course they were bluster, meant to establish control over someone who might cause future trouble for him.

Tony wasn't really a villain. What saved this supercharged Chicagoan was a basic innocence. "He talks into the telephone with the speed of an IBM machine but with the cherubic expression of a child still incredulous that the darned thing works," wrote John Crosby. What saved him was a kind of magic. "It was hard to be mad at him," said daughter Mary, "because he was so damned charming." He was also vulnerable in his unguarded emotionalism.

To some on the set, Tony seemed completely devoted to Donna. Every Monday he sent flowers to her dressing room. "She was precious to him, and not just financially," said Bill Roberts. And she was partly his creation, for without him *The Donna Reed Show* would have died aborning. He lent her cheer and boldness, she told the press. "Tony is a wild, wonderful man who is happiest when he is making others happy."

Off the set, at home, the children often sensed strain between their parents, though they never saw fights. "Not a lot of affection was shown outwardly," said Tim. But all the Owens were so active during the years of the show, the house was never quiet or empty, and Mom and Dad were partners in an enterprise that supported many people.

If Tony was seldom home, well, he was not unlike the traditional German Jew who was often out with his poker buddies. Anyhow, sex roles were more blurred then; men weren't really expected to be nurturing. Timmy did attend football and baseball games with his father. Occasionally, the boy would tag along to the Friar's Club, where Tony took the steam, got a rubdown, and played gin rummy. "The thing about Dad was, his friends—famous and rich and influential—were very important to him. He wasn't around much."

Like Tim, Mary related to her father through sports. He was fifty when she was born, and supposedly more settled, but she missed knowing him well. She was her momma's girl, and doted on. "Our little bonus gal," Donna called her. "I was her baby," said Mary, "but I think she was exhausted and very distracted as a mother. She loved us all and did the best she could, but there was a lot going on in her mind. She was always extremely busy."

Arriving a decade after her siblings, Mary grew up feeling by herself. As a preschooler, she communed with pet animals and talked on a toy phone with an imaginary person. "A lot of my childhood was unreal," she realized later. The Alpine house was on a crest, and she liked to ride a four-wheeled lion down the slope, swerving at the bottom to avoid the street and onrushing cars. Exuberant, yet sweetly fragile, Mary disliked anything smacking of glitz, annually saying "Ick!" to the Christmas lights hung outside the house. "Spock doesn't include a chapter on seven-year-old dissenters," wrote Donna to a friend in 1964.

The mature Mary would appreciate her mother's midwestern honesty and directness, her extraordinary intelligence, her capacity for caretaking. But Mary felt that before the show ended, her mother "sort of became her television persona." The entire family "bought into protecting the Donna Reed Show image—that was absolutely an unspoken agreement." And that meant the children *had* to be good.

Though Donna was very family-oriented, Mary had little sense of family cohesion during the sixties. Penny achieved independence quickly; Tony Junior bonded outside with a religious group; and Tim and Mary, genetically linked, were wilder, more rebellious. Visiting the TV soundstage, Mary often felt that the hairdresser Trudy Wheeler, the cameraman Clay Campbell, and other staffers were her real family. During these years, when interviewers routinely forced a comparison between Donna's real and television families, the Owens were rarely all together, Mary recalled, except to watch *The Donna Reed Show*.

Some of Mary's best memories centered on family vacations at Coronado, the seaside hotel in Queen Anne style near San Diego. Ronald Reagan's children were playmates there, and Donna befriended Doris Day and other regulars. "We had so much fun playing tennis and swimming," recalled Mary, "but Mom would be locked up in the room all day to catch up on her reading. She hardly ever came out. I think she desperately needed privacy."

Even during those letdown times at Coronado, Donna's mind raced. She brought along armloads of books, mainly nonfiction, from Martin-dale's. Whenever she traveled overseas, she immersed herself in local culture and history. Thrilled to be in romantic Florence, Donna wanted to spend time at the Piazza della Signoria and the Church of San Lorenzo, but Tony wanted to gab with strangers and keep moving. "He didn't enlarge his horizons as Donna did," said Mary Lou Daves, the widow of director Delmer Daves.

The tour that all the Owens remember came in July 1962, when they saw President Kennedy at the White House. Tim was "awfully nervous" as he manfully shook hands with JFK, who was "charming as could be." The president asked Donna about her sister Heidi. During his bachelor days Jack Kennedy had dated Heidi a few times. ("I wouldn't let him kiss me goodnight," she recalled.) In a casual way, that moment at the White House gauged the distance that had been traveled by two country girls from Iowa.

A top-flight model, Heidi had been married since 1957 to Dr. Michael Flynn from Ireland, a prominent plastic surgeon. During the forties and fifties her classic, well-scrubbed face looked out of ads for Ivory soap, Colgate toothpaste, Camel cigarettes. After a hundred or so television commercials, she played a spoiled rich girl in a TV drama with Jeanne Crain. Once was enough; she disliked the business of acting, having observed the demands on Donna, especially the time spent on the telephone. Heidi always thought she had more fun, though modeling could be "nerve-shattering."

As the firstborn, Donna took a mother-hennish interest in her siblings, contributing generously to the education of several of them, keeping posted on their doings. By the sixties, Keith Mullenger had passed his bar exams and joined a big patent law office in New York City. His wife, Adrienne, was a model and former Miss Rheingold. The younger Bill Mullenger was still in Iowa, farming on the homeplace, and married to Sandy, "a darling." All of Donna's new nieces and nephews were cooed over in letters.

Karen had always been "Donna Reed's little sister," often the object of pointing and whispering. She developed into a pretty and popular young woman, but was rather aloof, feeling that she wasn't judged on her own merits. An excellent student, she won a major scholarship to Stanford University in 1960.

Donna was overjoyed, but Karen was cool about the chance to attend Stanford in California. She murmured that she might stay in the Midwest. Perplexed, Donna flew to Denison, joining other family members one evening at the Mullenger house. Lights were turned off so that neighbors and autograph seekers would not interrupt, and in the darkened living room Donna led the push: Karen simply must not let Stanford slip away. It would be foolish not to go. Feeling cornered, Karen finally agreed. Later she appreciated Donna's nudging.

At Stanford she felt liberated and for three years never told a soul that she was Donna Reed's sister. That restraint was remarkable, because Donna was a television superstar now. When Karen married in June 1963, Donna gave her a fancy wedding. Being kids of the sixties, Karen and her groom wanted to make a change in the nuptial vows. "Absolutely not!" said Donna. "But it's *our* wedding," they said. "But I'm giving it and I'm the one who will be judged if things aren't done right—not you," replied Donna. Today Karen remembers: "For all her generosity and goodness, she had a very stringent side. There were lines that just didn't get crossed."

Karen was a quiet watcher, influenced by Donna's ideas about child-rearing (which were hard to practice with an acting career and uncompanionable husband). In some funny way, *The Donna Reed Show* provided an alter-life for her celebrated sister, who believed in its underlying ideals and never allowed cynicism to creep into the tired format. "She wanted a high moral tone to seem like real life."

Real life had its grief. During the years of the show Donna lost her mother by inches to Parkinson's disease. "There just doesn't seem to be any new relief in sight. She is secluded at all times," Donna wrote to Joyce Fisk in 1961. No longer able to feed herself, Hazel was cared for by Bill Mullenger, a prince of patience. Some winters they sought warmth in Douglas, Arizona.

The spring of 1962 brought the elder Mullengers to New York and the home of Keith and his wife, Adrienne. Hazel entered St. Barnabas Hospital for a surgical procedure that had been tested and improved by a famous specialist. Still, it was a frightening experience. The operation involved drilling a hole on the top of the head and freezing nerves to control shakiness. Only one side of the body could be treated at a time, and general anesthesia was impossible. The surgery was a qualified success, and by early 1963 Hazel had gained ten pounds. But the doctors wouldn't "do" the other side because of possible complications.

All through this period Donna worried about her mother, once leaving the set of the show and flying out to Iowa for a day. "She was always extremely good to her folks," said Sandy Mullenger.

Tony Junior was the only little Owen to appear, in bit parts, on *The Donna Reed Show*. It wasn't a family affair like *Ozzie and Harriet*, which picked up viewers in 1957 by parlaying Ricky into a musical sensation. Ricky Nelson's success gave the producer of *Donna Reed* an idea. One day Tony Owen asked Shelley Fabares and Paul Petersen if they would like to return next season. "Oh yes, Mr. Owen!" Well, then, they would have to sing.

Shelley was doubtful, Paul eager to experiment. They made some demonstration records—of solos and duos—at Columbia with Freddie Karger playing piano, and these were sent to Stu Phillips in New York. "I was awful," said Shelley. She expected this Stu person to listen and agree, "She's right, she can't sing." To her astonishment and dismay, he said, "Oh well, we can make anyone sound like anything. Bring her into New York."

When she got there, Stu Phillips asked, "Now, what's your range?" Shelley replied, "Nobody's getting what I'm saying. I don't *have* a range. I *can't* sing." She returned to the West Coast, followed by Phillips, who wanted her to try a certain song. But Tony Owen vetoed it as too sophisticated, and Phillips threw in something about a Johnny. So Shelley recorded "Johnny Angel" in an echo chamber to enlarge and enhance her voice. She sang softly to maintain control while the violins played. Then she repeated the lyrics, and technicians dubbed this rendition over her first—it was called double-tracking. Stu Phillips was proved right.

Lip-synching the words, Shelley introduced her record on *The Donna Reed Show* in January 1962. "Johnny Angel" quickly sold a million copies, and ultimately over three million. "It's a lovely record and I'm proud of it," says Shelley today, "but I'm still not a singer."

Paul Petersen also became an idol in the youth culture's last bubble of homogenized innocence—just before the advent of the raunchier Beatles and the politically aware Peter, Paul, and Mary. In 1962 he sang twice on *The Donna Reed Show.* The novelty "She Can't Find Her Keys," which was named worst song of the year by the *Harvard Lampoon,* occurred in a dream sequence, and "My Dad" was a moist-eyed tribute to Dr. Alex Stone.

Both recordings placed high on the charts, but Paul never made a dollar from them. Instead, he ended up owing $27,000 to the music company for promotion and other costs! "Managers are sharper today, and you have a right to inspect the books, but that wasn't so then, and there was no union to protect me." Shelley's experience was similar. "Most if not all the profits went to the recording company, and that's just the way it was set up," she said. "Fair, no, but . . ." Donna, whose own past labor had enriched faceless entrepreneurs, could do nothing.

Not always at center stage, Donna was content to look on adoringly as Shelley and Paul did their musical turns. She was a bit more relaxed about the show and was on the verge of remarkable personal changes. But at the moment she stuck to her Iowa conservatism; her flirtation with FDR liberalism had ended with Bill Tuttle. In a 1961 letter she clearly felt that Kennedy was leading the country into foreign perils. "How about that mess in Cuba, Asia, and the one brewing in Iran? I'm beginning to wonder if it is at all possible now to stem the Communistic tide; have we goofed forever our chance to help the have-not countries where political reform is the answer, not billions of U.S. dollars?" Tony worked for Barry Goldwater in 1964, and Donna sympathized with the Republican presidential candidate who "had the media against him."

In April of that election year, Donna attended the opening of the World's Fair in New York at the request of her new sponsor, Singer Sewing Machine. She was a guest in the amphitheater where President Johnson spoke. "There was an ominous feeling in the air," Donna told the right-wing columnist Hedda Hopper. "Secret Service men were stationed every three or four feet, and they looked grim. Just before the arrival of the helicopter carrying the president, an ambulance drove into Singer Bowl and stayed with the motor running during the entire program. You could hear such ugly, angry voices—an explosive kind of atmosphere." The newspapers reported that police arrested three hundred civil rights activists who protested the government's slowness in pursuing racial integration.

It was a disturbing experience for the normally insulated Donna. Her political transformation would come after her tenure on television, and through the exercise of an open mind. Unlike many people, she didn't restrict her reading to commentary that agreed with her. The director Andrew McCullough, a liberal, brought books and articles to Donna, knowing that they were alien to her philosophy. But she waded into them. A week or so later she might say, "Oh yes, about that Lippmann piece," and raise her considered objections. The more she read, the less she was ruled by emotional partisanship. McCullough observed how Donna "grew, changed, came to life in spite of a totally mindless environment." She was becoming, more deliberately, a citizen of the world.

Certainly the great social changes of the sixties—the effects of escalated cold war, sexual revolution, and the civil rights movement—barely made a dent on *The Donna Reed Show*. Like *Father Knows Best*, it focused on everyday crises in the nuclear family and belonged spiritually to the fifties. Even so, Donna Stone was not a plaster-perfect woman-manqué, smiling vapidly and wearing pearls and high heels while cleaning the house. Yet that image of her—of Donna Reed—is perpetuated by commentators and analysts of American popular culture.

While *The Donna Reed Show* was making an impression that would later be scorned by feminists in particular, Donna herself was riding a chartered bus toward feminism. "She began thinking for herself and realizing she didn't need a man to run her because she was brighter than anyone on the show and doing all the work," said McCullough. "She took control of her own life."

More than ever, Donna felt that the movies belonged wholly to men. "There are maybe a dozen top leading men, and the pictures are all written for them. There are very few good roles for women," she had told an interviewer in 1958. In a business now run by daredevil actors who owned their companies, women were subordinate on the screen to mountains, rivers, and cities. She thought that movie moguls revealed hatred for women by making them so unattractive. "It seems now when a woman is starred, she is playing a domineering type or is completely addlepated," Donna said in 1962. Or she was cast in a never-never land of glamour and not taken as seriously as a man. If her name was bankable, it was probably linked to well-publicized scandal and sensation. Veterans like Bette Davis and Joan Crawford had survived as horror queens.

The new wide-screen movies seemed dehumanized, concentrating on scenery and technology. Actors in a love scene looked ten miles apart, observed Donna. The epics—Biblical or not—were tasteless, awash in mayhem and perversion. Clearly, the Hollywood that had produced her was gone. She blamed James Bond for a new level of seductive, almost cartoonish violence. It was disturbing to see what was awarded as the best Hollywood could do. After *The Apartment* was honored with Oscars in 1960, she wrote to Joyce Fisk: "I found it as immoral a hodgepodge of comedy—not so funny—and tragedy—far too stark—as anything I've ever seen." Happily for the children, there was Walt Disney. Darryl Zanuck was about the only industry giant left to uphold the old standards of entertainment for all ages. In 1962 Donna wanted to quit acting and produce movies for a vast, half-forgotten audience.

Some producers still wanted Donna for movie roles, though her series allowed little time. She rejected the part of a prostitute because it had no redeeming quality and Campbell's Soup would have disapproved. In 1960 she accepted a cameo in *Pepe*, starring the Mexican comedian Cantinflas and directed by old friend George Sidney. The one-minute spot was nostalgic because she was reunited with Dan Dailey, an early leading man, but the movie was a bloated bore.

Pepe was, however, tied in with a memorable segment of *The Donna Reed Show*. The Stone family, visiting Hollywood, meet the famous director Sidney, who happens to be shooting a musical number with dancing sombreros—from *Pepe*. That night in a hotel room, Donna Stone dreams that she is a supremely self-centered actress. In dreamland, with hardly any distortion, Donna gives a devastating imitation of Bette Davis.

Following the success of *The Benny Goodman Story*, Donna had signed, in April 1956, an eight-year contract with Universal. She was promised top starring roles in three pictures. They never materialized, and in 1961 she filed a breach of contract suit against Universal. When she refused to play a minor role in *The Wild Innocents*, the studio slapped her with a countersuit. Finally, in 1963, Donna received a settlement out of court. It was a nasty foreshadowing of her later travail on *Dallas*.

In the summer of 1964, Donna was sought to play yet another wife in a picture, but she returned the script with a note pointing out that every character except the wife was interesting and she would never again play one who was dull and flat because the married women she knew were vital and versatile. The success of *Donna Reed* had proved to her that the public wanted to see "a healthy woman, not a girl, not a neurotic, not a sexpot." One could be reasonably normal *and* personally provocative.

An aging series required continued Vitamin B-12 shots, or the creative equivalent. Donna would beseech Tony to fight with Seymour Friedman of Columbia (known on the set as the Beast of Beachwood, a street by Screen Gems) for more money—the weekly budget was only about $50,000. "Tony, we're getting bogged down again," she could be heard saying on the phone.

Tony had hoped to film a few episodes in Russia, showing the lives of ordinary citizens there. That sounds like an agent's pipedream, but an overture was made to Soviet officials, who turned "very uncooperative" after the U-2 spy plane flown by Francis Gary Powers was downed in 1960.

The following year a dog was brought in—135 pounds of shaggy, slaphappy, spoiled uselessness. When the poodle joined the Stone family, a photographer from *Life* was there. A national contest was waged to find a name—mercifully, Coco was chosen over Diagnosis and Sir Yipsalot.

In one episode, Jeff asks his mother to take care of Coco. She says, "What good am I going to get out of this if I have to do all the work?" He replies, "Well, you get the use of the dog." Donna thought that was one of the funniest lines Jeff ever spoke. "Over the years it became a joke between us," said Paul Petersen. "You get the use of the dog" was the tag response to any implication of "I'm doing you a favor—what are you doing for me?"

Teenage problems were wearing down Donna by 1963. Before the camera she dealt with those of Mary and Jeff; on the set, those of Shelley and Paul; at home, those of Penny, Tim, and Tony Junior. "You can see where teen concerns might become overwhelming, to say the least," she told Joyce Fisk. Besides, it was harder for her, as Mother Stone, to hover over Mary and Jeff because they had grown much taller. "Have you ever tried to hover over someone you have to stare up at?"

As Shelley Fabares blossomed, many viewers remarked how much she resembled Donna Reed. "The fact is, if you dissected us facially, we looked nothing alike," said Shelley. "Donna had a square jaw and I have an entirely different-shaped face. She had that lovely long slender nose and I have an Irish pug nose. I have thin lips, she had a full lower lip. She had wide-set eyes and I—feature by feature, we didn't conform, but a combination of things linked us—my dresses, a similar hair style, eyebrows pencilled in to be more like hers."

If Shelley was a Donna seem-alike, that was mainly due to her attitude. "In playing Mary today I would consciously imitate Donna's way of using her hands, her walk, voice inflections, and so on. But back then I didn't know enough about acting to do that. I imitated her mannerisms unconsciously because I wanted so much to be like her."

Rumors were bruited in the trade that there was tension between the two actresses, one flowering and the other past her first flush. Donna quickly nipped them. "I love Shelley as I do my own daughters," she told a reporter. "She's so talented and well-mannered and thoughtful and un-actressy." When Andrew McCullough suggested conflict between mother and daughter in the stories, common enough in real life, Donna wanted nothing to do with it.

At the end of a five-year contract in 1963, Shelley felt ready to fly the Stone coop. She had worked all her life, and craved more time to be young. While appearing as Mary she wasn't aware of making any impact—television wasn't ruled by mouthy youngsters then as it is now. Much later she was astounded to hear prominent men say, "As Mary Stone, you were my very first crush." Nineteen years old in 1963, Shelley was receiving movie offers (she would be Elvis Presley's leading lady thrice). The next year she cashed in government bonds worth $32,400—her entire savings from *The Donna Reed Show*.

With Mary "away at college" (she would come home to the show periodically), the vacuum was filled by Trisha, an orphan who attached herself to the Stones. Tony Owen gave the role to Patty Petersen as a present for her eighth birthday, after she had pestered him for a chance to appear with her brother, Paul. An endearing gamine, Patty could have played the comic-strip character Nancy. Before the camera, she behaved rather than acted, speaking always as a child and never patronizing adults. "Being on the show was like playing at the house next door," said Patty, who now spells her name Patti. "Everyone was so good to me. I was little, they were big. Everyone had big hands."

Feeling protected and cared for, Patty visited other sets on the lot—*Hazel* and *I Dream of Jeannie*. At the commissary Carl Betz taught her how to roll spaghetti on a fork. Donna, good-natured, real in her tiredness, instituted "a family feeling down to the grips and lighting technicians." Once on the show, they never wanted to leave. The general warmth sustained Patty, separated from Paul and living with her single mother, who operated a typing service from home. Sometimes she had to forget the sheltered Trisha Stone and face a typewriter because "we needed the money."

No one connected with a television series could ever feel too secure. After the third season, the trade papers announced annually that Donna was quitting. Always she was lured back with the promise of more money or shorter seasons or expense-paid vacations. But she needed no coaxing to return in the fall of 1963. "For the first time in six years I have *time* to do a TV show, and I'd like to see what that is like! The kids have longer school days now—what am I going to do all day?" Donna wrote to a friend. "Of course my husband thinks I'm crazy and really doesn't want to do any more; aren't men perverse?"

Donna was excited by the prospect of more adult stories when Bob Crane and Ann McCrea were hired to play the next-door neighbors, Dr. Dave Kelsey and his wife, Midge. "I had been brainwashed to think our audience is mostly kids," she told the press. (Actually, a poll would reveal that young black women were the most fervent followers of *The Donna Reed Show*.)

Like Carl Betz, Bob Crane was established by *Donna Reed*. In 1963 he was a disk jockey on wake-up radio. About seven-thirty, he left the CBS building and crossed over to Screen Gems for a day of shooting. "He was a weird guy, a terrible actor, but he behaved himself on the show," recalled Andrew McCullough. "Bob never came on to me," said Ann McCrea. She saw nothing to suggest the sexual obsessions that eventually led to his murder; in fact, he expressed strong disapproval of the lusty movie *Tom Jones*. Crane did bring a nutty, manic energy to his scenes, and helped lift *Donna Reed* to the top ten in the Nielsen ratings.

The first shows involving the Kelseys were rather off-the-wall to suit Crane's personality. Then the writers began switching back to the quieter humor expected of *Donna Reed*, and some air went out of the Gracie Allen–type character played by McCrea. Midge remained a little ditzy, but the revised role allowed the actress small chance to develop her comedic talent. Gene Nelson thought she was, technically, a better performer than Bob Crane.

She was born Ann McCreight in the Allegheny mountain town of Dubois, Pennsylvania, to a Greek mother and Scottish father. He idolized W. C. Fields and used to appear with the circus at Madison Square Garden dressed to look exactly like the comedian. Ann, often sick, would be carried by her father to a porch swing, where she wrote penny postcards to movie stars, requesting their photographs. She mailed one to Donna Reed, and got no response. Finally, Ann reached New York, became a Powers model, and changed her name to McCrea, after the actor Joel McCrea. It was easier to pronounce, and she could keep the initials *McC* on her luggage. Ann had already appeared on television, often as a bargirl headed for trouble, when she auditioned for *The Donna Reed Show* early in 1963. Back from a trip to Rome and flat broke, she competed with several hundred actresses for Midge.

Though her character was soon collared, the redheaded Ann added snap. A sidekick for the sensible Donna, she was prone to fortune-telling, pleased to share a mink coat won jointly in a raffle. But when Bob Crane left after two seasons to star in *Hogan's Heroes*, Ann knew the odds were against a comedy series of her own. It was a shame, because in maturity she had a funny slant on things that kept friends laughing. With Crane out, Tony Owen wanted to drop Ann—if unconnected women had less social status in suburban America, they were also harder to fit into stories. At Donna's insistence, Ann stayed on.

Besides Paul Petersen, Carl Betz was the only regular to remain for the duration. He had intended to leave after the fourth season, but re-signed to dig out from the expense of a divorce. His second marriage, to Gloria Sokol in 1963, provided the stability he needed to stick with Dr. Alex Stone. He did not feel challenged by the role, except perhaps in creating the illusion of effortlessness.

Much to his credit, Carl never unleashed his frustration on the set. To rid his brain of vapors, he acted for the Stage Society of Los Angeles. In the evening he dashed from *Donna Reed* to the theater and was transformed into the aged man of *Krapp's Last Tape* or some other character. The pay was forty dollars a week. When he played the alcoholic, unfrocked clergyman in *The Night of the Iguana*, a man in the audience was heard to say, "That's Dr. Stone, but you wouldn't know him."

During the last years of the show, Carl and Paul Petersen grew close. After a night out, they might arrive at the studio red-eyed, but they never missed work. Paul bought a $15,000 Cobra sportscar in 1964. It was the perfect symbol of his fix on fleeting fame. To alleviate Donna's worry, he parked the powerful car some distance from the studio.

Some former associates like Paul West thought "it was sad that sponsor pressure kept the show running too long." Ratings declined by 1965, but *Donna Reed* survived conspicuously in a medium that had swallowed up hundreds of other sitcoms. It was shown in twenty-six countries; was least popular in England, where noisy Jeff was considered a bad example for children.

Donna had been honored by the American Medical Association and the National Education Association. She was, in 1965, national chairman of the Direct Relief Foundation, which shipped donated clothing, food, and medical supplies to needy areas of the free world. That year Lady Bird Johnson invited her to the White House for the opening conference on Head Start and the problem of school dropouts.

The very last *Donna Reed Show* was shot in December 1965; it would be telecast in March of the following year. Featuring the singer Lesley Gore, who stops in Hilldale, the episode has no distinction. The emotional ending for the cast and crew came a week earlier when the story focused on the sale of the Stone house. During the filming, news came of the sudden cancellation of the show, which had been scheduled for thirteen more weeks. The script called for Donna to reminisce about life in the old house, and she couldn't get through her scenes without crying. The sadness spread around the set.

Andrew McCullough, who had directed the first show in the summer of 1958, returned from New York to do the last ones. He remembered the wrapup party given by the executive producer. "It was the cheapest drugstore affair I've ever seen—a terrible ptomaine place catered cheese, bologna, Spam. Someone asked if *that* was all, and Tony told him where to go. A bar was set up with three bottles—no favorite white wine for Donna, who was gallantly thanking everyone. I ran out and bought a bottle of Dubonnet so she'd have something to sip at her own farewell party." Finally the star said her good-byes to the cast and crew and was photographed exiting the soundstage.

Through 274 episodes spanning eight seasons, Donna Stone was a soothing presence. She was in American homes almost as long as some real mothers are remembered as being there. To faithful viewers, she represented something beyond her manufactured media role. Among the poignant letters that Donna kept in her scrapbook was one written by a girl in 1967. It read: "I've always pretended in my heart that you were my mother because you're so pretty, understanding, thoughtful, warm, kind, and gentle, something I've never had in a mother and I've needed so deeply. During five awful years it was you who helped me." Karen Moreland, on being introduced as Donna's sister, has heard over and over, "Oh, I had such a horrible home life, and I would watch the show and imagine Donna Reed as my mother."

Eight springs and falls brought her home. The passing of time was reflected in the changing style of the show's opening credits. During the early period, the title and names were classically lettered; the players came out in a medium long shot; the theme song, "Happy Days," was slow and touchingly sweet; Donna had dark hair; and the children were smaller. The credits for the heyday middle period were less formal: The camera moved in closer as Donna answered the telephone, her hair was lighter, the children larger, the lettering bolder and asymmetrical, the music livelier. That the show had taken still another turn was suggested by the credits in the final period: Donna was dressed in street clothes, her hair (or wig) was professionally arranged, she glided with self-possession to the smoother music, still kissed hubby and kids good-bye as they left the house—but now she checked her wristwatch and walked out the door to keep her own appointment with the world. Though the credits changed stylistically, the introductory movements of the actors remained almost the same, and so did the setting—the stairway, telephone table, wall hanging, and latticed door were familiar and secure.

Through 137 hours, the equivalent of about sixty feature-length movies, many images remain firm in memory: Donna resembling Marie Antoinette after dyeing her hair white-blonde, Jeff smelling a rose (through his baseball catcher's mask) for the inspiration to write an English composition, Donna perspiring prettily while canning pickles, Alex confronting a lumbering version of his youthful self, Mary timidly approaching a waiter when her date can't pay a restaurant bill, Donna reading ghost stories by firelight to small boys on a camping trip . . .

Through a cavalcade of images emerged some stories that stand out because of their different modes: an eerie mystery about a Chinese carousel horse, a damsel-in-distress tale with Donna apparently imprisoned in a dark mansion, a satire proving that a monkey can obtain a credit card, a bit of Theater of the Absurd with a women's chorus supporting Donna as she perches in a carob tree to protest its removal by the city, Donna making a loose and Lucylike spectacle of herself at a medical convention after dosing on sleeping pills . . .

The long-running show placed tremendous demands on ingenuity and spirit and physical energy, but Donna left it feeling unfulfilled as an actress. Andrew McCullough begged her to do a funny Broadway play. "She would have dazzled everyone in the house, and I don't think she believed she was that good."

Anyway, how much life was to be sacrificed to acting? Actresses, at least married ones, didn't enjoy the flexibility of actors. "There are many things I should have done to become a really magnificent actress," Donna told a journalist in 1964. "I should have done something on the stage, I should have been involved in summer stock, but I didn't want school interrupted for the children and certainly there was nothing in the East for my husband, and so, you know, I've just kind of muddled through in the acting department."

After the last show was in the can, she wrote to Joyce Fisk: "I am *happy* to have finished that eight-year episode of my life. I was eight years at MGM, four years at Columbia, four years at Universal; wonder what the next four or eight years will bring?"

CHAPTER EIGHT

After the Show

The greatest luxury was being able to sleep late and wake up with two cups of coffee. Since the age of seventeen Donna had been going to college and working, then filming and raising a family. At forty-five she was tired beyond telling.

She missed Shelley, Paul, and Carl, so they lunched at the Bistro in Beverly Hills every month or so, causing heads to turn. Now she could do more charity as a member of the Colleagues and civic duty as one of the Blue Ribbon 400. She was photographed for the society pages with Mrs. Jules Stein. Blessedly, she could read saved-up books instead of scripts with thankless parts for women. She could travel, and did—to Europe and the Greek Isles. Without Tony, she joined old friends bound for India and Pakistan. Mary Lou Daves noticed how Donna loosened up, drew people to her during that jaunt. "It was almost a new experience. She had always fronted for a studio, or been married, and had never gotten around much by herself."

Briefly, all the Owens were at home. Early in 1967 they moved up the street to 919 North Alpine, which afforded elegance and enough space for antiques. Donna was ecstatic because for the first time in her life she had a room of her own. Tony might have preferred their second home in Palm Springs, but the desert never satisfied Donna's Nordic soul. "And it's so boring down there," she told a friend.

Before long, Donna was slipping into the well-known "empty hands" syndrome. Though she didn't miss acting, she needed "something creative to do." Producing a picture with Tony was out because he was sick of the business and wouldn't even look at a script. Lunching, clubbing, tripping, redecorating were fun but not terribly fulfilling. Surely there was something she could do besides performing. Something that would engage her mind.

The war in Vietnam escalated in 1966, with the United States changing from an advisory to a combat role. Nearly a hundred American troops were killed during just one week in April. Come summer, 125,000 of them were in Vietnam, with 35,000 being drafted every month. Watching the war on television, Donna was overwhelmed by despair. "I sat and suffered silently, but felt absolutely paralyzed, except for voting," she said later.

That year Donna voted against her friend Ronald Reagan, the Republican candidate for governor of California. During the campaign she complained to Reagan about his attacks on "the kids" who were massing antiwar protests. He shrugged his shoulders and replied, "But that's what people want to hear!" She was horrified when he advocated using "full technological resources," meaning nuclear, to end the fighting in Vietnam. The GOP was moving "too far right" for her, but she remained a registered Republican "in order to vote against the worst of the lot in the primaries."

Soon Donna's two sons would be fodder for the Viet maw. Without any urging from her, both resisted the draft. Tony Junior's distrust of the government had led Donna to question the American involvement in Vietnam. She thought he should serve as a noncombatant until he convinced her of the moral hypocrisy of that stance. Even as a conscientious objector he experienced turmoil that caused high blood pressure. Timothy, several years younger, tried to stay in college while the draft board eyed him every minute. "It was a time of great pain for all of us," Donna recalled after the war.

A Beverly Hills group called Another Mother for Peace asked Donna to join, and after months of hesitation she did. It was remarkable for her to link up with an organization that people close to her labeled "radical" or "feminist." Tony certainly did not approve, and neither did relatives, but she realized that women might be a reasonable force in ending the Vietnam War. Early in 1967, sixteen women had gathered around Barbara Avedon's dining room table to form Another Mother for Peace. In a few years its national membership was 285,000 and growing. Donna served as cochairman.

The mothers were civilized protestors. They didn't march or picket or call names. They wrote letters to congressmen, blizzards of letters, and based their public positions on careful research. Appearing at a press conference with Dick Van Dyke in June 1968, Donna launched a campaign for the creation of a cabinet-level department headed by a secretary of peace. The idea was first suggested by one of the signers of the Declaration of Independence, but it seemed new in this century of total war. The mothers mailed thousands of prepared cards to Washington, where they fell like snowflakes. While meeting with the press, Donna realized she had not done her homework. She returned to her reading, adjusting her thinking cap more tightly.

Donna proved vital to AMP as a researcher. Because she was a famous actress, the organization also called on her for PR work. She did some, but often resisted, knowing the general lack of respect for entertainers who ranted about world affairs. No Jane Fonda, she. "It's difficult for show people to get involved in politics in a satisfactory way," she said. "It's one thing to be passionate, it's another to be informed, equipped. But actors are citizens, and it's everyone's duty to speak up."

Donna had supported Richard Nixon in 1960, but eight years later she simply could not. He was "packaged and coached and staffed and presented right out of Madison Avenue." One day the veteran actress Norma Connolly, best known as Aunt Ruby on the daytime soap *General Hospital*, approached Donna about working in the presidential campaign of Eugene McCarthy. So the woman who stood for Mom and apple pie joined the Children's Crusade to end the war in Vietnam immediately. Donna adored McCarthy, "a good and fine, superior type man." One evening she sat by him for two and a half hours at dinner, and stayed up half that night making notes on all he had said.

With Norma Connolly, Donna was drawn to the Democratic National Convention in August 1968, though their man McCarthy was shunt of the nomination. Donna was disgusted and frightened by the proceedings in Chicago. She stayed at the Hilton and barely escaped tear gas in the lobby as the police battled demonstrators in the street. Trying to reach the amphitheater where balloting was beginning, she was jostled, pushed, swirled, sickened. Once inside, she was overcome by "the rising and falling volume of noise—anger, applause, boos—an ugly crescendo, phony cheers and signs for Humphrey." Cameras on the convention floor occasionally focused on her, but she was oblivious to them.

Next morning, Donna fled Chicago with a severe pain in her stomach that lasted four days. "If I had had my passport, I'd have left the U.S. for a few weeks," she said later. Back home, Donna reported to the steering committee of Another Mother for Peace. "She spoke of feeling she was in Nazi Germany in Chicago, with tanks in the streets and barbed wire and soldiers," recalled Barbara Avedon. "She was scared and furious."

Never before involved in politics, Donna was momentarily repelled by the hurly-burly. Those who thought she had totally succumbed to the siren call of politicking were wrong, she insisted. "This much I got out of Chicago—I couldn't stand to work with the average political hack, who is tough, insensitive, and thoroughly unattractive."

But she was increasingly committed to the antiwar effort. That meant actively supporting congressmen who voted to cut off war appropriations. Donna worked hard for Representative George Brown of California. In the 1970 senatorial race, he ran against John Tunney in the Democratic primary and lost his chance to unseat the incumbent, George Murphy. Donna held fundraising dinners for Brown at her home and cochaired his Southern California campaign. His defeat left her drained and disappointed. The Democratic hierarchy had rejected Brown, "a man of pure gold with an impeccable voting record," in favor of John Tunney, "a good-looking pure plastic fellow with a record only slightly to the left of George Murphy's." Charisma and money seemed victorious—and also "a smear campaign of the most flagrant vicious kind." Many years later George Brown remembered Donna Reed as "a warm and caring person deeply concerned about the course our country was taking." He wrote, "While I lost the race, the cause of peace won, in no small part because of the change in national public opinion brought about by Donna and her friends in Another Mother for Peace."

"I feel that we taught a whole generation of women how to make their voices heard," said Barbara Avedon. Donna believed it was up to women to build a constituency for peace by writing strong, informed letters. "I don't think men come home and write to their congressmen," she said. The thousands of women joining AMP every month in the late sixties and early seventies were urged by a newsletter to speak out. Donna did most of the research, reading widely in the most obscure sources, synthesizing useful information. "She knew the Defense Department's statistics backward and forward," said Barbara.

Donna was exercising her mind to good effect. She preferred the study to the stage. In 1969 she and Barbara—accompanied by Paul Newman, Joanne Woodward, Bess Myerson, Betsy Palmer, and others—went to Washington to lobby for the creation of a secretary of peace and against a new antiballistic missile system soon coming to a vote. "We went from office to office telling congressmen what we thought about the war. Donna and Dorothy Jones had the chapter and verse, and I had the punch in the nose," recalled Barbara. Donna was to give a speech in the Senate auditorium and show a film called *Another Family for Peace*. At the scheduled hour the place was packed with big shots, including senators and representatives, but Donna was nowhere to be seen. Barbara hurried to the hotel and found her paralyzed with fright. She had to be coaxed out of the room.

The Senate approved the "Safeguard" ABM system later in the year, but the closeness of the vote signified to Donna the influence of her organization. Another Mother for Peace was now omnipresent, its symbols and messages hard to ignore. Much in evidence was the sunflower poster with its handwritten slogan: "War Is Not Healthy for Children and Other Living Things." Syndicated newspaper articles often showed Donna standing by that poster and wearing a sunflower medallion necklace, one of the articles sold by the AMP to meet expenses. Another Mother for Peace was ultimately a global organization, but it never lost the personal touch of a neighborhood bake sale. Members felt a warm solidarity, mailing in their concerns and gathering with high purpose.

Donna was always moved by the annual Mother's Day assembly, especially the one that formed in San Francisco in 1970. She shared the podium with Bess Myerson, the New York commissioner of consumer affairs and former Miss America. The keynote speech by Myerson indicted large American corporations that were in the war business—General Motors, Dow Chemical, Whirlpool, General Electric, and Bulova Watch among them. "The companies that provide us with shiny beautiful laborsavers for our happy homes are at the same moment manufacturing products designed to destroy lives and homes in another part of the world. We never get a chance to see the rest of the line," said Myerson. She urged the women to complain to the company presidents and board chairmen: "Tell them how you feel about Pentagon Products." Donna listened raptly to the litany of facts and the refrain "You don't have to buy war, Mrs. Smith." She had just filmed similar messages for AMP. In one, the erstwhile Donna Stone looked into the camera and said, "Wouldn't it be surprising if a factory that can make a good toaster couldn't make a good bomb?"

From that San Francisco meeting was issued a worldwide *Pax Materna*. "War is obsolete," it declared. "We can no longer sustain war by our silence or with the lives of our sons. For now, forever, there is no mother who is enemy to another mother." Arnold Toynbee, one of Donna's favorite historians, didn't underestimate the power of united women. He saw them as the Pentagon's most formidable adversary. "In the mothers of America I do still see some hope for the world," he said at that time.

Donna volunteered full days to AMP, reading, writing, phoning— from her home and the organization's busy rented office. The weekly steering committee meetings were "exhausting, funny, and often productive." The women all talked at once, except Donna, who raised her hand to speak. She was clear about her part: "I try to keep my contribution scientific (arms race) and political (keeping track of Washington), and if I must say so myself, my Iowa common sense comes in very handy."

For Donna, Another Mother for Peace was "an amazing experience, better than any postgraduate course in political science." The rewards were "the greatest of my life." Quite simply, she had always wanted to help people. She told reporters, "As a human being you long to do universal things, as a woman first of all." During the last year of her television show she guessed that henceforth "scripts were not going to be enduring things for me." What she was doing in AMP "felt important." Still to come, in the early seventies, was her confrontation with Henry Kissinger and her crusade for safer nuclear plants. At the moment, she looked back on her years in movies and TV as "being trivial," adding, "as good as the industry is to women financially, it's a man's business."

In her earlier Hollywood days Donna was supposed to do what the studio asked and swallow any opinion she might have. As a wife, her thoughts really counted for little. In various situations, she was chagrined to find men recognized for ideas that had been ignored when she expressed them. Linking Donna with Vanessa Redgrave, Jane Fonda, and the Iowa-born Jean Seberg may at first seem ludicrous. But is it? *From the Journals of Jean Seberg* by Mark Rappaport asserts that Redgrave, Fonda, and Seberg in some sense resembled other actresses playing a public role in the sixties. They were (quoting reviewer Stuart Klawans) "treated as empty vessels, allowed themselves to be filled with men's ideas about ·women, and eventually sought to fill themselves through political action." Donna, seldom asked to be anything but pretty on the screen, married to a man with "childish ideas about what a woman should be," was finally filled up by her surprising activism.

The price was alienation from some old friends. "It's so bad out, I can't even have lunch with half of my girl friends anymore, and dinner including their husbands is completely out," said Donna. In 1970 she was "absolutely overjoyed" to hear that Joyce Fisk shared her opinions "regarding the war, our president, the arms race, the kids." Her siblings and in-laws certainly did not. Neither did Tony. Mary Owen remembered, "My mother blossomed when she got involved with the antiwar movement. My father was a Republican and didn't approve. I think it drove him crazy."

One evening in the late sixties Norma Connolly made the rounds in a beat-up station wagon, picking up Harry Belafonte and Marge Champion and her kids and finally Donna and Mary. They were on their way to a candlelight parade at UCLA to protest the war. "We rattled out of Donna's driveway, looking like the traveling Okies from Steinbeck's novel," said Norma. Just then, Tony came out of the house and got into his Rolls Royce to go to a fundraiser for Ronald Reagan. Something told her the Owen marriage was kaput.

The Owen household was breaking up as 1969 wound down. In September Donna and Tony decided to divorce. Late in the month Tim, deeply alienated from the mainstream culture, eloped with a girl who resembled Brigitte Bardot. Then, in November, Penny married and departed for San Francisco. The same week, Tony Junior moved out of the house on Alpine.

When twelve-year-old Mary came home from Westlake, a private school for girls, everything was unnaturally quiet. Her parents didn't talk, period, at least not in front of her. "The vibes in the house were very bad." The girl took refuge in riding horses, finding pleasure in preparing for local shows. Early in January 1970 at Will Rogers Park she was astride a misbehaving horse that fell during a jump, rolling on top of her. She was seriously injured—surgery repaired her damaged lower intestine—and Donna's own emotional pain increased.

While mending, Mary learned from schoolmates that her parents were divorcing; they had read it in the trades. At the dinner table Mary broached the subject, encountered silence at first, and was finally asked how *she* felt about the impending divorce. "I said it sounded okay, but inside I didn't feel it was." Donna and Tony and Mary would go to Palm Springs the following weekend and talk there and then.

But that family time in the Springs was canceled because Tony suffered a severe stroke. For several days he couldn't speak, and brain impairment was feared. He had been organizing a move from the house, and now Donna took the stricken man back in, nursing him for six months. In the summer of 1970, she wrote to Joyce Fisk: "He's nearly 100 percent now, and I am sad to say we are divorcing—after much soul-searching and pain, there doesn't seem to be any other way for me." Splitting after twenty-five years was, she told Heidi, "like climbing a mountain and falling all the way back down."

By August Tony was truly gone from Alpine. Donna planned to be away when he walked out the door. She took a flying trip to England with Norma Connolly, a trip marked by melancholy and the joy of release. "Donna was my gypsy girl friend," said Norma. "Suddenly we two ladies were like eighteen-year-olds." Once in London, Donna decided on impulse to take in Paris. Norma was to travel there later with her husband, the writer Howard Rodman, but Donna insisted, "I want to see your reaction to Paris." At dawn the women flew to the City of Light and rode in a cab to the Alexandre III Bridge. Norma, enthralled by the view, twirled about on the bridge, laughing. Unbeknownst to her, Donna had arranged the entire day. They attended a Matisse exhibit, lunched at the Bistro Allard, reveled in the Gallic atmosphere. "It was an extravagant day Donna treated me to, and had to be enormously expensive," said Norma, remembering.

When their divorce became final in June 1971, Donna and Tony divided the property and parted amicably. During his remaining years, Tony would mellow out in Palm Springs and marry a much younger woman who looked like Donna Reed.

Now Donna and Mary were alone in the house. Though a woman was hired to clean, mother and daughter did some of the daily chores. When Mary went to the horse stables in Pasadena three times a week, Donna was her chauffeur and most nervous booster.

The girl stuffed envelopes for Another Mother for Peace. Donna was beginning some of her most important work for the organization. In the fall of 1970 a midwestern member discovered a map in a specialized journal showing rich petroleum deposits off the shores of Vietnam, Thailand, and Cambodia. Was there a connection between American foreign policy and potential oil profits? Donna and Dorothy Jones, a veteran of the Office of War Information, investigated the situation for months, digging through obscure publications and consulting with experts at Stanford, UCLA, and the Bay Area Institute. Offshore drilling rights were about to be awarded by the government of South Vietnam, and American developers were salivating. Donna thought Nixon was in bed with the oil interests. "It's a big bad ugly picture!" she confided to a friend. "We are gathering facts, which are hard to get. Did you know oil companies keep dossiers on *all* office holders (political) and *all* persons speaking against them, oil?"

The winter of 1971, Donna and Dorothy published their research in the AMP newsletter. The headline read, "Are Our Sons Dying for Offshore Oil?" The women posed a hard question: "Do we continue to sustain the highly unpopular Thieu-Ky regime in order to allow U.S. oil companies to obtain the offshore oil leases?" Privately, Donna thought the whole issue was "very pertinent to the Vietnam foot-dragging." Publicly, she said, "We haven't accused anyone of going into the war because of oil. We just want to be sure we're not compelled to stay in Vietnam because of it."

It was pressure-point politicking at a popular level, and effective. The newsletter was mailed to 240,000 subscribers, who swamped J. William Fulbright with thousands of letters and cards urging him to hold hearings. Little was likely to *happen*, given the ways of Washington, but the efforts of Donna and Mrs. Jones certainly raised national awareness of a possible reason for being in Vietnam, and one for *getting out*. Newspaper columnist Mary McGrory marveled that Donna, "who used to be America's favorite TV housewife," was now an antiwar activist. Another Mother for Peace might have struck oil, McGrory said, but Fulbright was busy and maybe some other senator would "listen to the ladies."

The oil companies were silent, and the State Department denied there was any oil in those waters. In Washington, Donna confronted Henry Kissinger with her findings. The newsletter was just about to be published. "Well, we know there's oil all through Indonesia," Donna told Kissinger. "What does that have to do with Vietnam?" he asked. "Nothing, unless you believe in the domino theory," she replied. "Ridiculous," said Nixon's foreign policy adviser. "There is no oil in Vietnam."

Later that day Donna was dining with friends at a French restaurant, the Rive Gauche, when Dr. Kissinger arrived. His party had to pass directly in front of Donna's table and Kissinger found it difficult to ignore her without falling into a nearby waiter's cart.

Frustrated because peace was not at hand, Donna deplored the secretiveness of the government and its refusal to admit mistakes. She looked forward to a time when "nineteen-year-old boys will no longer be taken away to fight in old men's battles." Her passion against the war in Vietnam increased. So friends were shocked when she started dating a man who had been a military adviser there.

Colonel Grover Woodrow Asmus first saw Donna across a crowded room at a birthday party for the architect William Pereira. Really. There were no introductions, and the colonel didn't recognize her for a while. He kept looking at her. Finally she waved her hand (without a wedding ring) to the nice-appearing stranger.

Grover, himself divorced and senior aide to General of the Army Omar N. Bradley, told Mrs. Bradley that he had seen a lady whom he would like to meet. Then Kitty Bradley phoned Donna and said the *general* wished to meet her. Offered a choice of three dates, Donna chose the one furthest off—in two weeks she would join Kitty and the general for a day at the racetrack. Kitty added, "By the way, a Colonel Asmus will pick you up." Donna, who had done a little checking, said, "Ah, yes, Colonel Asmus."

Because it was "good practice to make a personal reconnaissance before any operation," the colonel stopped at her house several days before the big date. It would be closely chaperoned and last thirteen hours. Grover drove Donna to the Bradleys' for late-morning coffee. Then the foursome took a limousine to Hollywood Park, where the five-star general was greeted with fanfare. They sat through nine horse races and went directly from the track to a dinner party at Chasen's, then back to the Bradleys' for a nightcap.

The colonel was sort of like a lovesick kid after that. He gave Donna a diamond solitaire ring (she baked him a loaf of delicious bread, but only once during the courtship). This was 1971, and he would propose marriage nearly every day for the next three years. Once, for her birthday, he mailed five hundred cards that he'd collected from different places.

Donna felt comfortable with Grover, who was not a kid after all but a sophisticated suitor. She wanted this man in her life, but was leery of marriage. Everyone had a dark side, she said, and she couldn't marry him until she knew his. And they had real disagreements about the Vietnam War. Later, Grover said that Donna was "anti–stupid-political decisions, never anti-military." True, but in 1972 their differences were "exacerbated even by the peace signing trauma," Donna conceded. It would take time to overcome them.

That year saw the end of Grover's military career. He was trying to readjust—feeling, as Donna realized, "the professional army man's agony over the war and dissent and disrepute of the army." Momentarily, he lost stride.

Grover's usual self-assurance owed much to a background very different from Donna's. He was born in 1926 in North Bergen, New Jersey, at the family mansion built by his grandfather, a noted horticulturist. This early childhood home was known as "the showplace of northern New Jersey" and often pictured on postcards. His father was occupied with hobbies, collecting stamps, coins, antique firearms, first-edition books, and such. Grover recalled, "He was an authority on the Revolutionary

War, but he specialized on Major John André, the British compatriot of Benedict Arnold." The woman who would be Grover's mother insisted that the hobbyist take a job before she married him, so he became bacteriologist-pathologist for Hudson County. That was a smart move because the comfortable life of the Asmuses came to a halt in 1932 when Grandfather's widow died and his will was contested in a long court battle enriching lawyers and no one else.

During those years of changed fortune, Grover attended public schools, skipping grades, facing high school graduation at the age of fifteen but delaying it a year by winning a scholarship to Randolph Macon Academy in Virginia. Too young for the military in 1942, Grover collected another scholarship, this one to Drew University, not far from home. At the end of his freshman year, to discourage the idea circulating among family friends that he should get "excused" from the draft, he applied for an appointment to the U.S. Military Academy at West Point.

Thus his youth was accelerated by school achievement and shortened by war mobilization. In 1943, at the age of seventeen, Grover entered West Point and graduated after only three years. He fought in the Korean War, serving as a unit commander in the 19th Infantry Regiment of the 24th Division, which was severely mauled by the enemy. During the breaking out of the Pusan Perimeter, he replaced a fallen company commander, and after the liberation of Seoul pushed northward with his men almost to the Yalu River. Nothing that followed could be as intense as that experience in Korea. Afterward, the Army sent him to school for a degree in petroleum engineering. He drew assignments (one put him in Paris for eight years) that required expertise in logistics. Later he arrived in Saigon as an adviser to the South Vietnamese Army. His tour was extended as the war intensified in Vietnam. This was in 1967 and 1968, the same years Donna began protesting the American presence there.

Like the great general whom he assisted in the early seventies, Grover was a gentleman. He and Donna loved to spend time together, "doing everything from movies to museums to Saturday shopping." They traveled to Portugal and to Grover's familiar Paris, the city Tony had disliked. During their long courtship, as Grover rebuilt his life, he relaxed more, Donna noticed. In February 1973 she wrote to a friend, "I'm beginning to suspect he has tolerated my activities in the peace movement, found it easy to look the other way, dismiss even, as something sort of feminine misled and cute." But a year later, she wrote, "He understands, sort of, and is totally agreeable (by now) to my activities—in fact, enjoys them."

With the Vietnam War over, Donna and Another Mother for Peace took up the cudgel for continued civilization. She and three other members went to Geneva, Switzerland, in September 1972 to attend a world disarmament conference. The bright minds at the Palace of Nations, particularly Barbara Ward and Philip Noel Baker, impressed Donna. She came home convinced that AMP had found "a good formula for talking about disarmament—bombs in the backyard." Its next Mother's Day program would focus on "the state of your state and what's buried in backyards everywhere." In Colorado, for example, radiation from bomb-building had tragically affected children.

Six years before the accident at Three Mile Island, Donna was crusading for safer nuclear power plants. She devoted much of 1973 to gathering facts about the situation in California. Largely as a result of her research, AMP could claim a volume of information about installations second only to that of the Atomic Energy Commission. Ralph Nader asked Donna and her organization to work in his Citizens Action Group on an initiative for the fall 1974 elections. The legislation would impose strict safeguards at nuclear plants and shift liability for accident damage from the government to the civilian nuclear industry. Donna and her friends were up against leviathans, and they knew it. "If nuclear power plants are safe, let the commercial insurance industry insure them," she said in the *Los Angeles Times*. "Until those expert judges of risk are willing to gamble with their money, I'm not willing to gamble either."

Although the initiative failed at the ballot box, Donna felt that AMP had alerted citizens of California and beyond to the issue of nuclear safety. She was gratified to see the *Times* now placed stories about it on the front page. Barbara Avedon's most lasting image of Donna had her addressing a rally in east Los Angeles, urging her listeners to write their representative, Roy Ball, about the perils of nuclear facility storage. The Hispanic audience adored her. "She was gorgeous and she was clearly, righteously pissed," said Barbara.

But millions remembered her as Donna Stone, hardly a firebrand, and even that comforting identification carried risks in these crazy times. One day Mary, opening her mother's mail, was stunned by a sinister letter containing a newspaper cutout of a handgun. Donna was more upset when, during the 1972 presidential campaign, the would-be assassin of George Wallace was revealed as fantasizing about her. *Time* published an excerpt of Arthur Bremer's high-school English composition. "The mothers of television always smiled at their kids and kissed their foreheads. My mother was not like that," said Bremer's persona, called Paul. "I used to hate those television mothers. Now I hate Mom. I dreamed about Donna Reed, my television mother, cooking dinner for me and kissing my forehead. If Dad were only married to Donna Reed! Man!" When his parents fought, Paul "tried to think about pretty Donna Reed." Realizing that his father would not buy him an expensive guitar, he looked down at his feet: "I dreamed my shoe laces were big snakes and they were crawling up my legs, and it was dark, and I was lost in Africa. . . . Donna Reed was pulling at the snakes to save me, but I did not care. I pushed Donna Reed away from me. I wanted to die." On reading that, Donna was saddened—and shaken. "It got her worried about kooks," said Grover.

During this period Grover was courting Donna without letup. Early on, he competed with a movie producer who had gained an edge. "Donna was rather in love with this producer, but I didn't think he was good enough for her. He was Tony Owen without Tony's charm and humor and generosity," recalled Doris Cole Abrahams. After her divorce, Donna was in psychotherapy. So was the producer. Doris, who was visiting, would hear at the breakfast table what each psychiatrist was saying. "It was really funny, almost as if the two psychiatrists were running the affair." At the same time Grover was sending Donna roses and driving around her block several times a day. The artistic Doris "couldn't imagine Donna mixed up with some dull military type," but on meeting Grover she was taken with his manners and cosmopolitanism. After that she rooted for the colonel.

Donna still had misgivings about marrying again. In January 1974, after reading Jane Howard's *A Different Kind of Woman*, she wrote to Joyce:

"I didn't realize, until I got out, how *deeply* submissive I was expected to be in my long marriage—and really, my opinions were 'worthless'— so were my desires, ideas. We all really had a big snow job done on us about cooking and housekeeping—began learning at seven years of age, as though one needed to be a genius to manage, when any idiot who is willing *can*." She gave glimpses of her single life at the moment, "I do the cooking and have only a cleaning man once a week and resent losing my privacy even then. Furthermore, I'm not fussy about a little dust. But I don't know any men who aren't."

One evening Donna and Grover were dining at LaGrange Restaurant on Westwood Boulevard. Over cocktails, before their friends Delmer and Mary Lou Daves arrived, he ventured, "It's time for my daily exercise: Will you marry me?" She answered, "You've worn me down. Yes. I still haven't found your dark side, but I think I can live with it when it does pop up." Dinner was something special.

On August 30, 1974, they were married at Donna's home, with only family members and a few friends—Norma Connolly Rodman and Ann McCrea Borden and their husbands—attending. After honeymooning at the Bel Air Hotel, they commuted for several months between Los Angeles and Seattle, where Grover was hired by Alyeska Pipeline Service Company, the consortium building the Trans-Alaska Pipeline. And so the former antiwar activist who was anathema to Big Oil was hitched to a former warrior who made his living in oil.

"While I doubt we need that oil, I frankly think the pipeline can be done safely, ecologically speaking," said Donna, who had seen the "formid-able" plans and precautions. Grover was in charge of logistics, and happy to be in the management rank. But Donna worried. She knew the oil com-panies in Alyeska had extensive holdings in nuclear energy. "What would you do if they threatened you in some way about your position because of my stand?" she asked her new husband. He was ready to resign if that happened, but it never did. "I respected Donna's honesty and integrity more than I would have any corporation, or for that matter the govern-ment," said Grover.

The Asmuses moved to Mercer Island, Washington, reputedly the largest body of land completely surrounded by fresh water. The island is connected to the rest of Seattle by a bridge, and their place boasted a fifty-foot dock but no boat. Here they lived for the next three years, enjoying what Donna called "the drama of the great outdoors." She wrote, "Life is *good* with Grover. We have the nicest, best, closest, most contented relationship, which is sure *new* for me; in fact, it's miraculous and I'm grateful to say the least." A bonus was that Penny and her husband had been transferred to Seattle.

Penny was still at *Sunset Magazine* and Tony Junior in aircraft maintenance. Timothy, always very close to Donna, was the one most traumatized by the late sixties. He had been in Chicago, though not with his mother, during the 1968 Democratic convention. "By then I had given up on everything," he said. "Bobby Kennedy had been shot in June, Martin Luther King in April. I didn't want any part in this crap anymore." He dropped out, doing occasional drugs and "all the stuff that went along with the sixties." At that tumultuous time, smoking marijuana was equated with drug addiction. "When I was nineteen or twenty, Mom would always bust me if I smoked pot," said Tim. "She'd walk in and look at my eyes and right off the bat she'd start yelling at me because she knew I'd been smoking. She could tell by the glazed-over redness in my eyes. I couldn't fool her."

Tim's relations with his parents were often stormy during these years. "But even in my spacey days when I was a hippie, I could talk to Mom about stuff and she could relate. Mom was *naturally* high, almost like stoned." In the early seventies he learned how to play guitar well and began composing songs with titles like "Bandida" and "Pretty Lies." A bit later, when he was supporting his music by construction jobs and hefty newspaper deliveries, he would phone Donna to play a new song like "Fresh-Start Daisy" and find her sharp in suggesting snatches of lyrics. In 1977, Donna's last year in Seattle, she wrote to a friend: "Tim still strums his guitar, lives on the edge of poverty, but seems secure in belief in himself—it's really hard—but he stays devoted and helpful to his father, who just remarried."

After Mary gave up horses, much to Donna's relief, she took to music also, learning to play five instruments at Pasadena City College. Her teenage rebellion was directed against the whole Hollywood scene. "I swore a lot, tried to look as ratty as possible, and hated my mother's friends—thought they were all phony." She particularly couldn't stand the movie offspring who attended Beverly High. Reality—that's what she craved. Donna, undeniably real, couldn't circumvent the general falsity that Mary perceived. "Even though my mother was not a typical movie star and still had all those good Iowa values, my growing up in Beverly Hills wasn't normal," said Mary. Donna more or less let Mary's rebelliousness go (Penny had known more discipline); clearly she was tired after her television show and perhaps changing with the times. Oh, mother and daughter certainly tiffed, and much later Mary (thinking herself perverse) wished they could have been as uninhibited as the characters on *Roseanne*. Yelling implied intimacy.

Yet the two were very attached, to the extent that after her mother's death Mary struggled to find a separate identity. Today she understands her mother's sense of right and wrong, seeing it in herself, as well as the same tendency to be uptight and overcritical. "But as Mom grew older, she had a kind of regal, ethereal quality that drew people to her—it was in her eyes, something going on in the mind, mysterious," said Mary. "She was so bright." Turning pensive, Mary continued, "My mother did everything for everyone, but it was hard for her to let anyone take care of her—part of that is letting down your guard. She was very independent." As Mary was and is.

Near the end of 1977, back in Los Angeles, Donna divulged in a letter, "Mary's visits are briefer and briefer. I want to cry every time she leaves, and I know how Mom felt (she cried every time I left) and feel a bit guilty about all those five-day visits to Iowa. What I really want for Mary is a good warm marriage situation but she's not ready or looking even. All her friends are so independent too, unconcerned about getting married. (So was I at her age, but was made to feel I was wrong or bad or something! If only I had followed my instincts more—they were good, but I didn't count on them enough.)"

Following "The DR Show," as Donna called it, she felt "great tugs and pulls back" to her early life. On a Friday in 1967 she and Keith, Lavone, Bill, and Karen met on short notice with their parents in Palm Springs—

without any in-laws or children. "We relaxed to the point of indecency and reaffirmed our faith in the thought there's no tie that binds like the family tie," wrote Donna.

A sad note was that Hazel Mullenger was "deteriorating dangerously." Soon a new drug called L-Dopa was improving her mobility a bit, though her "quietness" alarmed Donna. By December 1972, Hazel had turned inward even more, refusing to come to Southern California for the winter. "So Pop stayed in Iowa to take care of her and risked losing his health," said a frustrated and worried Donna. "It's very hard to give up on them, and to give them up." Early in 1974, she expressed sympathy to Joyce Fisk, who had lost a family member. "That's ahead, but imminent, for me—Mom is in terrible shape, falls down, can't remember, can barely speak." When Hazel Jane Mullenger died on July 17, 1975, one day after her seventy-sixth birthday, Donna was at her bedside in Denison.

On her island in Washington, Donna was effectively out of Another Mother for Peace. For mental exertion, she got involved in the stock market, astounding her brokers by making money from options when experienced investors were losing. That required constant surveillance. It could be done anywhere—and when Grover's work on the pipeline ended in April 1977 she was eager to leave "the eternally grey skies" of Seattle behind, though not Penny. Donna was disenchanted, too, because "the state's commitment to nuclear power (madness! with all their cheap hydroelectric) and to the Trident sub base on the gorgeous Hood Canal (which will eventually be home to sixteen thousand H-Bombs and only one hour from Seattle) has, pardon the expression, mushroomed."

Though Donna missed her old friends in Los Angeles, she hated the stepped-up traffic there. Angelenos might find a way free, but only if the Redeemer appeared over the city and immobilized every third car. So she was happy when Grover was transferred to outlying Irvine. They bought a house on the beach at Corona Del Mar, nine minutes from his office. That was where she wanted to grow old.

Donna's letters turned more reflective. "I have great interest in gardens and birds and pets, and great overwhelming love for my Aunt Mabel, who writes me or phones as Mom might have, had she been well for the past fifteen years." In 1977 she also wrote: "I spend inordinate amounts of time keeping up with friends and family, which I find enormously satisfying—then I realize how difficult the years between seventeen and forty-five were and how *much* family and work took out of me. I am really only now feeling 'healed' and in balance. I have had enough of steam-cooker pressure! *L O W E R   S T R E S S*, pls."

Donna liked to watch the sun set on the water and dreaded the thought of ever moving again "because it does *not* get easier." Some of her things, and Grover's, were stored in various places. "Mine is mostly memorabilia which has become valuable, suddenly. Like some of those old films I appeared in, damned by faint praise at the time, which are now deemed classics by the experts. Makes my head spin—if only from all the accolades." She was surprised by an American Film Institute poll showing *It's a Wonderful Life*, but not *From Here to Eternity*, among the top fifty films. "What a turn around!"

During the seventies Donna moved imperceptibly toward a return to the screen. At first, she wanted to produce—a dramatic film about a grandmother in Creole country, and a documentary about Ishi, the last of his California Indian tribe. She wasn't tempted for a minute by television offers. However, Donna's friend Howard Rodman planned to write a TV movie specially for her, a modern version of Ibsen's *A Doll's House* to be called "A Beautiful Lady." Perhaps too recherché for the decade of *All in the Family*, the idea never developed.

The almost obligatory "Donna Reed Show Reunion" never jelled, either. In July 1977 a deal was made with Columbia and ABC to film a serious drama using the *Donna Reed Show* cast. The theme had been agreed on and a writer hired when Donna learned that Carl Betz was terminally ill with lung cancer. It was a terrible shock, all the more so because he had seemed happy and okay at their regular luncheon a month before. For more than a year after Carl's death in January 1978, scripts were written and rewritten, but there would be no fatherless reunion.

Donna wanted to make her comeback in *Friendly Fire*, the true story of an American soldier in Vietnam killed by an American artillery shell. She had met the victim's mother, an Iowa farmwoman named Peg Mullen, and completely understood, empathized with, Mrs. Mullen's bitter quest to learn from the government what happened to her son. In 1977 Fay Kanin was adapting C. D. B. Bryan's book and Donna was talking to ABC-TV about the mother's role. "I can't imagine anyone else being *right*—silly me," she told friends. But some other logic prevailed and the younger, dramatically untested Carol Burnett got *Friendly Fire*—and an Emmy.

So few middle-aged heroines like Peg Mullen could be found now in movies and television and literature. That angered Donna, and spoke volumes for the culture. "I think it's *obscene* that artists of all ages can't work at all stages of life, especially women," she said. It seemed that aging women stars had to settle for cameos or play monsters and freaks. She refused to be a victim. Better to hold out for a role that didn't degrade women. More than anything else, it was a *cause* that led her back to acting: a determination to represent an attractive, intelligent, strong middle-aged woman on the screen.

Her vehicle for doing that was, unfortunately, not the caliber of *Friendly Fire*, but still a landmark of sorts. Donna returned from Europe with Grover and Mary in the summer of 1978 to find an offer waiting for her. *The Best Place to Be* was an upgraded soap opera, scheduled for four hours of prime-time television. Donna at fifty-seven was playing the romantic lead, a woman her own age. She considered that a breakthrough. Ordinarily, the nervous network would have hired a younger actress (Audrey Hepburn had been first choice) and "matured" her with makeup and wig.

Though glad to be back, Donna didn't look forward to "the endless negotiating, manipulating, begging, demanding if necessary." So much was required "before you ever *begin* to *act!*" For a month before filming in October she trained like an Olympic athlete. She was filled with fear, after twelve years away from the cameras. But she *knew* more now.

The character of Sheila Callahan, widowed in middle age, realizing her worth and potential and coming fully alive only then, was familiar to Donna. "A good placid marriage, three children, nothing ever really stirred Sheila," she told an interviewer. "Then after her husband's death, the world opened for her like a flower." This exciting premise was doomed in spite of abundant talent.

The director, David Miller, whose movie successes had included *Sudden Fear* and *Midnight Lace*, hadn't seen Donna since *Saturday's Hero*. They met again in a crowded office, spontaneously and silently embracing. Helen Hayes, who had admired Donna since *Eternity*, was set to play her mother and had some influence on the scenario even after she fell ill and was replaced by Mildred Dunnock. Though the point has been forgotten, *The Best Place to Be* pushed an adolescent Timothy Hutton toward stardom, as well as Gregory Harrison and Stephanie Zimbalist, the daughter of Efrem Zimbalist, Jr., who was Donna's leading man.

The schedule was strenuous, with Donna traveling by trailer to various Los Angeles locations, arranging her own wardrobe and makeup in the evenings, often shooting ten or twelve hours at a stretch. Her first movies had demanded as much, but now the business provided no sense of continuity. "Once you leave it, even for a short time, you come back and feel you're in a strange land. You don't recognize anyone, and you're convinced no one recognizes you. That's no way to live, at least not for a girl from Denison, Iowa." And the new freedom was a little disorienting. In the seventies Sheila Callahan could be shown exploring her sexuality. A bedroom scene was de rigueur, so Donna went into it with good humor, recalled John Philip Law, cast as her younger lover. "Oh darling, the last time I did this scene," she told him, slipping into bed under the camera eye, "it was two hands outside the covers and one foot on the floor."

Donna had some problems with the script. Sheila's daughter is running with a nihilistic crowd. Her boyfriend, a hippie type, confronts Sheila and berates her middle-class morality. Donna complained that in this scene Sheila was beaten down. Instead of being a passive victim, the mother should be strong for her daughter's sake. The script gave her no moral authority. For help, Donna went to the acting coach Jeff Corey. He suggested that she silently recite "The Lord's Prayer" during the boyfriend's harangue. She did that when the scene was shot, conveying necessary strength without changing the script.

Donna Reed's comeback was loudly trumpeted, but the more cynical critics had a bang. "The spirit of Helen Trent rides again," said one, referring to an old-time radio heroine. "Oppressively chic and tasteful here, Reed approximates a statue, her coiffure seemingly bronzed to her head," said another, uncharitably. "Stuffed with enough plot and character for four months of soap opera," said a reviewer who was nevertheless hooked. *The Best Place to Be* didn't *feel* like soap opera to Donna, who anticipated the criticism. "It feels very legitimate and good," she told Robert Osborne during the filming. She was pleasantly surprised to discover that her emotional resources had increased with maturity.

Yet her performance didn't move deeply, perhaps *couldn't* because it was based on Helen Van Slyke's frothy novel and surrounded by Ross Hunter's stultifyingly lavish production. Everything about Donna still suggested quality and grace, but often in her performances from now on the admirable dignity is in danger of freezing the talent. Millions of fans were happy to see her again—they didn't make Donna Reeds anymore. Some would have liked to see her as the worn wife of an Iowa farmer standing up to foreclosing bankers, or as Ibsen's Nora slamming the kitchen door, or as Norma Rae unionizing exploited workers. She had more blood knowledge of beleagured Iowa country women than any younger actress; she had resisted being turned into a figurine and even slammed a few doors; and she had passionately rallied citizens to demand nuclear safety. Here she was trapped in Country Club ambience, and would be in later acting assignments.

Still, given the realities of network television, it was remarkable for her to head a big-budgeted miniseries after a long absence, especially when so many of her contemporaries were reduced to supporting roles and cold cream commercials. Donna's family especially liked *The Best Place to Be*, and it drew huge Sunday and Monday night audiences in the spring of 1979.

By this time Donna was living in Tulsa, Oklahoma, where Grover had taken a managerial position with the Williams Brothers Engineering Company. She saw Tulsa for the first time at the end of 1978, when she flew out to secure a house on South Oswego Avenue. Newspapers as far away as Wichita announced that Donna was now a neighbor.

Tulsa was not the best place to be for one used to a Mediterranean climate, but Donna felt comfortable with the people and "their basic Midwest-ness." She and Grover bonded with Rex and Jody Watkinson and Carl and Friday Leonard, who were truly neighbors. Rex was a real estate developer and Carl an insurance executive, and their lively, warm-hearted wives found much in common with Donna.

The three couples inhabited a kind of Knots Landing cul-de-sac without the alarming knots. They often ate together, taking potluck, whether spaghetti or meatloaf or beef bourguignon. "If one of us is ambitious and cooks a special dish, the others bring what they have and we all take supper together," said Donna. Hosting a Sunday night buffet, Grover wore his splendid dress white military uniform with gold braids and medals. That inspired Carl Leonard to retrieve from the attic his corporal's uniform, which he wore during his turn as host. Grover, a good sport, laughed hardest.

"We saw all the Iowa in Donna," said Carl. "She got back to old times in Tulsa." She wasn't on display there, and no one wanted anything from her—a double relief. Friday observed that she never talked about Hollywood unless asked. She might have been Donna anybody, at home in Joe's chili parlor or the finest place, or back at Cronk's in Denison before she was somebody.

But Donna felt exiled in Tulsa, far from family. After forty years, she was living in the Midwest again and finding the weather harsher than she remembered. She complained about the winter winds and suffered through the hot summer of 1980. Other things dragged on her spirit. Grover's experience gave her a glimpse of the corporate structure, perhaps the same as elsewhere but still disturbing in its concentration of salary at the top. Then, too, there was the prevailing political conservatism. Having, very recently, spent so much energy on liberal causes, she now found herself on the unpopular side of most issues published in the *Tulsa World*, but she didn't raise her voice, except privately in writing to friends. Donna's stress, bottled up for months, broke out in a December letter to Joyce Fisk: "Power is very savage and raw here—women frequently carry guns—everyone shoots to kill—Oral Roberts is a saint, there's a church on every corner, and the highest divorce rate of any city in the U.S."

Her opinion might have shocked her new Tulsa friends, who took justifiable pride in the city's schools, parks, museums, and symphony and opera and ballet companies. Donna, appreciative of culture wherever found, wasn't blind to the good things about Tulsa life. Her strong words to Joyce reveal her frame of mind at a particular time. Like many social activists of the sixties and seventies, she was drawing inward at the beginning of the Reagan era, in effect folding up her tent and decamping. Despite the friendliness of Tulsans, she and Grover were somewhat cut off from them. Referring to the Leonards and Watkinsons, she wrote, "If it weren't for our wonderful neighbors, we'd be miserable."

Donna retreated indoors. The fairly recent television showing of Alex Haley's *Roots* had spurred her interest in genealogy. Now she began tracing her own lineage with the absorption that had marked her political activism. More than playing bridge, which Grover taught her, genealogy kept her mind working, with a payoff. It appealed to her love of history and research and problem solving.

Some family mysteries intrigued Donna. Was her great grandmother, Sarah Shirk Herner, really an Indian, as rumored? Did her father's sister, Ruby, commit suicide at the age of twenty-eight, or was she murdered? Bill and Hazel Mullenger had always forbidden any questions about the matter. A more distant relative, Emma Mullenger, had vanished at the age of sixteen, never to be seen again by her family. What had happened to her?

Gradually Donna was pulled into constellations of long-past lives reaching into the present and connecting with her own. She combed records, visited graveyards, corresponded with anyone who might supply a missing link. Like many amateur genealogists, she experienced the strange sensation of being led to information, as if by a guiding spirit.

Some discoveries delighted her, some saddened. A search at the Library of Congress revealed that Eliza Coffin, the humble Quaker mother of Grandfather Charles Shives, was descended from English royalty— from Henry II. "Isn't that a *kick*?" Donna told a friend. "Well, there *have* been times when I felt, at least, like Eleanor of Acquitaine, slightly diluted!" She sent the information to sister Karen with a note: "I thought this might amuse you for a day or two—or for the rest of your life, even." Other aspects of genealogy brought sorrow and regret, especially the stories now coming to her of distant relatives, some experiencing hardship, who had tried without success to contact her in the past.

Eventually, in 1981, Donna and Grover would travel to England to meet her newfound Mullenger and Tyler relatives. On being introduced to a Tyler descendant named Emma Biggs, Donna felt that she was looking at herself—"not from a physical standpoint especially, but something psychic and deep." She could write: "Our family has been greatly extended through these searches, and I like everyone *very much*—a good feeling." Genealogy had answered Donna's craving for blood ties at a time when her more immediate family was scattered and dying out.

When she began the searches in 1979, she was still "feeling the great emotional loss" of her mother. She was worried about various family members. Tim had severely injured his right hand, which meant no guitar playing and emotional depression. Brother Bill, who had been conservator to their aging father, was struggling with alcoholism—Donna would plead with him in many tearful long-distance phone calls. The elder William Mullenger was now "greatly diminished mentally." He had cheerfully survived a lifetime of setbacks and tenderly cared for Hazel; had driven his car, jogged, chinned a bar, played horseshoe, and cut weeds in July heat until he was eighty-five. He still beat Donna in solving crossword puzzles, but no longer could be sure of her name or find the thermostat to his house furnace or his way around the neighborhood.

Donna helped move her father to a Denison nursing home in the summer of 1979. Then, sweating without air conditioning, she packed up things in the house where he had lived alone since Hazel's death. "My God, but I've been so sad ever since!" she wrote to a friend. "They lived with the barest necessities (by choice), surrounded by photos and memorabilia connected to their children (no really, *engulfed* by them) and Mom's brothers and sisters."

Pop Mullenger, who had handed down his intellectual curiosity to Donna, should have shared her excitement at the unearthing of an ancient Indian encampment west of Denison. Having coffee at Cronks, she listened to old friends from farm days talk about the pottery and weapons coming to light. "I can't wait to see something," she said. Back in Tulsa,

Donna looked forward to the autumn European trip that she was giving her Aunt Mildred, who had provided a roof when she first came to California.

Age had not withered Aunt Myl's eccentricity; at seventy-seven, she was preoccupied with sex. Strolling through the Louvre, approaching Winged Victory while clutching Grover's arm, Aunt Myl talked about recent skinny dipping with a boyfriend. "Well, whatever turns you on," wrote Donna, "but between Winged Victory and Grover's strong right arm, I'll take Grover too!" Later, during a bus tour of Paris, Donna urged Aunt Myl to look out the window for the Eiffel Tower about to loom up, and Myl said, "Have I told you I am acquainted with Baby Leroy?" Seems the former child actor also lived in Ventura, California, and saw her once a week. Donna shrieked, "There's the Eiffel Tower!" Aunt Myl glanced out the window and said "Uhhhh-Huuuuuh!" but kept chattering about Baby Leroy after the bus stopped. Finally, Donna asked, "Aunt Mildred, could you tell me what it is about the Eiffel Tower that reminds you of Baby Leroy?" And she answered pertly, "Oh nothing! But I saw his name on a building way back there; it said L-E-R-O-I!"

Donna wanted a relative of Mildred's generation along as she tried to trace ancestral roots near London. "I looked for more Mullengers on tombstones in ancient English cemeteries than I care to think about," recalled Grover. When he and Donna returned to England several years later to see live Mullengers and Tylers, she was prepared by her research in Tulsa. "Doing all four family lines at one time is a bit like playing two games of chess simultaneously," she said.

"I shall be sixty in January and am thrilled to have made it through my fifties without a major illness," wrote Donna in December 1980. Stranded in Tulsa, she missed her children and many California friends. She still wasn't acclimated to Oklahoma. In a rainy season, crickets and spiders got into the house through the heater and air vents. One night, while reading in bed, her eye caught the movement of a scorpion on the carpet. She asked Grover to get rid of it, and he obliged with the heel of his boot. "If I ever write a book about life in Tulsa, I can call it *Scorpions in the Bedroom!*" she told a penpal.

Late in 1980 Donna had planted hundreds of tulip bulbs in case their house went on the market the next spring. The red tulips had bloomed and begone, and the Asmuses were still in Tulsa. Then in July 1981 came the most dreaded of phone calls: William Mullenger was dead at the age of eighty-eight.

After the funeral in Denison, Donna and her brothers and sisters and the spouses and children spent some "magical" hours at the Mullenger farm, roaming through the old house, picking apples and mulberries, playing horseshoes, taking photographs. The siblings had not been all together in the farmhouse since Donna's departure in 1938. "Which gives me great pain, that thought!" she wrote to Joyce Fisk.

The calendar changed, as if stripped by a steady wind, and the Asmuses remained in Tulsa. Finally, after Thanksgiving 1982, Donna and Grover made their long-awaited exit, but not quite. Their Volvo, with trailer hitched behind, broke down in a place west of Tulsa called Sapulpa. An accelerator cable had to be ordered from Chicago, and the wait was just the icing on frustration. They were leaving a house that hadn't sold in the depressed economy, and going to one in Beverly Hills that needed enlarging and upgrading. Donna had come to realize how deep her roots were—in California.

With so many family members on the West Coast, reunions were easier to manage. Social life resumed in Sunny Cal. Donna had become "fiercely bonded" to old friends like Lillian Sidney and Ann Straus, both from her earliest days at MGM, and seeing them was necessary to her happiness. And here drama might await an actress past sixty: another top starring role in a television movie.

Five days before Christmas 1982, Donna started filming *The Girls of Starkwater Hall*, which would be shown as *Deadly Lessons* the following March. At first, she had trouble relating to the role of a cold, authoritarian headmistress at an exclusive girls' school. Grover described his experience with martinets in the military, and she drew on that, stretching dramatically. But not much, because the story—about murder visiting some snooty young—was less gratifying than it might have been. Donna noticed how the quality of television production had declined since the sixties. "Working conditions in TV are horrible, the schedules are tighter and shorter than ever—if you get the dialogue out, they print," she said. "It all makes the care and time given my show years ago seem like *Gone with the Wind*."

Mary observed that her mother was less confident and secure, both more feisty and passive, in the new Hollywood. She had returned to the business older, without Tony Owen to look out for her. She had contributed to a memory bank that paid no interest. Merely keeping her place required attention to a few rules that had never seemed important. It meant not going for job interviews, being seen in the right spots, sitting on the dais at testimonial dinners, and so on.

Tulsa friends, the Watkinsons and Leonards, visited in California and saw a different side of Donna. In Tulsa, she had been down to earth, but in Beverly Hills clubs and restaurants she was aware of flattering lighting and the status attached to certain tables. She had to be, because the industry people present were—and she hadn't entirely dropped out. Jody recalled that at the Bistro Donna politely but firmly asked to be moved three times to progressively more satisfactory tables, and finally the manager appeared, apologizing profusely. The game could be a contest. One night the Tulsa friends accompanied her and Grover to Spago's, a night spot surrounded by the paparazzi. It was *the* place to go, but the result might be a very candid shot in tomorrow's papers. That night Donna's party exited through the kitchen and past the trash cans to avoid the photographers, who came running after, crying "Miss Reed! Miss Reed!" Donna implored Grover to gun the car. "They'd just love to get a shot of my hindside climbing in," she told her astonished Oklahoma friends.

"Donna was incorruptible in a corrupt business and to some extent corrupted by it," said her sister Karen. "You can't come out of it intact. She stayed as clean in that business as possible, didn't fall prey to bad personal habits, was sexually faithful, didn't rely on drugs or drink, didn't kiss up to people, and yet she wanted to be successful. That means you're going to have to compromise yourself a bit. I think there was some tension in her life over that." Karen had met some movie stars who were heroes to their public, and knowing them through Donna she saw how they actually were. "But the reality of Donna was so much better than the

Hollywood fiction. I mean the reality of Donna the person, not necessarily her life."

The person was still growing, reaching out to others. Excited at the prospect of a national Shives family reunion, Donna wrote to Betty Massman: "I suppose I'm like my own dear mother, who never met a relative she didn't like!" Additions brought subtractions. A Shives kinswoman, 104-year-old Daisy Ellis of Dayton, Ohio, died before Donna could talk with her, a great disappointment. A family loss of another sort occurred in February 1983: The old Mullenger farmhouse burned to the ground. It had been occupied by a younger generation of Mullengers, who were absent when the furnace blew up. Donna was thankful for that, but devastated by the loss of her childhood home. Also destroyed was a beautiful elm tree that had been standing when Grandfather Mullenger moved to the place eighty years ago.

Early in May, Donna and Grover flew to Hong Kong, where she filmed a *Love Boat* special with Efrem Zimbalist and Gene Kelly. Donna played a double role convincingly, one half requiring a British accent. It was the last time she photographed well, thought her sister Heidi. The days of shooting in Hong Kong were "horribly long, hot, muggy, noisy, smelly, crowded." The almost daily rain was hard on wardrobe and hair. But the discomfort bought the opportunity to travel after production ended.

During a spring heat wave Donna and Grover flew from Hong Kong to Osaka, Japan, and then cruised on the *Royal Viking Star* down the southern Japan coast and on to China. The Great Wall, reached by bus, lived up to its billing, and Shanghai was colorful; but visiting China was a joke. "One sees so little in a Communist country where movement is constricted and people are polite but aloof." The cruise ship went up the Yangtze River in the dead of night "so no one would notice a measly little military installation on its banks." After this unromantic interlude the Asmuses flew back to Los Angeles and then directly to Tulsa, where their house had finally sold. While clearing out the furniture, Donna was in jet-lag haze, "my head on one side of the room, my body on the other."

For Donna, the coming months brought an increased sense of mortality. "I thank my lucky stars for every day of good health, that's for certain," she said in March 1983. At the end of the year she was abed with an infection following minor surgery on her ankle. It required bottles of antibiotics and more than eight weeks to heal. A spate of sad news didn't help. To paraphrase Willa Cather, after one's fiftieth birthday death seemed to rain all around one, and after sixty it became a veritable thunderstorm. In January 1984, Donna's cousin Joyce Glover, Aunt Mildred's daughter, died. In March, her Aunt Mabel Yankey, who had been like a second mother, died. And in May, her former husband, Tony Owen, succumbed to lung cancer in Palm Springs. Donna had visited him at the Eisenhower Medical Center, and there was great tenderness between them. "I really appreciate the way you raised the kids," he had told her. "He was very brave, never complained, and died a terrible death," she wrote a little later, shocked to realize that he was seventy-seven years old.

Life was dearer than ever with the devoted Grover, and the whole world came to visit. At North Linden Drive in Beverly Hills, she could enjoy her first really pretty California flower garden. The mail brought love letters after every televising of *It's a Wonderful Life*. When approached about doing a sequel with James Stewart for pay TV, Donna said, "Hurry!" But the project never had a chance because Frank Capra was vehemently opposed. Then at a vulnerable moment she accepted an amazing offer from another quarter. To a friend she said, "I lost my head," and to a reporter, "My book needed another chapter."

Donna couldn't imagine why the producers of *Dallas* would be calling her in the late spring of 1984. Intrigued, she met the people at Lorimar and learned they wanted her to replace Barbara Bel Geddes as Miss Ellie, a pivotal character in the big television series. After undergoing open-heart surgery, Miss Bel Geddes had decided not to return, and Philip Capice, the executive producer, saw in Donna the same "quiet authority and simple elegance." Maybe she looked a bit too young and pretty to be J. R. Ewing's mother, but Miss Ellie didn't have to be a wrinkled frump. She broke her rule in going for an interview and charmed the *Dallas* people, who had dismissed five hundred names from consideration before thinking of her. Early in June she signed a contract to play the matriarch of South Fork.

Donna understood the difficulty of stepping into a role already established by a well-liked actress, so she planned her own interpretation. "I'm creating Miss Ellie from bits and pieces of my family, the generations before me who survived all the hard times in the Midwest," she said. The accent was more on midwestern than southern. In spite of her wealth, Miss Ellie was in essence "country," as Donna was. For the first time an actress often cast as "society" could be true to her own origins. What was needed was the dignity of meaningful work, doing more than sitting around with a coffee cup and waxing homiletic. As she grew into the part of Miss Ellie, Donna hoped to make some changes. "She wanted a desk and some sort of activity other than nursing that bloody dad's coffee mug," said Grover.

Now, at the beginning, Donna's joy in being tapped for the role was evident in a parade of newspaper and magazine articles. She could relate to an American heroine like Miss Ellie, the linchpin of her family; and if the members plotted against each other, at least they all gathered round her dinner table. Far from being a victim, Mama alone had moral authority over the irascible J. R. And Donna's personal circumstances were perfect for this professional windfall. She wrote to Joyce Fisk: "The best part of the whole thing is being able to work in a top show, in the right role, *without* the responsibility of four children waiting for me at home (which is where I preferred to be anyway when they were little), as well as the difficult personality of poor Tony, who only got worse as the years passed. Grover is supportive and busy himself."

The heavy barrage of publicity raised expectations and made her nervous. "Donna Does Dallas," blared the press in headlines of a size generally reserved for Liz. It capitalized on the dramatic sleight of hand: the return of dowdy and rather plain Miss Ellie from her honeymoon, blissfully transformed into Donna Reed, who always personified glow. And no one was supposed to notice. How could they do that? Would the public accept Donna? Was this gentle soul from television's past tough enough to make J. R. behave? The media made sure that millions would watch the unveiling of the "new Miss Ellie."

Donna arrived in Dallas for location shooting in July. There was no good reason to film there at the hottest time of year, but she was used to the sadistic business and didn't complain. She was worried about fitting into the ensemble-acting group. The others were very comfortably allianced, and she might be resented by Barbara's partisans. But the welcome seemed friendly enough, and the off-camera highjinks between Larry Hagman (playing J. R.) and Patrick Duffy (his brother Bobby) amused her.

"The cast for the most part is extremely bright and clever," she wrote to a friend. "Everyone works hard and fights right down to the last inch of space on the film for his share. Hagman is funny and very dominant—he and I have done lots of testing each other." When Donna proved that she could still hold a master scene together in closeup after ten hours on her feet, he applauded. Early on, Duffy asked Donna, "Can I call you Mama?" She was delighted by the little-boy gesture, but heard Hagman muttering, "Well, she isn't my Mama."

Hagman clearly controlled the show, and that was fine. "Donna wanted to support him in every possible way," said Grover. She was simply happy to have a part in creating popular mythology. But there were muted signs that Hagman was not happy with her. The gradual result was a coldness on the set from actors who were afraid to cross him. In early November, when Donna made her much-publicized debut in *Dallas*, tension increased at South Fork.

Friends gathered at the Asmus house to watch Donna introduced as Miss Ellie, back from her honeymoon with Clayton Farlow, or Howard Keel. Donna was distressed and embarrassed when she saw herself on the TV screen. No key lights had been used, and she photographed terribly. Her hair, which had been sort of sandy in tests, had evidently been printed up to look a shocking bright gray. Now she understood why Philip Capice had prohibited her (but not the other actresses) from seeing any of the rushes. Confronting Capice, she said, "I do not mind being made to look old, but I object to monster lighting." She felt ambushed, remarking in a letter: "The harsh side lighting is deliberate and mean as can be."

Donna felt betrayed too, and with reason. In early photographic tests she had looked good, and the placement of key lights, considered important by every actor, had been promised. "It is a gentleman's agreement when you and the producer and cinematographer agree on the *result of a test*—which should not be *broken*, and never has been in my experience until now," she told a friend. The *Dallas* people were caught in a lie when they blamed the cinematographer, who revealed that he had not been allowed to shoot her as he had for the test.

To some, this business about lighting might seem unimportant and even suggest a bit of the prima donna. But Donna didn't indulge in tantrums. That was unprofessional. She had been studio-trained in the mechanics of her craft. (When Elizabeth Taylor appeared on *General Hospital* she too was always aware of lighting and camera angles.) She had quaint Iowa principles, word of honor being one. And for some time she had wanted to show on the screen that a deeply mature woman could be vital and attractive—not a victim. Ironically, in the male-dominated world of *Dallas*, she herself was to become a victim.

In the fall of 1984, Grover remembered, Donna was often in tears when she came home from work. Yet she was endowed with her father's basic optimism and always rallied quickly. In October she signed a contract for two more years on *Dallas*. That was surety of her worth. At Christmas, she gave cookies and gifts to cast and crew members but left a party tossed by Hagman because she clearly didn't fit in. When Grover commented that nothing was worth her suffering and she should consider leaving the show, she replied, "I am not a quitter!"

Early in 1985 she was being photographed better, but her screen time was whittled down. Fans began to notice that she wasn't involved in any ongoing story. She and Grover would rise at four in the morning, and he would drive her forty miles just so Miss Ellie could sit in a courtroom with her family. "Wish I were doing more!" she said. If Miss Ellie was the glue that held things together, as publicists liked to say, it was disappearing glue! Now Donna was scrambling with the rest of them for every inch of film, and pleased at any break. This was series television in the gilded era of I'll Get Mine. "What a snakepit out there!" she wrote to Betty Massman.

Donna's first season ended early in April, and after a wrap party for Patrick Duffy (whose character had temporarily died of injuries), she and

Grover flew to Paris for a long-planned vacation. She left with flu-like symptoms, fever and gastric upset, but looked forward to returning to work in mid-May. Next year would be better, as her father used to say.

Paris, May 11. Donna and Grover were in their hotel suite dressing for a dinner date with friends when the telephone rang. She was surprised to hear the voice of her agent, Wilt Melnick, on the line. He had lunched with the producers of *Dallas* and learned that the show was "returning to the core cast." Donna asked him to repeat. What did that mean? "They've fired you," said Melnick. But *why*? she wanted to know. And how could they? She had a contract for two more years. They didn't give a reason, he said, but Barbara Bel Geddes was coming back as Miss Ellie. While Melnick was gentle, the news was like a slap in the face. Worse. "I felt as if someone had opened a trapdoor and I was falling through, spinning crazily as I tumbled," Donna said later.

She was stunned and then angry. Forty-four years in the business, and she had never before been fired. The producers had offered her no options, no chance to negotiate. They didn't even have the courtesy or decency to phone her personally, though they knew where she was vacationing. It was a very public firing. Next day, the European media carried the story. Lorimar put a face on it: Donna has been dropped because of declining ratings. (This was patently false—the ratings rose for every episode that gave her some prominence.) Humiliated, Donna wanted to return home immediately, but Grover feared a brouhaha in Los Angeles and persuaded her to stay the tour, relaxing as much as possible and seeing old friends.

Paris was cold, and Donna hadn't really recovered from the flu. Crossing a street, she was knocked down by a motorcyclist who stole her purse. She was unhurt, but being robbed of her passport and money and personal articles was another violation. As soon as possible, she and Grover flew to London, where the weather was even colder. Incongruously, the trees were flowering. They stayed at the Alexander in Kensington, and the press was more intrusive than it had been in Paris. Feeling better some days, she did research on her British ancestors at the Mormon Library.

Home again in early May, Donna wanted to hide. Grover could hardly budge her from the house on North Linden. She had always taken superb care of herself, but now she slept fitfully and ate erratically. Her professional and personal pride had never been so hurt. The firing carried the suggestion that she was an incompetent actress, a woman who would bow ladylike to overweening power. The producers wanted Donna to issue a public statement that she never intended to play Miss Ellie for more than a year—it would be coordinated with their own, similar statement. Donna refused to participate in such dishonesty. She also refused Lorimar's ungenerous offer of twenty cents on the dollar to settle her contract, and its subsequent offer of thirty-nine cents on the dollar. "I signed a contract in good faith," she said, "and would hope that Lorimar did also."

Donna swallowed most of her anger, but bits of it spilled out in letters to friends and family. For months she had been dimly aware of maneuvering behind the scenes, cross-country flights, meetings taking place. In effect, she felt, she had been set up, and for reasons she could not spell out. "It's just a political thing," she wrote to her cousin Opal Whiteing the day after returning to California. "Also, I don't think Hagman liked a strong actress playing his mother—he wanted a fat, waddling brown wren of a woman who blinks a lot." She added a postscript: "Just remember, nobody ever said show biz was easy, fair, fun, or filled with nice people. *Dallas* is the pits, obviously."

Later in May, Donna and Grover hired a lawyer, Michael Donaldson. She filed a breach of contract suit against Lorimar and CBS Entertainment. There were moral and practical reasons for suing. She was fighting for all actors who signed contracts and worked in a professional manner, only to be dumped arbitrarily and callously. A contract was binding; she'd have been pinned to the wall for breaking hers. There was another aspect, perhaps only understandable to the gender that still got shafted in Hollywood. "It's my stand to show that no one, no matter how powerful, can treat women as if they don't have a say in their own lives," she declared.

Since Donna was legally under contract and drawing a salary, there was the complication of the "pay or play" provision. That meant producers had the right *not* to use players as long as they were being paid. It might seem nice to be paid for "doing nothing," but a player who could be called to act at a moment's notice could hardly take other assignments. It was a worrisome entanglement that Donna wanted resolved.

Meanwhile the Lorimar publicity machine, which had put her forward months before, went into reverse, throwing out tut-tuts about the public not accepting Donna as Miss Ellie, and her not fitting in with the cast, and the unfortunate necessity of shoring up ratings. Donna wrote to a friend, "The Dallas/PR stuff is very annoying and hurtful if you think about it." She tried not to, but was aware of the tabloids shouting her name to customers in food markets across the country. "This too shall pass—I hope." Only the angels, who sometimes neglected actresses, knew what might be printed—already a paper in Singapore had fabricated a $2 million settlement—and for the first time in her career Donna hired a publicist, Harry Flynn, to get out her side of the story.

The summer of 1985 was filled with court hearings. There were setbacks. Donna's lawyer asked for an injunction that would block any other actress from appearing as Miss Ellie (but not block the entire production, as widely reported), and in June a Superior Court judge ruled against the request. However, Donna felt that gains were being made behind the scenes. In July, even those seemed lost when CBS sent in a different top lawyer who "threw a monkey wrench" into the negotiations. "Disentangling oneself from the strings of a contract while getting full salary is no small feat," Donna realized. "Actors really get the short end of everything in these contracts!" But a week later, it seemed a settlement was in sight.

That came in mid-August. Three months after the firing, Lorimar's lawyer and Donna's agreed to terms. She would receive her regular salary for the next two years and be free to work elsewhere during that period. That was fair, and Donna was happy. It was fair contractually, but personally—what a toll!

Donna was increasingly ill during that hectic summer. "I have felt God awful, but I feel it is merely *all* the endless stress of the past three months—not to mention the previous year's work on that mean show— my gastric system is in an uproar, a first for me!" she wrote to Joyce Fisk in late July. Early in the month, she had gone for a physical exam, an ordeal because the nurse always struggled to find a vein for taking blood. She missed the reassuring presence of her longtime internist, who had retired. The diagnosis was bleeding ulcers, no surprise. The treatment was traditional: a bland diet that left her starving, Alternagel or Mylanta. "Pure misery," she wrote.

There were other worries. "I don't know what the good Lord had in mind for me the last months, but let me tell you, they have been rough!" Donna told Joyce. She was thinking not only of the *Dallas* fiasco and her health but of her brother Keith. In June he underwent brain surgery for Parkinsonism, the same procedure that her mother had endured, but now improved. The surgery was immediately followed by swelling in the brain. Keith's memory, speech, and coordination disappeared for four days, and the family feared the worst until, miraculously, all was restored. He returned to work six weeks later, the operation a partial success. But how much could anyone's nerves stand? "Sure helps put life in perspective, these terrors," wrote Donna.

Her younger brother, Bill, had been off alcohol for a year, and she was pleased and proud, but also upset because he didn't see any value in keeping up the old Mullenger farmstead. After the house had burned, only the barn was left and now it was falling down. "Soon, *all* will be gone!" she mourned.

In spite of everything, it seemed, Donna was beginning to feel her old relish for life. Her letters picked up genealogy again, revealing that Dr. Tom Shives, the head of orthopedics at the famed Mayo Clinic, belonged to her mother's side of the family. The Owen children were doing fine. Mary had stayed in the cottage behind the North Linden house, but was spending the summer in San Francisco and planned to attend the American Culinary School there. Penny had remarried and was busy with three stepchildren and her job at *Sunset Magazine*. Tony Junior, off from teaching for the summer, photographed Donna in August, and the resulting portraits were so good she planned to give out copies of them to publications and fans. To celebrate their eleventh wedding anniversary in early August, she and Grover visited their old haunts in Corona Del Mar and saw a lot of Tim, who lived in the vicinity. In September they were looking to buy a weekend retreat, perhaps an oceanfront condo in Oxnard, the last undeveloped area near Los Angeles. The beloved house at Corona Del Mar, where she had hoped to retire and read books and look at the sea, had been sold some years back.

Donna's stomach distress did not abate, and in September she went to another specialist for more tests. Again, an ulcer was implicated. She returned home and tried to carry on as if nothing were happening to her. Friends from Paris visited, and she and Grover took them to see the stage play *Cats*. Early in October, final papers were ready to be signed with Lorimar/CBS. Donna wouldn't watch *Dallas* this fall. "Nor do I read things said about me, though friends insist on giving me the gist of them," she dropped. A cast member had said rather unflattering things about her in some tabloid; too silly to think about. "I thought he was a friend—but then *no* actor is your friend, I guess."

No one knew how ill she was. About this time she asked Grover to contact a relative in Los Angeles who might catalog and organize her memorabilia. On October 23, Donna told a cousin, Clyde Shives, that the doctors had diagnosed her condition: "multiple duodenal ulcers, much edema, polyps in the stomach—benign, thank God." A week later she showed an alarming symptom, and Grover rushed her to the specialist, who ordered her to Cedars-Sinai Medical Center. There, a CAT scan and ultrasound test revealed a mass on her pancreas. It was cancerous. That evening, October 31, the doctors told Grover that Donna had six months to live.

An operation was performed to ease discomfort. Some days later the surgeon told Donna about her pancreatic cancer but didn't give a death sentence, leaving her some hope. Donna, being Donna, wanted to read about what ailed her, and a friend brought a book that described one of the most deadly of cancers. Grover was sorry that she saw the book because from then on she seemed to lose her will to fight.

Yet she kept up appearances, was always carefully groomed and dressed in a robe. Though her energy was down, she tried to keep everyone's spirits up. "She was her usual exquisite, considerate, darling self," said Shelley Fabares, who came to the hospital every day.

As Thanksgiving neared, Shelley, married to actor Mike Farrell, was faced with cooking dinner for the Fabares and Farrell families. So from her bed Donna directed the neophyte cook, advising her on recipes. Donna asked about the size of the turkey. Would it fit into her oven? Shelley replied, "Why would they make a turkey that couldn't fit into the oven?" Grover spoke up: "I once had to oversee a dinner for General Bradley, so the day before I had the entire meal cooked—a dry run." Donna looked at him balefully: "Grover dear, so military." Shelley said, "Donna, it may be military, but Grover and I are both Capricorn and it appeals to me greatly." So she did it his way, with Donna's help. "Last night I was thinking about this stuffing you're doing," she said to Shelley. "Now, you should try . . ."

Shortly after Thanksgiving, Donna went home, but soon collapsed and returned to Cedars-Sinai. While at North Linden, she wrote in a shaky hand to Opal Whiteing, thanking her for flowers and prayers. "I do need *all* your prayers, plus every piece of Iowa backbone I have left. Grover has been a prince through it all and nurses me now. My kids are angels of goodness to me." She had wanted so much to return to Iowa that fall, but didn't have the strength. "I saw pretty pictures on TV yesterday of the ducks and geese flying south from Iowa."

In December she was failing rapidly, but remained lucid. She worried about not communicating. "I just hate it when I can't think clearly," she said. One day she wanted to know what Penny was reading. "*Town and Country.* Mom, listen to this ad: 'Mediterranean villa, Costa del Sol, fully furnished, maid's quarters, boat ramp, only one million, three.'" Donna looked at her intently, "Oh, you could get it for less." Penny knew how much her mother enjoyed sizing up real estate, calculating the buying cost, expense of improvements, and potential profit through resale. "She was still wheeling and dealing in her mind," said Penny. "Her mind was really clicking."

It was a painful time for everyone. Heidi and Karen came to the hospital whenever possible. One day, talking to Karen by phone, Donna observed, "All my life I've worried about money." To her sister she said, "I wish I knew how much time I have left," but never to the children. Penny reflected later, "We were pretending for her. She was pretending for us. She knew exactly what was going on." In nightly phone calls, Mary could hear that knowledge in her mother's voice saying good-bye.

Close friends like Barbara Avedon and Norma Connolly tried to offer maximum support without intruding. Barbara, who had just read Norman Cousins' book about his miraculous recovery from illness, brought Donna a videotape of *Tobacco Road*. Norma, whose grief was compounded because her husband was dying, also tried to make her laugh. In a poignant moment, Donna asked Norma, "God, am I going to be remembered for the firing from *Dallas*?" Norma assured her: "No, no, my darling. You made some legendary films that will be remembered long after *Dallas* is forgotten. *It's a Wonderful Life, They Were Expendable, The Picture of Dorian Gray, From Here to Eternity* will be in the archives forever. *Dallas* is for making money, not for posterity."

An actor friend came to the hospital to pray for Donna. He was accompanied by his guru. "She was a religious lady with a hotline to the Big Guy upstairs," said Tim, who was deeply touched by her. So, he thought, was his mother, who started to feel better. Tim was grateful to this magnificent woman, who seemed to radiate electricity. "For me and Mom, she was a comfort, an awakening. Ever since, I've worn a cross. I feel like there's something to it—I *know* there is."

On December 20, Donna's illness was made public. Her publicist was quoted as saying, "The doctors are very optimistic since they caught it [malignant growth on pancreas] fairly early, and it seems to be slow-growing." At almost the same moment, Donna's physician was telling Grover that she had less time than first thought. One detail of news reports was correct: She was taking massive doses of vitamins. They were being administered intravenously because she couldn't swallow pills.

Donna was allowed to leave the hospital on Christmas Eve. The house on North Linden had been brightened with decorations by her old friend Pat Scott and the houseboy, Nino. Knowing what was important to a woman, Grover arranged for a hairstylist to come by. On Christmas Day a nurse dressed Donna and brought her out to the living-room couch for a while. The children were there—and Lillian Sidney, who had always eaten Christmas dinner with the family.

After the first of the new year, Donna's deteriorating condition didn't encourage visitors. Pat Scott offered to bring her husband, Randy, over to North Linden, but Donna said, "Oh no, I'm so jaundiced I think it might upset Randy." She sounded very weak when speaking with friends and relatives on the phone. On the evening of January 11, Tony Junior visited and watched a television game show with her. When it was over, she complained of tiredness and they said goodnight. "As I walked out of the house that night I knew it would be the last time I would see my mother. I also realized that she knew the same. I sat in my car and cried." Next day, a Sunday, the local Presbyterian minister saw Donna, who was concerned about getting a birthday gift for Shelley Fabares. That evening she had what turned out to be her last phone conversation with Penny, ending with, "You've been a wonderful daughter."

Monday morning, Shelley, on her way to Canada with Mike, stopped by without seeing her. "Give her this rose, and tell her I love her," she said to Grover. That day he drove Donna to the doctor's office and she seemed perkier. In the evening Grover had to attend a board meeting of the West Point Society. When he returned, she seemed the same.

In the middle of the night the nurse alerted Grover to Donna's turn for the worse. The nurse advised him against going to the sickroom because Donna was rational and might see his appearance as a signal of the end. He couldn't sleep, and in the morning—it was January 14—waited for the doctor to arrive. Grover asked Donna if she wanted to go back to the hospital and she said yes, another sign that the pain had increased. The doctor gave her a shot and called Cedars-Sinai to arrange for a bed, but one would not be available until afternoon. After he left—the clock said about nine—Grover went to Donna's bedside and expressed his eternal love, which she returned in a soft voice. Then he left the room to write some checks for the special-duty nurse. Before he finished the third check, the nurse appeared in the doorway and said, "I think we've lost her." Donna was two weeks short of her sixty-fifth birthday.

During the past terrible months, no one had talked much about "courage" because it was present in everything said and unsaid, realized and done. A husband who had seen death on the battlefield, children who had been more privileged than they knew, friends who had viewed Donna as indestructible—so many people who loved her perhaps in the end required more courage than she did. For who can say when peace surpasses panic in the dying loved one, and everything beyond the familiar shapes of external reality is changed?

The words spoken at Donna's funeral service were inadequate, as words always are, but necessary and true to memory. "She was a woman of hope and vitality and verve, a lady of grace, a lady of life," said the Reverend James Morrison at the Beverly Hills Presbyterian Church. "Over the years, through her upbringing in Iowa and through triumphs and disappointments, she learned that life was a gift. That's why she always had time for others. She spent her life giving."

Burial was in a most unlikely spot for a cemetery—a manicured square of grass between tall buildings in downtown Westwood, not visible from the commercial thoroughfare, recessed and reachable through a wrought-iron gate. Donna's grave, marked by a modest stone, is only a few feet from Natalie Wood's. Also adjacent are the mausoleums of Daryl Zanuck and his wife, Virginia. To the north, almost directly in line with Donna's resting place, is the vault containing the remains of Marilyn Monroe.

Because Donna went so fast—almost as if she'd been in a car wreck—many were shocked. No one in the family was more devastated than Timothy, who couldn't play his guitar for a year after his mother's death. "Anything life has to throw at me after that is like a picnic, like a walk in the park," he said later. And no friend grieved more than Lillian Burns Sidney, who remembered the day in early 1941 when a frightened girl with striking eyes came to MGM—with no experience to smooth a screen testing, no nice clothes to bolster confidence, no money for lunch if she rode the bus. Lillian, the former drama coach, remembered.

When *Field of Dreams* played at the Academy, Lillian attended with Grover, who had weathered his own difficult passage. At the end of the movie, after a baseball diamond had been built in a cornfield to bring back the players of yesteryear, Lillian was quietly sobbing. "It was the greatest catharsis for me," she said. "Because even when I go by myself to visit Donna, the ground is not where I want to picture her. In the movie James Earl Jones is wonderful and you know he's dead—when he goes he hesitates, and as he walked through the corn I could just see—that's where Donna is—I could see her on that farm in Iowa. Just walking . . . and the cornfield became eternity, the road to it."

A few days after Donna's death, the Irish playwright Hugh Leonard wrote about "the love of my life." Donna Reed had kept thousands of men single for years, he said. "When Donna looked at you with those steadfast, unflinching eyes, you knew you were capable of anything. And I tell a lie: she did not look at you: she *shone*. She had a faith that could move mountains and that mountains could not move. For her, you would eat brussels sprouts, give up saying 'Jasus' and, if the occasion demanded, fight an alligator."

Back in 1968 an embattled character in a Leonard play mused aloud: "Whatever happened to Donna Reed?" Audiences in Dublin and London reacted warmly to that line, indicating to Leonard that it had struck a nerve.

Since then, and especially since her death, the legend of Donna Reed has grown. The home-starved heroine of the remade *Little Shop of Horrors* sings about "cooking like Betty Crocker and looking like Donna Reed." The producer of *Serial Mom* says his title character is a combination of Donna Reed and Lizzie Borden. A commercial for Jif peanut butter gets stuck on Donna Reed. A male in the soap opera *Another World* tells his girlfriend, "Well, you're no Donna Reed!" A poem about Donna Reed (Donna Stone) appears in the high-brow *Paris Review*. Writers as diverse as Erma Bombeck and Erica Jong have used her name to signify the changes in American womanhood. Listing all the ways that "Donna Reed" has entered into the culture would require many pages.

The revival of her television show on Nickelodeon from the mid-eighties to the mid-nineties helped to perpetuate her image as the old-fashioned homebound wife and mother. The network cleverly (and affectionately) marketed her as the perfect specimen of her era: a weeklong "Donna-thon" of her shows was titled "Seven Days to Tidy the World." If she was never as rude as Roseanne, she was never the repressed Donna Stone described by detractors.

The Donna Reed image is strengthened by its one-dimensional simplicity, evocative of daisies and faux pearls. But the woman's long run with the public has depended on indefinable, irreducible qualities that go beyond the fixed image. Not many screen faces so romantic convey such gentle kindness, not in the star rank. If the fire in her sometimes seems stoked down, it is nonetheless there, transmuted into that famous glow. She might be Guinevere, and with her intelligence make the queen a bit too studied. Donna Reed's essential screen self is rather unapproachable. She is an enigma, yielding and yet subtly forbidding, warmly feminine in her familiar middle-class way and yet cooly self-contained. On the screen she doesn't cry like June Allyson or fence verbally like Barbara Stanwyck or purr like a needy Marilyn Monroe. Some dynamic is held in reserve. It's in her eyes, in her controlled body movements. To every role she brings a luminous quietude. The perfection that attaches to her public image, falsely though understandably, inspires in some a counter image of her as gone monstrously awry in perfection. Perverse minds are tempted to carry any seeming extreme to its opposite extreme. (For example, a once beautiful blonde woman is turned into the ghastly beauteous Resurrection Mary, the blonde ghost that haunts a Chicago cemetery.)

As James Agee said of Teresa Wright, she was one of the few women in movies who really had a face. If Donna Reed's face, magnified ten times, is not the tabula rasa favored by French New Wave filmmakers, who claim that the inexpressiveness of a Gene Tierney causes the audience to supply the needed emotion, it is still a face that connects with something deep in the national psyche. The old sexist labels—Girl Next Door, All-American Girl, Eternal Female, Queen of Valentine Tarts—are inadequate and no longer matter anyhow. The real cultural significance of Donna Reed, sometimes aka Donna Stone, eludes words and belongs to the realm of fragmented dreams, where dwell unadmitted yearnings for tender embrace, for mutual comforting, for mutual mental stimulation that is not aridly mental as between men. For beauty, too, in its various forms—and any "sexism" in the use of the word doesn't really matter, either. So Donna Reed—in her unique combination of sympathy, intelligence, and beauty—speaks to powerful inarticulated dreams. She would be amused at this romantic notion, being tough-minded in real life, but did she not pursue a life of dream production?

"Pretty girls often aren't as strong as she was," said her sister Heidi. Donna refused to sign a movie contract until she finished college, refused to continue at MGM and Columbia when kicked downstairs with poor parts, refused to falsify her television show in order to boost ratings, refused later to play a role that degraded women. She was an early feminist who confronted the patriarchy at MGM, and she always said plenty about the unfair subordination of women in Hollywood. Yet she never became cynical or self-destructive, and never soured on men, despite a trying marriage to Tony Owen. She was sort of a postfeminist, adapting to the male hierarchy on *Dallas* but upholding her own identity and fighting when it was stepped on.

Even so, her life and career offers little comfort to the more programmatic and rhetorical feminists, who would see her as inconsistent and uncommitted. She enjoyed too much—friends, travel, gardening, photography, books, art—ever to live on a single track. She lived one of the richest lives on this planet. With more concentration, she might have been a bigger movie star, but she saw the price paid by those preoccupied with stardom: personal emptiness. Similarly, she could have been limited by the political activism of her later years. But, in conducting her almost scholarly research, she weighed facts and other points of view and kept on learning.

Donna's intelligence sometimes gave her published interviews a rather sharp edge. The words don't capture her essential sympathy, which, the children remember, was oddly connected to her tendency to be overcritical, of herself as much as others. Of course, no words can ever substitute for actually meeting her. "I think it would take anyone meeting Donna quite a few minutes to simply stop being bowled over by her physical beauty," said Steve Allen. A natural beauty warmed by a healthful temperament.

I never met Donna Mullenger Reed Tuttle Owen Asmus, but feel that I've arrived, finally, at some detailed sense of this public icon and very private person. It has come from many sources. From interviews that took me among people in places that I (still at heart a Kansas farmboy) never expected to see—so strange it was to eat breakfast at McDonald's and then spend a morning at the Bel-Air mansion of Mrs. Delmer Daves. It has come from hours spent in cavernous archives guarded by sentries and from repeated viewings of her work on film. Even her minor movies have been described here because they are a point of reference for readers with their own memories and a surprise in store for viewers who know only *It's a Wonderful Life*, *From Here to Eternity*, and maybe *The Benny Goodman Story*. Now her oldies like *Gentle Annie* and *Eyes in the Night* are being shown on the Turner Classic Movies network. Donna's voice has come mainly from her literate and expressive letters, especially those saved by Joyce Anderson Fisk over nearly fifty years. Ultimately, any coherent sense of her had to come out of my own gut.

My search for Donna Reed began on the backroads of Iowa, where Yankeys and Shiveses and Mullengers demonstrated the same friendliness that had been bred into her. A cousin recalled a very young Donna playing the piano at her wedding. Another relative described Donna's pecan pie. From Iowa, my search spread out and gradually circled ever closer to the core of a personality as impenetrable as Citizen Kane's, or anyone else's. All the time the search was really inward, for hundreds of images of Donna Reed were somehow attached to different times of my own life. Having come all this distance, I still can't explain her hold on my lost youth. But writing her story has regenerated a simple faith in decency that had declined for me as the media projected a world growing more ugly, cynical, and mean. Surely her special life-affirming quality deserves remembrance. And maybe now I have some kind of hold on *her*. My own Donna Reed.

Notes

Page 1: "symbolized the heartland virtues of American womanhood": "Milestones," *Time* (Jan. 27, 1986): 78.

Page 2: holiday parties: "Still Wonderful," *New Yorker* (Jan. 12, 1981): 29–31; Patricia Braus, "Donna Reed Is Still Dead," *American Demographics* (Sept. 1995): 13–14; "women still want to be Donna Reed": "Psycho-Gs," *Mediaweek* (Mar. 11, 1991): 2, 10; "the Donna Reed armchair": Marilyn Bethany, *New York* (Mar. 29, 1993): 38 ff.; Donna's feminist consciousness: interview with Barbara Avedon, Denison, Iowa, June 3, 1989.

Page 3: "intriguingly covert": interview with David Miller, Los Angeles, Nov. 22, 1989.

Pages 3–4: Lewis and Clark crossed Boyer: F. W. Meyers, *History of Crawford County, Iowa: A Record of Settlement, Organization, Progress, and Achievement*, vol. I (Chicago: S. J. Clarke, 1911), p. 12.

Page 4: two red oaks planted: obituary of William Richard Mullenger, *Denison Review*, July 1981.

Page 5: Denison's economy: editorial by Chuck Signs, *Denison Review*, Jan. 23, 1990.

Page 6: In writing this section, I consulted Donna's own genealogical charts, kindly provided by relatives; 250,000 foreigners arrived: Marcus Lee Hansen, *The Atlantic Migration, 1607–1860*, edited with a Foreword by Arthur M. Schlesinger (Cambridge, Mass.: Harvard University Press, 1940), p. 301; Iowa resembled south of England: Jacob Van der Zee, *The British in Iowa* (Iowa City: State Historical Society of Iowa, 1922), p. 27.

Page 7: "always reaching for something unattainable": letter from Donna Reed Asmus to Janet Mullenger Auburn, July 7, 1981; biographical sketch of William G. Mullenger, *History of Crawford County, Iowa*, vol. II, pp. 558–59; mail delivery and phone service: Anna Marie Schneller, *Crawford County, Iowa, History, 1850–1925*, vol. 1, pp. 72, 82.

Page 8: experience marked him: interview with Keith Mullenger, Lavone (Heidi) Mullenger Flynn, and Karen Mullenger Moreland, Denison, June 11, 1988;

younger William faced future wife: interview with Lavone Mullenger Flynn, Rancho Santa Fe, Calif., Aug. 18, 1990.

Page 9: on Shives forebears: letters from Betty (Mrs. Charles) Massman, Jan. 1, 1992, and Aug. 1997. See also Albert Bernhardt Faust, *The German Element in the United States*, vol. I (Boston: Houghton Mifflin, 1909), pp. 230–31.

Pages 9–10: obituary of Charles Alexander Shives: *Denison Bulletin*, Mar. 1, 1905.

Page 10: "much funnier than most entertainments": typewritten report on Mary Etta and Charles Shives by Donna Mullenger Asmus, Dec. 16, 1979; Mary Etta at cookstove: letter from Donna Reed Asmus to Ferne Lipp, Apr. 9, 1984; "boats against the current": F. Scott Fitzgerald, *The Great Gatsby* (New York: Charles Scribner's Sons, 1925), p. 182.

Page 11: wedding announcement: *Denison Review*, July 7, 1920; "many who used to eat sirloin": *Denison Review*, Feb. 9, 1921; "Born to": Ibid.; seeing baby Donna in town: letter from Leona Rollins to author, Aug. 8, 1990; midwife Belle McCord: letter from Vernette (Mrs. Lilburn P.) Taylor to author, Aug. 7, 1990; William Reform's gifts to firstborn: letter from Donna Reed Asmus to Janet Mullenger Auburn.

Pages 11–13: details of Mullenger house and daily life: letter from Keith Mullenger to author, Aug. 31, 1990.

Page 12: "Little Mother": interview with Earl Shives, Denison, Oct. 17, 1987.

Page 13: influence of father's attitude: Meredith Brown, "Mother Knows Best," *Soap Opera Digest* (Feb. 12, 1985): 116; sensitivity of Shiveses: interview with Roberta and Donald Yankey, Opal and Frederick Whiteing, Denison, July 8, 1990; "fearfully maternal": Karen Mullenger Moreland, Denison, June 11, 1988.

Pages 13–14: Hazel's washday: letter from Keith Mullenger to author, Aug. 17, 1990; oiling kitchen floor: interview with Lavone Flynn.

Page 14: men ate first at family dinners: Kitte Turmell, "Family Holiday with Donna Reed," *Los Angeles Times Home Magazine*, Dec. 24, 1961; Daisy disliked Donnabelle: interview with Lavone Flynn.

Page 15: Lincoln's farm: The government granted Abraham Lincoln 120 acres of land 6 miles northwest of Denison for his service in the Black Hawk War; his son, Robert, sold it in 1892. See Schneller, *Crawford County History*, vol. 1, p. 105; cutouts of movie stars on bedroom wall: interview with Opal Yankey Whiteing, Denison, Oct. 31, 1987; fan letter to Anne Shirley: interview with Lavone Flynn; I am indebted to Roberta Yankey for supplying the words to "Put My Little Shoes Away."

Page 16: Donna suffering chilblains: interview with Marian Drake Justice, Denison, July 10, 1990; studied Elson Readers: letter from Lillian Luvaas to author, July 2, 1991; Donna questions test answer: interview with Marian Justice; "special gifts in English": the quote comes from Irene Storm, "When the Heart Goes Home," *TV Radio Mirror* (July 1964): 56.

Page 17: "let's talk this over": interview with Yankeys and Whiteings, July 8, 1990; Westinghouse scholarship: letter from Keith Mullenger to author, Sept. 28, 1990; wholewheat yeast rolls: Opal Whiteing, Oct. 31, 1987; "A boy with a bankbook": quoted in Schneller, *Crawford County History*, vol. 1, p. 225.

Page 18: reference to delinquent tax list: Schneller, *Crawford County History*, vol. 2 (1988): 15, 25; farm prices dipped in 1932: *Years of Struggle: The Farm Diary of Elmer G. Powers, 1931–1936*, ed. by H. Roger Grant and L. Edward Purcell (Ames: Iowa State University Press, 1976), p. xiv; cows tested for TB: letter from Keith Mullenger to author, Sept. 28, 1990; horse dies from clover: conversation with William L. Mullenger, Denison, May 18, 1991; "the drought that withered crops": Donna Reed, "The Courage to Face Today," *Guideposts* (Sept. 1962): 3; livestock crying for water: Donna Reed quoted by Tom Seligson, "Everybody's Mom?" *Parade* (Feb. 3, 1985): 4–7; "She didn't know where they were going": Reed in *Guideposts*.

Page 19: Hazel in hospital in 1930: letter from Keith Mullenger to author, Sept. 28, 1990; "laboring hard with no returns": Reed in *Guideposts*; "They won't grow": phone conversation with Col. Grover W. Asmus, Oct. 19, 1990; German shepherds back home in two days: interview with Arden Amman, Denison, July 11, 1990; "Bill did a little jig": interview with Earl Shives; a bit of a laughing stock: interview with Donna's siblings, Denison, June 11, 1988.

Page 20: Spode bone china: letter from Lavone Flynn to author, Mar. 23, 1992; "may have been good training for life": Donna quoted in "The Farmer's Daughter Who Went to Town," *TV Guide* (May 6–12, 1961): 14; "Poverty as we know of it today": letter from Lavone Flynn, Apr. 15, 1991.

Page 21: reminiscences of high school days: phone interview with Joyce Anderson Fisk, Aug. 9, 1990; also letter from Joyce Fisk to author, Aug. 10, 1990; churches mobilizing: Schneller, *Crawford County History*, vol. 2, pp. 45, 48.

Page 22: "my favorite girl": phone interview with Dr. Thomas Hutcheson, Sept. 7, 1990; interesting people strayed through: *Denison Review*, Oct. 25, 1934; Oct. 7, 1937; May 19, 1938.

Page 23: Donna's eyes: letter from Margaret Anderson Carbee, July 24, 1990; "anytime you were around her": interview with Arlen Gemeroth, Denison, July 7, 1990; version of play Ayn Rand disowned: Introduction to *Night of January 16th*, Final Revised Ed. (New York: New American Library, 1987), pp. 13–14; Jack Nau recalled: interviews with Harold Auld, Arlen Gemeroth, and Donald Yankey, Denison, July 7–8, 1990; "only one outside the movies": phone interview with Hutcheson.

Page 24: cheese and onion sandwich: interview with Ervin Mohr, Denison, July 10, 1990; destitute farmers met: "July 1936," Schneller, *Crawford County History*, vol. 2; Ammans lose land: interview with Ervin Amman; Donna borrowing formal: interview with Virginia Richard Powell, Denison, Oct. 17,

1987; mock wedding, listening to Dutch Reagan: phone interview with Joyce Fisk.

Pages 24–25: movie made in Denison: interview with Donald Yankey, July 8, 1990. See also *Denison Record*, Aug. 6, 1936.

Page 25: "Mothers of Men": *Denison Review*, Feb. 25, 1937; for an account of the Miss Denison contest, see *Denison Review*, Oct. 7, 1937; going to dance at Carroll: letter from Kenneth Langer to author, Aug. 28, 1990.

Page 26: working after school: letter from Lucille Kepford Tomey to author, July 31, 1990; interview with Gemeroth; classmates affected by the depression: Ervin Mohr, Donald Jensen, and Ila Bledsoe Wiebers in group interview, Denison, July 10, 1990; Donna's coronation described in *Denison Record*, May 19, 1938; "Her ability to sustain": letter from Margaret Anderson Carbee.

Page 27: "He was so bitter": interview with Harold Auld, Denison, July 7, 1990; Donna rattled into LA in sedan: "Campus Queen Comes to Hollywood," *The Lion's Roar*, Jan. 1942; Donna's obituary in the *Los Angeles Times* (Jan. 15, 1986) repeated the legend as fact; "I know we can rely on you": Hazel quoted in *TV-Radio Mirror* (July 1964): 82.

Page 28: "I can still see my mother crying": interview with Lavone Flynn.

2. TO CALIFORNIA

Page 29: My background reading on California included Harry Carr, *Los Angeles: City of Dreams* (New York: Appleton & Century, 1935); Matt Weinstock, *My L.A.* (New York: A. Wyn, Pubs., 1947); and Carey McWilliams, *Southern California: An Island on the Land* (1946; reprinted by Peregrine Smith, Santa Barbara, Calif., 1973).

Page 30: The phrase "golden age of crackpotism" comes from Andrew Rolle, *Los Angeles* (Materials for Today's Learning, Inc., 1981); Mildred Van Kampen described: phone interview with Nanette Linden, Mar. 20, 1992; "always searching for something": interview with William L. Mullenger, Denison, July 28, 1990; "Gosh, if you were only": letter from Donna Mullenger to Joyce Anderson, Nov. 1938. Note: Donna's letters to her Iowa friend are hereafter cited as *Donna to Joyce* because their last names changed over the years.

Page 31: "You've spent too much time": interview with Jerry Blunt, Los Angeles, Aug. 17, 1990; "to act or die!": letter from Ardath Atkinson McLean to author, Aug. 3, 1991; "Part of her charm": interview with Jerry Blunt; on Donna's looks and Alexis Smith's clothes: phone interview with Kelly Quinn (Marie Legér), Mar. 4, 1992; not a "darn new stitch": letter from Donna to Joyce, Sept. 22, 1939.

Page 32: Donna's glasses: letter from Donna to Joyce, April 1939; "takes an audience so fast": undated typed paper written for cinematography class by Donna Mullenger; "*Up* came the oysters": unpublished vocal exercises by Vocha Fiske, courtesy of Moria Turner Bruck; "Queen Elizabeth could": interview with Jerry Blunt; "a struggle, and I do mean": letter from Donna to Joyce, Nov. 1938; "it was all so hard": interview with Moria Turner Bruck, Los Angeles, Dec. 9, 1991; beginners spoke only to: letter from Ardath Atkinson McLean.

Page 33: "I'm prepared for this": interview with Harvey Tietzell, Santa Monica, Calif., Nov. 25, 1989; a pattern for Mildred: phone interview with Nanette Linden; boarded with Baumeister family: phone interview with Virginia Ricks Hill, Aug. 31, 1991; enrolled in fifteen and a half hours: Donna to Joyce, Sept. 22, 1939. Donna gives her daily schedule in her July 1939 letter.

Page 34: "totally focused": phone interview with Virginia Hill; "I work like a fiend": Donna to Joyce, Nov. 1938; "It would cost a fortune": Donna to Joyce, July 1939; Earl Carroll's theater restaurant: Donna to Joyce, Jan. 1939.

Page 35: taking Donna downtown: phone interview with Virginia Hill; "I have a terrible cold": Donna to Joyce, Nov. 1938.

Pages 35–36: visit to MGM described: Donna to Joyce, Ibid.

Page 36: accumulate a "good pile": Donna to Joyce, Jan. 1939; homesickness: Donna to Joyce, April 1939; suffering from heat: Donna to Joyce, July 1939; trip home in 1940: biographical form filled out by Donna for MGM, Apr. 5, 1941, from file on Donna Reed at Margaret Herrick Library, Academy of Motion Picture Arts and Sciences, Los Angeles.

Page 37: Donna on Rose Bowl float: phone interview with Virginia Hill; Donna rehearsing dialect: letter from Mendie Koenig to author, May 10, 1991; lacked ethnic European spirit: letter from Helen Katz Mann to author, July 15, 1991.

Pages 37–38: on way to a reading: letter from Sam Sebby to author, Nov. 29, 1991.

Page 38: Carradine advised students: letter from Elberta Casey Hunter to author, May 11, 1991; forgot Shakespeare: "Cinderella Has No Cinch," *The Lion's Roar*, Sept. 1943; Donna began to read from: letter from Mary Huston Jaco to author, July 2, 1991; "This will be my last year": Donna to Joyce.

Pages 38–39: life at Johnsons' described: phone interview with Virginia Hill, March 31, 1992.

Page 39: movies seen, Red Cross review, Heidt show: Donna to Joyce, Nov. 1940. See also "Miss Mullenger on Horace Heidt Show," *Denison Review*, Oct. 17, 1940; photographer arranged for: phone interview with Milton Dobkin, Nov. 7, 1991.

Page 40: "I might not be any good": Kate Holliday, "Farmer's Daughter," *Collier's* (June 27, 1942): 13 ff.; Donna's interview with Grady: Billy Grady, *The Irish Peacock: The Confessions of a Legendary Talent Agent* (New Rochelle, N.Y.: Arlington House, 1972), pp. 76–77; for a general view of the MGM lot in its heyday, see James Kotsilibas Davis, *The Barrymores: The Royal Family in Hollywood* (New York: Crown Pubs., 1990), pp. 112–13.

Page 41: "She was brought in": phone interviews with Lillian Burns Sidney, Feb. 18,

1990, and July 19, 1991; "It will be ready when I say": phone interview with Sidney, July 19, 1991. See also article on Mrs. Sidney by Sandra Shevey in *Los Angeles Times*, Dec. 18, 1977.

Pages 41–42: screen test and Mayer response: phone interviews with Sidney.

Page 42: "Maybe you think I can't use": Donna to Joyce, Apr. 8, 1941; Denison newspaper wouldn't print news: Donna Reed quoted in *Denison Bulletin*, June 28, 1979; "luckiest person alive": Donna to Joyce, Apr. 8, 1941.

3. LEARNING WITH LEO

Page 43: "It's all like a fairy story": letter from Donna to Joyce, Apr. 8, 1941; makeover: "From Campus Queen to Film Heroine Overnight, Donna Reed's Miracle," *Hollywood Star*, July 1941; sent to Palm Springs: interview with Danny Desmond, Aug. 1990, Los Angeles; "awful time finding a name": Donna to Joyce, Apr. 8, 1941.

Pages 43–44: name change: "Donna Mullenger Becomes Donna Adams, Screen Star," *Denison Review*, May 1, 1941.

Page 44: "a cold, forbidding sound": Donna quoted in David Ragan, *Who's Who in Hollywood* (New Rochelle, N.Y.: Arlington House, 1976), p. 380; first time on set: "Her First Year," *Lion's Roar*, Sept.–Oct. 1942.

Page 45: "Lou and I hung on": Donna to Joyce, June 2, 1941; "Donna Reed arrives": review of *The Get-Away* by Edwin Schallert, *Los Angeles Times*, June 11, 1941; "still in a daze": letter from Hazel Mullenger to Donna Mullenger Reed, June 15, 1941.

Page 46: seeing herself on film: Lydia Lane, "Donna Reed Says Success and Beauty Depends on Happiness," *Los Angeles Times*, Aug. 23, 1953; "I was so happy": Donna to Joyce, Apr. 8, 1941; "I've seen too many summers": Inez Wallace, "Film Star Donna Reed Tells Why She'll Never Starve," *Cleveland Plain Dealer*, Feb. 27, 1944; Ayn Rand and black stockings: phone interview with Marie Windsor, Mar. 1992.

Page 47: life at Studio Club: Zeanette Moore, "Studio Club Bolsters Film Novice's Courage," *Los Angeles Times*, June 24, 1945. See also "Donna Reed on the Star Trail," *Lion's Roar*, Mar. 1942; Donna's only extravagance: Donna to Joyce, June 2, 1941.

Pages 47–48: visitor to MGM: Bob Crossley, "I Was Just Terribly Lucky," *Denison Review*, June 24, 1941.

Page 48: "happiest I've ever been": Donna to Joyce, June 2, 1941; "aura of sadness": phone interview with Virginia Ricks Hill, Aug. 31, 1991; called down for going out in bluejeans: interview with Mary Owen, Dec. 5, 1992; "Everyone getting married": Donna to Joyce, Oct. 16, 1941.

Page 49: "a premonition": Donna to Joyce, Aug. 6, 1941; "Emphasis is laid on the fact": "School for Glamour," *Lion's Roar*, 1941–42; Burns on Stanislavsky: interview with Lillian Burns Sidney, Feb. 18, 1990.

Page 50: role "drippy at times": Donna to Joyce, Aug. 6, 1941; "much as I hated to quit college": Donna to Joyce, Oct. 16, 1941.

Page 51: drove to Laguna Beach: interview with Moria Turner Bruck, Dec. 9, 1991; fought dream battles: undated interview with Gladys Hall, Gladys Hall Collection, Folder 404, Margaret Herrick Library, Academy; "rare camera poise": Dorothy Manners, undated review of *Courtship of Andy Hardy* in Donna Reed memorabilia, Denison; "Reed going places": Wanda Hale, *New York Daily News*, 1942; "Donna seems destined": John McManus, *PM*, 1942; name in lights: Donna to Joyce, April 5, 1942. See also "Her First Year," *Lion's Roar*, Sept.–Oct. 1942.

Page 52: Blake remembered first hug: Steven Cole Smith, "Actor Returns from Oblivion," *Sunday Omaha World-Herald*, Jan. 24, 1993; "a very intelligent, deep-thinking": Donna to Joyce, Apr. 5, 1942; one unkind critic: *Motion Picture Herald*, June 27, 1942.

Page 53: "can bake a cherry pie": "Small, Terrific and Cornfed," *Photoplay and Movie Mirror*, Oct. 1942; "Donna's hair and eyes": Herb Howe, "Wonderful Life with Donna," *Photoplay* (July 1947): 65.

Page 54: Mayer as "sentimental tyrant": interview with Ann Straus, Dec. 14, 1991, Los Angeles; "never had an aging moment": phone interview with Esther Williams, May 23, 1989.

Page 55: Donna at Crawford County Fair: "Donna Reed 'Bonds,'" *Denison Bulletin*, Aug. 20, 1942. See also "Iowa Girl Home from Hollywood," *Des Moines Register*, Aug. 1942; night train back to California: "Sweetheart of the Army," *Lion's Roar*, Apr. 1944; "By the way, what happens": interview with William Tuttle, May 1989, Los Angeles.

Page 57: married producer in pursuit: interview with Lillian Burns Sidney; one weekend in San Diego: phone conversation with William Tuttle, Aug. 28, 1997; apartment at Beverly Glenn: Donna to Joyce, Mar. 2, 1943.

Page 58: movie historians seize on name Dull: Jay Robert Nash and Stanley Ralph Ross on *The Man from Down Under* in *The Motion Picture Guide, L–M, 1927–1983* (Chicago: Cinebook, 1986); "capable and attractive actress": review by Theodore Strauss, *New York Times*, Sept. 27, 1943; Donna losing roles: interview with William Tuttle, May 1989; "Billy is a swell guy": Donna to Joyce, Mar. 2, 1943.

Page 59: "It paints a clear picture": Donna to Joyce, Mar. 2, 1943; "silly little skit": Donna to Joyce, Jan. 24, 1944.

Page 60: "very, very happy": Donna to Joyce, Ibid.; incident as bad omen: interview with Tuttle, Dec. 1991. See also Bee Bangs, "There Are No Rules," *Silver Screen* (May 1946): 87; when Donna became pregnant: interview with Bill

Tuttle; "Donna was like a Dresden doll": letter from Angela Lansbury to author, Sept. 13, 1993.

Page 61: 102 takes required for scene: interview with Tuttle, Dec. 1991; memo of Aug. 29, 1944, from Berman quoted, MGM file, Cinema-Television Library, University of Southern California; ten players to star category: "Metro's Ten New Stars on 20th Anniversary," *Variety* (June 21, 1944): 3; Tony would invite them to beach house: phone conversation with Tuttle, Aug. 28, 1997; discouraged her from doing Lassie film: interview with Tuttle; to impersonate bass fiddle player: Edwin Schallert, *Los Angeles Times*, May 8, 1944.

Pages 61–62: character in *Gentle Annie*: Joanne D'Antonio, *Andrew Marton* (Metuchen, N.J.: Director's Guild of America and the Scarecrow Press, Inc., 1991), pp. 122–23.

Page 62: "He can do anything": letter from Donna to Joyce, Oct. 10, 1944; tensions but no blowup: interview with Tuttle; "To BA from BA": phone conversation with Tuttle, Aug. 28, 1997.

Page 63: "This has been coming": "Divorce Won [last Tuesday] by Donna Reed," *Los Angeles Times*, Jan. 13, 1945; everyone was killed: "Airliner Crash in Fog Kills 24," *Los Angeles Times*, Jan. 11, 1945.

4. A WONDERFUL LIFE

Page 65: Tony Owen in New Orleans and Chicago: interview with Sukie Mergener, Nov. 25, 1989.

Page 66: young Tony in Chicago: interview with Ann Straus, Los Angeles, Dec. 14, 1991; "Standard Club's John Barrymore": "Star in Recent Revue," *The Standard Club Magazine* (Mar. 5, 1929): 2; "I started this world wrong": John Crosby, "Just Try to Turn Off Tony Owen!" *Chicago Sun-Times*, Dec. 13, 1959.

Page 67: veep and business manager of the Lions: interview with Sukie Mergener; called Pop Owen: Herb Howe, "Wonderful Life with Donna"; "I'm going to marry": Crosby, "Just Try to Turn Off."

Page 68: "fought like cats and dogs": *TV-Radio Mirror*, July 1964; "I was longing for excitement": Jane Ardmore, "The Hidden Truth about Donna Reed's Marriage," Jan. 24, 1961; "hide the tan of": Howe, "Wonderful Life with Donna"; Donna confided to family member: interview with Mary Owen, Los Angeles, Sept. 16, 1993; Ford's treatment of Donna on *Expendable*: interview with Robert Montgomery, New York, May 1980, in Lindsay Anderson, *About John Ford* (New York: McGraw-Hill, 1981), p. 227; "typical as a Liberty-head dime": Ford quoted in "Donna Up to Date," *Lion's Roar*, 1946.

Page 69: Ford presented Donna with pearls: phone interview with Grover Asmus, Dec. 1996; Washington premiere of *Expendable*: "The Hollywood Scene" by Lowell E. Redelings, *Hollywood Citizen-News*, Jan. 7, 1946; "Visually, and in detail": James Agee, review in *Nation*, Jan. 5, 1946; Donna "extraordinarily touching": review by Bosley Crowther in *New York Times*, Dec. 21, 1945; lawsuit over *Expendable*: *Los Angeles Times*, Dec. 4, 1948. See also "Damages 'Excessive,' Judge Orders New Trial," *Variety*, Aug. 3, 1949. Also: discussion of *Expendable* lawsuit in *The Motion Picture Guide, T–V, 1927–1983*, pp. 3362–64.

Page 70: Ford put troupe through paces: Louella O. Parsons, *Los Angeles Examiner*, June 12, 1945; married to Tony: "Judy Garland, Donna Reed Become Brides," *Los Angeles Times*, June 16, 1945; Tony hosted reception: interview with Lillian Sidney; newlyweds stopped in Iowa: George Mills, "Donna Tries Her Cooking Skill but Doesn't Trust Tony on a Tractor," *Des Moines Sunday Register*, June 1945; honeymoon in New York: Donna to Joyce, Aug. 1, 1945; barrels of Ohnstein family silver: Bee Bangs, "There Are No Rules," *Motion Picture* (Feb. 1946); beach house: Donna to Joyce, Aug. 1, 1945.

Pages 70–71: Scotts are neighbors: letter from Mrs. Randolph Scott to author, Oct. 25, 1989.

Page 71: Donna spent day in department store: *Lion's Roar*, 1946; "talent for comedy indecision": review of *Faithful in My Fashion* in *Variety*, June 11, 1946; Arthur and Rogers spurned role of Mary Bailey: Joseph McBride, *Frank Capra: The Catastrophe of Success* (New York: Simon & Schuster, 1992), p. 525; "She looked like she'd fall in love": Frank Capra quoted in "Americans Still Hear the Gospel of Frank Capra," *Tulsa World*, Mar. 19, 1982; "Everybody was looking for approval": Donna Reed quoted in Doug McClelland, *Forties Film Talk: Oral Histories of Hollywood* (Jefferson, N.C.: McFarland & Co., 1992), p. 312.

Pages 72–73: script versions of *Wonderful Life*: notes on script changes by Michael Wilson, Jan. 10, 1946, file at Margaret Herrick Library, Motion Picture Academy of Arts and Sciences, Los Angeles.

Page 73: telephone scene with cake: first draft continuity, June 3, 1946, file at Motion Picture Academy; phone scene in single take: Jeanine Basinger, *The It's a Wonderful Life Book* (New York: Alfred A. Knopf, 1986), p. 40.

Pages 73–74: Denison called "tiny": "Donna Reed: James Stewart's New Leading Lady Spends a Weekend in a Small Town," *Life* (June 10, 1946): 133; citizens object to "tiny": Anna Schneller, *Crawford County History*, vol. 2, p. 99.

Page 74: "I'm rather shy and gentle": Donna Reed quoted in *TV-Radio Mirror* (Dec. 1963); time off from *Wonderful Life*: "Donna Reed to Adopt Girl," *Los Angeles Times*, May 18, 1946; "exciting way to get a baby": interview with Karen Moreland, Mendocino, Calif., August 6, 1991; Heidi named after Swiss heroine: interview with Lavone (Heidi) Flynn.

Page 75: loss of foreign markets: "More Metro Studio Economies Expected," *Variety*, Nov. 12, 1947, and "Metro Contrives to Chill Video," *Variety*, Dec. 10, 1947; Donna blamed for financial failure of *Wonderful Life*: Robert Osborne, "Rambling Reporter," *Hollywood Reporter*, Jan. 15, 1986; Stewart "thinking of his professional life": *Parade*, Feb. 3, 1985; "a hurt that lasted for years": Col. Grover Asmus in Jimmy Hawkins and Paul Petersen, *The It's a Wonderful Life Trivia Book* (New York: Crown, 1992), p. 66; "Have you asked Miss Allyson?": interview with Col. Asmus, Beverly Hills, Nov. 20–21, 1989; Paramount in 1947: Bob Stahl, "Postwar Pains, Strikes Keep Televison from Public," *Variety* (Jan. 8, 1947): 119.

Page 76: "Marguerite reacted": Donna Reed, "The Role I Liked Best," *Saturday Evening Post*, Mar. 3, 1951; "Who's going to believe that?": Donna quoted in Robert Osborne, *Hollywood Reporter*, Jan. 15, 1986; Karen sang "Fuzzy Wuzzy": interview with Karen Moreland; "very quiet, observing": letter from Donna to Joyce, Oct. 5, 1948.

Page 77: after "living in dreary houses": Ibid.; atomic bomb story: "Donna's Atomic Age," *Lion's Roar*, Aug. 1946. See also *Los Angeles Examiner*, Oct. 14, 1966, and "Inside Stuff: Pictures," *Variety*, Feb. 12, 1947; Donna marched into Mayer's office: interview with Mary Owen, Sept. 16, 1993; "sweet . . . tough dame": Mickey Rooney, *Life Is Too Short* (New York: Villard Books, 1991), pp. 152–53; "I want to do the things": Donna quoted by Faith Service, "What's Happened to Donna?" *Silver Screen* (Dec. 1947): 80.

Page 78: one night she shouted at him: biographical file at Margaret Herrick Library, Academy of Motion Picture Arts and Sciences; Donna ordered to West Point: interview with Ann Straus; "patrons hate pictures to backtrack": exhibitor quoted in *Motion Picture Herald*, Nov. 13, 1948.

Page 79: *Beyond Glory* "pretty silly": Donna to Joyce, Oct. 5, 1948; studios cut budgets and payrolls: *Variety*, Dec. 31, 1947, p. 1, and Mar. 31, 1948, p. 9; Movietone cameras: "On-Scene Filming Innovations Used for *One Woman*," "Paramount News," *Motion Picture Herald*, Aug. 30, 1948. See also review by Edwin Schallert in *Los Angeles Times*, July 1, 1948; "spectator is made to feel": review of *Chicago Deadline* in *Variety*, Aug. 31, 1949; "carefully avoid me": Donna to Joyce, Nov. 10, 1949.

Page 80: "Everything I have done": Donna quoted by George Blumenson, "Much Ado-o-o-o," *Richmond (Va.) Independent*, Sept. 5, 1949; "next part I play must have": Edwin Schallert, "Donna Reed Declares Self in Revolt against Sweet, Simple, Negative Roles," *Los Angeles Times*, Oct. 23, 1949; what contract had meant to her: Ibid.; "In a few years": interview with Ann Straus; rebelled against *Bride Goes Wild*: *Parade*, Feb. 3, 1985; left *Scene of Crime*: *Los Angeles Examiner*, Jan. 31, 1949.

5. TO *ETERNITY*

Page 81: home movie: interview with Timothy Owen, Costa Mesa, Calif., Sept. 17, 1993; "a very husky healthy guy": Donna to Joyce, Nov. 10, 1949; bout with rheumatoid arthritis: Donna to Joyce, Ibid.; went to bedside: interview with Lillian Sidney.

Page 82: "pushed into doing" *Saturday's Hero*: Donna to Joyce, Nov. 6, 1950; boasted of paving Gower Street: interview with William Roberts, Denison, June 11, 1988; wooing Tony away from Feldman-Blum agency: Bob Thomas Papers, UCLA library; "greatest respect for Donna": interview with Lillian Sidney.

Pages 82–83: "She had something inside her": interview with David Miller.

Page 83: difficulties in filming *Saturday's Hero*: Ibid.; agreement blocked screen credit: *Variety*, Aug. 2, 1950; advertisement for movie: undated (1950) Los Angeles newspaper, file for *Saturday's Hero*, Margaret Herrick Library, Motion Picture Academy.

Pages 83–84: Buchman before HUAC: Larry Ceplair and Steven Englund, *The Inquisition in Hollywood, Politics in the Film Community, 1930–1960* (Berkeley: University of California Press, 1979), p. 382.

Page 84: movie theaters picketed: *Variety*, Oct. 24, 1951; groups not easily identifiable: letter from Alexander Knox to author, May 24, 1993; "sidetent of Americana": review by Tim Cohane, *Look* (Sept. 25, 1951); all this hurt: "Un-American Raps vs. Some of Its Pix Seen Key to Columbia's Net Slide," *Variety*, June 11, 1952; "To all intents": Donna to Joyce, Nov. 6, 1950; "self-sufficient" Penny: Donna to Joyce, Oct. 5, 1948; "You'd better decide which": Donna quoted in Bob Thomas, *King Cohn: The Life and Times of Harry Cohn* (New York: G. P. Putnam's Sons, 1967), p. 210.

Pages 84–85: Cohn promised Tony: interview with Tony Owen, July 24, 1965, in Bob Thomas Papers, UCLA.

Page 85: attended meeting of Professional Football League: *Los Angeles Examiner*, Jan. 23, 1951; Holden had rejected *Scandal Sheet*: interview with Phil Karlson, July 24, 1965, in Bob Thomas Papers, UCLA. *Scandal Sheet* is better regarded today—Danny Peary lists it as "essential viewing for the true film lover" in *Guide for the Film Fanatic* (New York: Simon and Schuster, 1986), p. 514; "Busy, busy": Donna to Joyce, Sept. 17, 1951; Donna on friendship: Donna to Joyce, Oct. 9, 1951.

Page 86: festival "a joke": Donna to Joyce, Apr. 9, 1952; movie attendance down: David Robinson, *The History of World Cinema*, rev. and updated (New York: Stein and Day, 1981), p. 248; "swimming pools are drying up": Herbert Clyde Lewis quoted in Garth Jowett, *Film: The Democratic Art* (Boston: Little, Brown and Co., 1976), p. 342; Tony asked Randy: letter from Mrs. Randolph Scott to author, Oct. 25, 1989; Donna's refined prettiness: letter from Claude Jarman Jr. to author, Dec. 11, 1992; only fifty-four corpses: review of *Hangman's Knot* in *Cue*, Dec. 12, 1952.

Pages 86–87: radio comedy "fun": Donna to Joyce, April 9, 1952.

Page 87: Heidi on *Blind Date:* Donna to Joyce, July 19, 1952; "merely collecting a weekly paycheck": Donna to Joyce, Apr. 9, 1952; "after I get a few more pics": Donna to Joyce, Sept. 17, 1951; adopted into Flathead Indian tribe: Donna to Joyce, July 19, 1952; *Raiders of Seven Seas* filmed nowhere near water: letter from Anthony Moreno to author, Sept. 18, 1993.

Page 88: "Stenographers make the best wives": Warner Bros. press release by Ned Moss, Warner file, USC library; earned $30,000: Warner file, USC; phantom of James Dean: Randall Riese, *The Unabridged James Dean: His Life and Legacy from A to Z* (New York: Wings Books, 1991), p. 532; testing for *Eternity*: Bob Thomas, *King Cohn*, pp. 311–12; "No one at Columbia even called": Donna Reed quoted by William H. Brownell Jr., "The Way to Eternity: Donna Reed Reflects on Past and Prize Roles," *New York Times*, Apr. 25, 1954; "Don't ask any questions": Thomas, *King Cohn*, p. 312; Donna's virus on day of test with Clift: Brownell, *New York Times*; Cohn ran test for Lillian: phone interview with Lillian Sidney, July 19, 1991.

Page 89: competing with Roberta Haynes: Bob Thomas Papers, UCLA; Cohn called Donna about midnight: Ibid.; "One could not forever": Fred Zinnemann, *A Life in the Movies: An Autobiography* (New York: Macmillan, 1992).

Page 90: no close-ups being shot of Donna: Thomas, *King Cohn*, p. 334, and Bob Thomas Papers, UCLA; Family members say Donna outsider on set: interview with siblings, Denison, June 11, 1988; "We seldom met": letter from Deborah Kerr to author, July 1993.

Pages 90–91: Cohn irate because Donna not on plane: Thomas, *King Cohn*, caption for photo showing cast at planeside, following p. 108.

Page 91: Cohn's cutting suggestions: March 24, May 22, May 28, 1953, Fred Zinnemann File, Margaret Herrick Library, Motion Picture Academy; "no great shakes as actor": Donna to Joyce, Apr. 5, 1953; Monty moved her to tears: Hedda Hopper, *Chicago Tribune Magazine*, Nov. 13, 1955; "Women were completely overshadowed": Ibid.; "easiest thing I ever did": Donna Reed quoted in "An Interview with Donna Reed," *Denison Review*, May 22, 1976; "What was subtle about Joan Crawford?": Jeanine Bassinger discusses "the exaggerated woman" in *A Woman's View: How Hollywood Spoke to Women, 1930–1960* (New York: Knopf, 1993), pp. 169 ff.

Page 92: "This was to make me look not so good": Donna to Joyce, Apr. 5, 1953; "Pish and tosh!": Donna Reed quoted by Dorothy Manners, *Los Angeles Examiner*, Sept. 20, 1953; "Madonna face": James Jones, *From Here to Eternity* (New York: Charles Scribner's Sons, 1951), p. 854; "poetic playing of": Alton Cook, *New York Telegram*, 1953; Donna and Frank best things about movie: Manny Farber, *Nation*, Aug. 22, 1953.

Page 93: Donna ran to stage: William L. Mullenger, Denison; severe headache: Allen Rich, "Listening Post and TV Review," *(San Fernando) Valley Times*, Apr. 7, 1960; "I've been beside myself": Donna to Joyce, Mar. 29, 1954; "Well,

I don't think": Hazel Mullenger quoted by Karen Moreland; Timmy aware mother had public face: interview with Timothy Owen.

6. FROM *ETERNITY*

Page 95: studio "hysterically happy": Donna to Joyce, Apr. 5, 1953; "agony" of those months: Bob Thomas Papers, UCLA; "a little dictator": Donna to Joyce, Apr. 5, 1953; "dog" Westerns: Donna quoted in *St. Paul Dispatch*, Oct. 15, 1958.

Page 96: "not a single peaceful moment": Roy Ringer, review of *Gun Fury* in *Los Angeles Daily News*, Oct. 29, 1953; "Miss Reed's artistry": review in *Variety*, Oct. 23, 1953; "it isn't impossible to love you": letter from Donna Reed Owen to Tony Owen, Sept. 5, 1953; "it really is ridiculous": Donna Reed Owen to Tony Owen, Sept. 21, 1953; "wait until you hear details of Kinsey Report": Donna to Tony Owen, Sept. 5, 1953.

Pages 96–97: A December letter was half-teasing: Donna to Tony Owen, Dec. 12, 1953.

Page 97: "Daddy Wise Eyes": Donna to Tony Owen, Sept. 6, 1953; "Don't run out": Donna to Tony Owen, Sept. 8, 1953; Donna fed headlines: Donna to Tony Owen, Ibid.; "It seems we're always in a financial mess": Ibid.

Page 98: "How I hate": Donna to Tony Owen, Sept. 9, 1953; "preceding two lines": Donna to Tony Owen, Sept. 7, 1953; "clipping in which you are featured": Donna to Tony Owen, Sept. 21, 1953; thought every plane that flew over: Donna to Tony Owen, Dec. 20, 1953.

Pages 98–99: Tony's prank: MGM biography by Howard Strickling, 1954, file at Motion Picture Academy.

Page 99: on Choufleur: Donna to Joyce, Feb. 13, 1954; "What Miss Reed is doing": review of *The Caddy* by Philip K. Scheuer, *Los Angeles Times*, Aug. 27, 1953; Westerns she never saw: *St. Paul Dispatch*, Oct. 15, 1958.

Page 100: wanted to costar with Kirk Douglas: Reba and Bonnie Churchill, Hollywood Diary, *Beverly Hills News Life*, Dec. 10, 1955.

Page 101: Donna's acting called "vapid": Bosley Crowther, review of *The Last Time I Saw Paris*, in *New York Times*, Nov. 19, 1954; her "unique" attractiveness: John O'Hara, "Appointment with O'Hara," *Collier's* (Jan. 7, 1955): 12; Tony was sharp: interview with Gene Nelson, Sept. 12, 1993.

Page 102: "Donna took her parenting seriously": interview with Karen Moreland.

Page 103: dyslexia and tennis game with father: interview with Tony Owen Jr., Denison, June 10, 1988, and letter to author, Aug. 22, 1997.

Page 104: Timmy craved hugs: interview with Timothy Owen, Sept. 17, 1993; "brought up by a zillion nannies": Ibid.; Mom on set of *Far Horizons*: interview with Tony Owen Jr., Los Angeles, May 1989. See also Phyllis Pope, "Love and Marriage," *Motion Picture* (Jan. 10, 1956).

Page 105: Sacajawea for Hall of Fame: Emily Belsen, "Seek Hall of Fame for Indian

Maid," *Los Angeles Herald*, Mar. 14, 1955. See also *New York Times*, Apr. 3, 1955; Donna best thing about picture: review in *Variety*, May 25, 1955. The same point is made in *Hollywood Reporter*, May 20, 1955; James P. Ronda, author of *Lewis and Clark among the Indians*, in conversation with author.

Page 106: Donna hoped to make a movie: letters from Col. Grover Asmus to author, May 30, 1988, and July 24, 1997; medical emergency: "Donna Reed Has Surgery in Salt Lake," *Los Angeles Examiner*, July 27, 1954; Bill Mullenger invested in sheep: interview with Karen Moreland; "I have lots of time to think": letter from William Mullenger to Donna Reed Owen, Aug. 16, 1955.

Pages 106–107: "She appears to be calm": Sidney Skolsky, "Hollywood Is My Beat," *Hollywood Citizen-News*, Mar. 24, 1955.

Page 107: "a dame men kill for": Hedda Hopper, *Chicago Tribune Magazine*, Nov. 13, 1955; "silly darned thing": Donna to Joyce, Nov. 15, 1954; Donna wanted to buy *Bad Seed*: DR interview with Hedda Hopper, 1955, in Hedda Hopper Collection, Margaret Herrick Library, Motion Picture Academy; offered *Around the World*: interview with Sukie Mergener, and letter from Col. Asmus, July 24, 1997.

Page 108: Donna interested in widow in *Backlash*: Hedda Hopper Collection, Margaret Herrick Library; filmed at Vaca Ranch: Universal-International Production File, USC library; gift of amulets: Ibid. (June 23, 1955); salary: Ibid.; "paid off like a slot machine": Widmark quoted in Michael Buckley, "Richard Widmark," Part Three, *Films in Review* (June–July 1986): 32.

Page 109: "I might never have got to high": Donna to Joyce, Apr. 5, 1953; Goodman and musicians jammed for Reed: U-I publicity release, *Benny Goodman Story* file, USC library; letter from Steve Allen to author, Apr. 13, 1990; "Almost everyone here looks like a gangster": interview with William Roberts, Denison, June 10, 1988.

Pages 109–110: Goodman's personality: letter from Steve Allen to author, Apr. 13, 1990.

Page 110: "Finally someone's life without June Allyson": report on preview comments, Oct. 27, 1955, *Benny Goodman Story* folder, Valentine Davies Collection, Margaret Herrick Library, Motion Picture Academy; "What a provincial soul": Donna Reed quoted by Hedda Hopper, Nov. 13, 1955.

Page 111: review of remake of *Ransom*: Molly Haskell, "Look-alike Dudes Descending a Staircase," *Film Comment*, vol. 33 (Jan.–Feb. 1997): 82; readying London flat for Donna: phone interview with Doris Cole Abrahams, Oct. 29, 1989; "All I wanted to do was": interview with Timothy Owen.

Page 112: "stubbornness is shocking": Donna to Joyce, Oct. 4, 1956; meeting with Garbo at airport: letter from Hillary Watson to author, May 3, 1990; "it all looked and felt": Donna to Joyce, Oct. 4, 1956; Marshall drank Pernod: interview with William Graf, Los Angeles, November 1989; Marshall treated Donna like a novice: letter from Col. Grover Asmus to author, August 23, 1989.

Page 113: "cast is smoothly professional": review of *Beyond Mombasa*, in *Los Angeles Times*, 1957; "Donna put me out of business": Tony Owen quoted by David Ragan, *Movie Stars of the '40s: A Complete Reference Guide for the Film Historian or Trivia Buff* (Englewood Cliffs, N.J.: Prentice-Hall, 1985), p. 178; "not another goddam castle!": interview with Timothy Owen; "pure French" hotel: Donna to Joyce, Oct. 4, 1956; "reading some dreadful scripts": Ibid.; Donna feared nothing left to give fourth child: Donna to Joyce, Jan. 31, 1958.

Pages 113–114: real estate transaction: "Jack Benny Kin Sued Over Home, *Los Angeles Examiner*, Nov. 14, 1957.

Page 114: "should have a nervous breakdown": letter from Virginia Hill to Col. Grover Asmus, Feb. 13, 1990; "When we lived in Coldwater Canyon": Donna quoted by Don Dornbrook, "Hollywood Homebody Donna Reed," *Milwaukee Journal*, Aug. 2, 1959; "effort expended to get there": Donna to Joyce, Jan. 31, 1958; "Time is a terrible enemy": Donna to Joyce, Ibid.

Page 115: Paris irritated Tony: Donna to Joyce, Ibid.; "the money involved": Donna to Joyce, Ibid.; first time since 1942 Mullengers reunited: "Donna Reed's Career on TV," *Des Moines Register*, March 1958; Mildred blamed elder Mullengers: interview with Karen Moreland.

7. THE DONNA REED SHOW

Page 117: "All the family shows": Donna to Joyce, Dec. 3, 1958; casting ideas: "Mother Was Almost a Bullfighter: Donna's Real Family," *TV Times*, Oct. 9, 1963; Mitchell noticed photo: "World-Herald Magazine Launched Donna's New Career," *Omaha World-Herald Magazine*, Feb. 1, 1959.

Page 118: cute titles like: Steven H. Scheuer, "Much Thought Went into Naming Donna Reed Show," TV Keynotes, *Paterson (N.J.) News*, Oct. 20, 1958; Donna Stone inspired by Mrs. Molony: interview with William Roberts, Denison, June 10, 1988; Roberts in his treatment: "The Donna Reed Show Presentation" (typewritten), by William Roberts, Feb. 7, 1958.

Page 119: "Heading back to begin filming": postcard from Donna to Joyce, July 6, 1958; "last time Frank Sinatra and I": "Turns Down Choice Role for Security," *St. Louis Globe-Democrat*, Nov. 9, 1958; "a cheap lot": interview with Andrew McCullough, Sept. 14, 1993, Los Angeles; "Clearly, Paul and I": telephone interview with Shelley Fabares, July 12, 1994.

Pages 119–120: she hated phrase: *Birmingham (Ala.) Post-Herald*, Aug. 25, 1962.

Page 120: Screen Gems productions shared: interview with McCullough; Donna had worked with since early fifties: Donna to Joyce, Dec. 29, 1965; felt guilty about deserting Mary: Rose Perlberg, "My Husband or My Children—I Had to Choose," *TV and Movie Screen* (undated), pp. 27–29, 64–66, in Donna Reed memorabilia, Denison; "right off the bat": Kay Gardella, "Donna Recalls

Shaky Start of Her Hit TVer," *New York Sunday News*, May 15, 1960; Lemmon saw pilot: interview with McCullough.

Page 121: hash not well mixed: Andy Wilson, *TViews* (undated), in Donna Reed memorabilia, Denison; "best thing to come from Iowa": Terrence O'Flaherty, "Hollywood Knows Best," *San Francisco Chronicle*, Sept. 28, 1958; "I always forget to tell you": letter from Hazel Mullenger to Donna, Nov. 6, 1959; "My mother loved having me on TV": Donna Reed quoted in Jane Ardmore, "She's Catching Up with Herself," *Photoplay* (Mar. 1973): 70+; rating of 8 recalled: "Donna Reed Eyes Producing Career," *Richmond (Va.) Times Dispatch*, Nov. 11, 1962; mark of success for new shows: *Variety*, Nov. 19, 1958; scheduling snarl: Donna to Joyce, Dec. 3, 1958; Nielsen sank to 6: Dwight Newton, *Oakland (Calif.) Tribune*, Aug. 11, 1959, and "Never Argue with a Woman," *TV Guide* (Aug. 8, 1959): pp. 8–11; "people would say hello": "Donna Has Last Laugh," *San Francisco News*, July 4, 1959.

Page 122: "guess you saw the Nielsen": interview with William Roberts; Mrs. Campbell loved show: phone interview with Shelley Fabares, July 12, 1994; Donna and Tony feared that ABC: Donna to Joyce, Dec. 3, 1958; Nielsen rating in January: "Never Argue with a Woman," *TV Guide*; "In an era when wisecracking": review in *TV Guide*, Feb. 14–20, 1959; "antiseptic oatmeal": Bill Fiset, "These TV People," 1959, in Donna Reed memorabilia, Denison; "bleary bit of blancmange": Harriet Van Horne, *New York World-Herald Telegram*.

Page 123: "Everyone says . . . our stories": Donna to Joyce, Dec. 3, 1958; Shelley recalled rapport: interview with Fabares, July 12–13, 1994; Paul's mother born near: interview with Paul Petersen, Denison, June 4, 1989; "I was incorrigible": Ibid.; "absolute joy to play a scene with": Donna to Joyce, Dec. 29, 1965.

Page 124: "I was really snippy": interview with Fabares; "I lived in a sheltered": Ibid.; "wanted to grow up to be": Ibid.; "thought I'd never": Ibid.

Page 125: dedicated Anglophile: "A Mere Matter of Life or Death," *TV Guide*, Apr. 13, 1968; "Carl was a ball": interview with Petersen, June 4, 1989; "Carl would have been a very popular professor": phone interview with Gloria Betz, July 30, 1994; "He loved being an actor": interview with Fabares.

Page 126: "as for my husband": Donna to Joyce, Dec. 29, 1965; second shift began: Perlberg, "My Husband or My Children" (schedule also described in letter from Donna to Joyce, Dec. 3, 1958); "This is about as glamorous": "Every Day Is Mother's Day," *New York Mirror Magazine*, May 10, 1959.

Pages 126–127: she looked drawn: Dwight Newton, "Second Year Assured for Gay Situation Series," *Oakland (Calif.) Tribune*, Aug. 11, 1959.

Page 127: "when I should have been thinking": Gardella, "Donna Recalls Shaky Start"; "She wasn't overseeing": interview with McCullough; she feared that different scriptwriters: J. D. Spiro, "A Star in the Kitchen," *Milwaukee Journal*,

Oct. 26, 1958; Donna thought she overacted: "The Farmer's Daughter Who Went to Town," *TV Guide* (May 6, 1991): 12–15; Carl got into off-beat: interview with McCullough; "There was so much bad film": Donna to Joyce, Feb. 6, 1960; "There's too much of me": interview with Bill Roberts.

Page 128: a strong personality: Wallace A. Grimes, "Stay Home, Girls, Says Donna Reed," *TV Times*, Aug. 20, 1960; Donna winced at West German title: *Los Angeles Times*, Dec. 4, 1970; "You used maybe three percent": interview with Nate Monaster, Los Angeles, Nov. 26, 1989; Donna loathed his first: Donna to Joyce, July 16, 1959; "Four people on my block": interview with Monaster; "I know you're a commie": Ibid.

Page 129: "felt like Abraham Lincoln": Ibid.; "When I got back": Donna quoted in Jane Ardmore, *Photoplay* (March 1973): 126; "I'm quitting": Monaster quoted by McCullough in interview; "Tony knows me!": interview with Monaster, and also quoted in interview with Alfred Levitt.

Page 130: the Levitts always felt: interview with Alfred and Helen Levitt, Los Angeles, Nov. 27, 1989. See also "Children of the Blacklist," *Los Angeles Times Magazine*, Oct. 15, 1989; "a Southern Baptist lady": Helen Levitt; James Wong Howe, who had to go outside Los Angeles: Todd Rainsberger, *James Wong Howe, Cinematographer* (San Diego: A. S. Barnes & Co., 1981), p. 58; Phil Sharp predicted: interview with the Levitts; "No one had ever done that": Ibid.

Page 131: Paul West's Capralike sensibility: interview with Jeffrey Hayden, Los Angeles, Dec. 11, 1991; Sharp's con scenes: interview with McCullough; "steel fist in the velvet glove": letter from Paul West to author, Nov. 14, 1989; "In conferences she picked up": interview with McCullough; "a bright, bright story mind": interview with Hayden; "murder of Donna Reed": Dalma Heyn, *The Erotic Silence of the American Wife* (New York: Random House, 1992).

Page 132: "My TV series certainly aggravated men": Donna quoted in Cliff Jahr, "Great Hollywood Comebacks," *Ladies Home Journal* (June 1985): 163; "Early during the show she tried nicely": letter from Col. Grover W. Asmus to author, Aug. 23, 1989.

Page 133: visible game for Paar: Hal Humphrey, "Donna Reed Square? Never," TV section, *Los Angeles Times*, May 30–June 5, 1965; visible game for Susskind: Donald Freeman, "Donna Reed: Fire and Ice," *Saturday Evening Post* (Mar. 28, 1964): 20; "many family sitcoms . . . were so far out": Joe Hymans, "Tiger Is Shining Bright," Lively Arts, *New York Herald Tribune*, Apr. 9, 1961; "I got sick and tired of hearing": Betz quoted in Marian Dern, "Carl Betz as Judd—A Defensible Case," TV Week, *Hollywood Citizen News*, Mar. 22–29, 1968; When a staff member asked to direct: interview with McCullough.

Pages 133–134: on Oscar Rudolph: phone conversation with Paul Petersen, Aug. 27, 1997.

Page 134: "informed and caring" point of view: interview with Hayden; "The moral of it": interview with Shelley Fabares; "Everyone had to come up to her": interview with McCullough.

Page 135: experience of making *Coach*: interview with Fabares; Donna believed her right jaw: interview with Hayden; "She was never bitchy": interview with Gene Nelson, Los Angeles, Sept. 12, 1993; "Lower the key lights!": interview with McCullough; "She could have been a lot more out there": interview with Mary Owen, Los Angeles, Dec. 5, 1992.

Page 136: "She had good coloring": interview with McCullough; one scene called for infant: interview with Virginia Christine, Los Angeles, Nov. 25, 1989.

Pages 136–137: Kathleen saw her as the type who: phone interview with Kathleen Freeman, Sept. 12, 1994.

Page 137: Keaton impersonating Santa: interview with Bill Roberts; "We were completely without artifice": phone interview with Esther Williams, May 23, 1989; Donna worshiped Bainter: phone conversation with Andrew McCullough, Aug. 29, 1997.

Page 138: During the filming Hamilton: interview with Bill Roberts; "I couldn't breathe": interview with Shelley Fabares; Donna the only woman: Jack O'Brian, "Last of TV's Top Gals," *New York Journal-American*, June 23, 1961; criticism by *Newsweek*: "From Eternity to Here," *Newsweek* (July 31, 1961): 75.

Page 139: complaint from Michigan Council of Churches: letter from executive director G. Merrill Lenox, spring 1960; complaint from U.S. Park Service: Bob Williams, "Donna Reed vs. Role of Ideal Wife," Around the Dials, *Evening Bulletin*, Nov. 5, 1958; light comedy less likely to be awarded: Bob Lardine, "It's Still a Man's World," *New York Sunday News*, Aug. 13, 1961; eulogy to mothers at Waldorf: Hal Humphrey, "Donna Is Not All-Out for Togetherness," *Los Angeles Mirror News*, May 25, 1959; "Doing more for American motherhood": *Daily Variety*, May 20, 1960; "When you assume you are worthless": Dora Albert, "Donna Reed Talks about Faith," *Good Business* (April 1965); Some walked to the front door: interview with Mary Owen, Dec. 5, 1992.

Page 140: at Chasen's he claimed front table: interview with Penny Owen Stigers, Mary Owen, and Bill Roberts, Denison, June 1988; "He lived high": interview with Karen Moreland; gift of turquoise necklace: letter from Donna to Joyce, Feb. 6, 1960; gift of diamonds: Donna to Joyce, Dec. 25, 1964; "She didn't like ostentation": interview with Barbara Avedon; Timmy would duck down: Shelley Fabares, "What Mothers Are the Last to Know about Their Daughters," source of published article unidentified, in Donna Reed memorabilia; family cook was mightily impressed: interview with Timothy Owen, Costa Mesa, Calif., Sept. 17, 1993; "No one ever really knew": interview with Sukie Mergener, Los Angeles, Dec. 1992; "They can be turtle-dovy": Dwight Newton, "Second Year Assured," *Oakland Tribune*; "charming Chicago hood":

interview with Barbara Avedon; imitation of a bad guy: letter from Paul West to author, Aug. 9, 1997.

Page 141: "He talks into a telephone": John Crosby, "Just Try to Stop Tony Owen!" *Chicago Sun-Times*, Dec. 13, 1959; "hard to be mad at him": interview with Mary Owen, Sept. 16, 1993; "She was precious to him": interview with Bill Roberts; "Tony is a wild, wonderful": "The Wonderful Way I Learned about Love," *TV Radio Mirror* (Dec. 1963); "not a lot of affection was shown": interview with Timothy Owen; "The thing about Dad": interview with Timothy Owen; "our little bonus gal": Donna to Joyce, Dec. 3, 1958; "I was her baby": interview with Mary Owen, Dec. 5, 1992.

Page 142: "Spock doesn't include": letter from Donna to Joyce, Dec. 25, 1964; "sort of became her television persona": interview with Mary Owen, Dec. 5, 1992; "we had so much fun": interview with Mary Owen, Dec. 5, 1992; Donna brought stacks of books: interview with Mary and Penny, Denison, June 10, 1988.

Page 143: thrilled to be in romantic Florence: Marilyn Beck, "Men! You Can't Live with Them, You Can't Live without Them!" *TV & Movie Screen* (March 1966): 32+; "He didn't enlarge his horizons": interview with Mary Lou Daves, Los Angeles, May 23, 1989; visited White House: interview with Timothy Owen; dated JFK, wouldn't kiss goodnight: phone conversation with Lavone Flynn, Aug. 26, 1997; Heidi modeled for Ivory Soap: interview with Lavone Flynn, Rancho Santa Fe, Calif., Aug. 18, 1990; modeling "nerve-shattering": Jack Springer, "The Life of a Model," *Des Moines Sunday Register*, Dec. 2, 1951; "a darling": Donna to Joyce, Feb. 13, 1954; "Donna Reed's little sister": interview with Karen Moreland.

Page 144: Lights were turned off: Ibid.; "It's *our* wedding": Ibid.; "doesn't seem to be any new relief": Donna to Joyce, Dec. 4, 1961.

Pages 144–145: The operation involved: interview with Sandra (Sandy) Mullenger, Denison, Nov. 1987.

Page 145: Hazel gained ten pounds: Donna to Joyce, Jan. 6, 1993; "She was always extremely good": interview with Sandy Mullenger, Denison; recording of "Johnny Angel": interview with Shelley Fabares.

Page 146: Paul ended up owing money to record company: interview with Paul Petersen; "Most if not all profits": interview with Fabares; "How about that mess": Donna to Joyce, May 26, 1961; Tony worked for Goldwater: Donna interviewed by Hedda Hopper, June 25, 1964, in Hedda Hopper Collection, Margaret Herrick Library, Academy; "There was an ominous": Ibid.

Page 147: arrests reported: *New York Times*, Apr. 23, 1964; Donna "grew, changed": interview with McCullough. Note: My background reading on the sitcom genre included a number of books, but they all perpetuate a one-dimensional, sometimes parodic image of Donna Stone; and the only book that even mentions (in passing) Donna Reed's own feminism is Nina C. Leibman, *Living Room Lectures: The Fifties Family in Film and Television* (Austin: University of Texas Press, 1995), p. 182; "There are maybe a dozen": Will Jones, After Last Night, "She's a Reed in the TV Wind," *Minneapolis Tribune* (date missing), in Donna Reed memorabilia.

Page 148: "seems now when a woman is starred": Hal Humphrey, "Mom Knows Best—Donna to Quit," *Los Angeles Times*, July 4, 1962; actors in a love scene: TV section, *Chicago Tribune*, Oct. 14–20, 1961; tasteless, awash in mayhem: Mary Hopkins, "Donna Deplores Poor Taste Exhibited by Movie Makers," *Norfolk-Portsmouth (Va.) Ledger-Star*, Sept. 16, 1961; Donna blamed James Bond: Janine Jons, "Reed Comeback Is Television Film Landmark," *Denison Review*, May 22, 1976; "I found it as immoral": Donna to Joyce, May 26, 1961; Zanuck about only giant left: Robert McMorris, "Donna Reed May Quit TV to Produce Films," *Omaha World-Herald*, Nov. 11, 1967; seriously considered producing movies: McMorris, and also Aleene Macminn, "Donna Reed, Producer," *Los Angeles Times*, May 27, 1962; rejected part of prostitute: Will Jones, "She's a Reed in the TV Wind."

Pages 148–149: Universal promised her: "Donna Reed Sues Film Company," *Los Angeles Times*, June 21, 1961. See also "Settles Out of Court with Film Studio," *New York Daily News*, July 5, 1963.

Page 149: she returned script with note: Hedda Hopper, "They Love Donna Even If Emmy Ignores Her," *Los Angeles Times*, Sept. 6, 1964; "a healthy woman, not a girl": "Donna Reed: Fire and Ice," *Saturday Evening Post*; "Tony, we're getting bogged down": interview with Gene Nelson; Tony hoped to film in Russia: *TV Times*, Aug. 20, 1960; dog brought in: interview with Paul Petersen, Denison, June 4, 1989; photographer from *Life* there: "A Lot of Dog for Donna," *Life*, Aug. 4, 1961.

Page 150: "You can see where teen concerns": Donna to Joyce, Jan. 6, 1963; "Have you ever tried to hover": Humphrey, "Mom Knows Best," *Los Angeles Times-Mirror*, July 4, 1962; "If you dissected us facially": interview with Shelley Fabares; "In playing Mary today": Ibid.; "I love Shelley as I do my own": Donna quoted in Bob Salmaggi, "Honesty: The Better Part of Ratings," *New York Herald Tribune*, Oct. 23, 1960; suggested conflict between mother and daughter: interview with McCullough; "As Mary Stone, you were": interview with Fabares.

Page 151: cashed in government bonds: *Los Angeles Citizen-News*, Aug. 7, 1964; gift for eighth birthday: interview with Patti Petersen, Denison, June 12, 1993; "For first time in six years": Donna to Joyce, Dec. 18, 1963; "I had been brainwashed": Donna quoted in Hal Humphrey, "Donna Reed Giddy Over Her Nielsen," *Los Angeles Times*, Nov. 28, 1963.

Pages 151–152: A poll would reveal: interview with McCullough.

Page 152: Crane "was a weird guy": Ibid.; "Bob never": interview with Ann Mc-Crea Borden, Denison, June 12, 1993; Ann technically a better performer: interview with Gene Nelson; wrote penny postcards: interview with Ann McCrea.

Page 153: He had intended to leave: Tom Mackin, "Betz to Play Hot Lawyer," *Newark News*, May 21, 1967; did not feel challenged: interview with Gloria Betz; "That's Dr. Stone": Hal Humphrey, "*Iguana* Therapy for TV Doctor," *Los Angeles Times*, Feb. 2, 1964; arrived at studio red-eyed: interview with Paul Petersen, June 4, 1989; show least popular in England: Humphrey, "Mom Knows Best," *Los Angeles Times*; sponsor kept show running: letter to author from Paul West, Aug. 9, 1997; national chairman of DRF: "Actress Heads Direct Relief Foundation," *AMA News*, May 17, 1965; Lady Bird Johnson invited her: Louella O. Parsons, *Los Angeles Herald-Examiner*, Feb. 20, 1965.

Page 154: emotional ending for cast: interview with McCullough; "cheapest drugstore affair": Ibid.; "I had such a horrible home life and": interview with Karen Moreland.

Page 155: "She would have dazzled": McCullough.

Page 156: "many things I should have done": Donna quoted by Perlberg, "My Husband or My Children"; "I am *happy*": Donna to Joyce, Dec. 29, 1965.

8. AFTER THE SHOW

Page 157: photographed with Mrs. Jules Stein: photo accompanying article by Maggie Savoy, "The Blue Ribbon 400 Defines Its Cultural Goals, *Los Angeles Times*, Aug. 14, 1968; "It was almost a new experience": interview with Mary Lou Daves; "it's so boring down there": Donna to Joyce, Dec. 1969; Tony sick of business: Donna to Joyce, Jan. 7, 1967.

Page 158: "I sat and suffered silently": Donna quoted in Michelle Willens, "A Bright New Force for Peace," *Des Moines Register*, May 26, 1971; Donna complained to Reagan about attacks on young: Donna to Joyce, June 6, 1970; "a time of great pain": Donna quoted in Jane Ardmore, "Donna Reed: She's Catching Up with Herself," *Photoplay*.

Page 159: Donna realized she hadn't done homework: interview with Grover Asmus, Los Angeles, Nov. 20–21, 1989; "difficult for show people to get involved": Donna quoted in Michelle Willens, "Miss Reed Starring for Peace," *Los Angeles Times*, May 6, 1971; Nixon packaged and coached: Donna to Joyce, Oct. 27, 1968; "a good and fine, superior type man": Donna to Joyce, Ibid.; "rising and falling volume": Donna to Joyce, Ibid.

Page 160: "spoke of feeling she was in Nazi Germany": interview with Barbara Avedon; "couldn't stand . . . average political hack": Donna to Joyce, Oct. 27,

1968; "man of pure gold": Donna to Joyce, June 6, 1970; "warm and caring person": letter from Rep. George E. Brown to author, Dec. 11, 1995; "we taught a whole generation of women": interview with Barbara Avedon; "I don't think men": Donna quoted in Nancy Baltad, "Her Goal: A Secretary of Peace," *Los Angeles Citizen-News*, Sept. 1968; "she knew the Defense Department's statistics": interview with Barbara Avedon.

Page 161: "We went from office to office": Ibid.; "The companies that provide us": Another Mother for Peace newsletter for June 1970.

Page 162: "In the mothers of America": Arnold Toynbee quoted from *New York Times* in AMP newsletter, Ibid.; steering committee meetings described: Donna to Joyce, June 6, 1970; "amazing experience": Donna to Joyce, Ibid.; rewards "greatest of my life": Donna quoted in Gene Handsaker, "Former Actress Fulfilled in Home and Peace Work," *Montana Standard*, March 1971; "As a human you long": Donna quoted in Ardmore, *Photoplay*; "felt important," years in movies and TV "trivial": Donna quoted in Willens, *Los Angeles Times*.

Page 163: women treated as empty vessels: Stuart Klawans, "Empty Vessels of the Self," *Nation*, March 18, 1996; "childish ideas" about womanhood: letter from Donna to Tony Owen, Sept. 5, 1953; "It's so bad out": Donna to Joyce, June 6, 1970; "My mother blossomed": interview with Mary Owen; "rattled out of Donna's driveway": interview with Norma Connolly, Denison, June 3, 1989; girl who resembled Bardot: interview with Timothy Owen.

Page 164: bad vibes in house: interview with Mary Owen; "He's nearly 100 percent": Donna to Joyce, June 6, 1970; "like climbing a mountain and falling": interview with Lavone (Heidi) Flynn; "my gypsy girl friend": interview with Norma Connolly.

Page 165: married a woman who looked like Donna Reed: interview with Sukie Mergener; "big bad ugly picture": Donna to Joyce, December 1970; "We haven't accused": Donna quoted in Willens, *Los Angeles Times*.

Page 166: McGrory marveled that Donna: Mary McGrory column, "Oil on Troubled Waters," *New York Post*, March 16, 1971; Donna-Kissinger confrontation: Blake Green, "AMP: Are Our Sons Dying for Offshore Oil?" *San Francisco Chronicle*, March 12, 1971, and letter to author from Grover Asmus, Aug. 12, 1997; "nineteen-year-old boys": Donna quoted in Willens, *Los Angeles Times*.

Page 167: Grover meets Donna: interview with Grover Asmus, and Tom Seligson, "Is Donna Reed the Ideal Mother?" *Parade* magazine, Sunday, Feb. 3, 1985; Donna was "anti–stupid-political decisions": interview with Grover Asmus; differences "exacerbated even by the peace signing": Donna to Joyce, Feb. 7, 1973; "professional army man's agony": Donna to Joyce, Ibid.

Pages 167–168: Grover's background: interview with Grover Asmus in Los Angeles; interview in Denison, Oct. 23, 1993; and letter to author, Aug. 12, 1997.

Page 168: "doing everything from movies to": Donna to Joyce, Jan. 7, 1974.

Pages 168–169: "I'm beginning to suspect he": Donna to Joyce, Feb. 7, 1973.

Page 169: "He understands, sort of": Donna to Joyce, Jan. 7, 1974; "good formula for talking about disarmament": Donna to Joyce, Feb. 7, 1973; "If nuclear power plants are safe": Donna quoted by Lee Dye, "Initiative to Cut Curbs on Atom Plants Started," *Los Angeles Times*, 1974; "She was gorgeous and": interview with Barbara Avedon.

Page 170: "The mothers of television always smiled": "Arthur Bremer's Notes from the Underground," *Time*, May 29, 1972; "got her worried about kooks": interview with Grover Asmus; "Donna was rather in love with": interview with Doris Cole Abrahams.

Page 171: "I didn't realize . . . how submissive": Donna to Joyce, Jan. 7, 1974; "It's time for my daily exercise": interview with Grover Asmus; "While I doubt we need": Donna to Joyce, Jan. 7, 1974; "what would you do if they threatened": interview with Grover Asmus.

Page 172: "Life is good with Grover": Donna to Joyce, Dec. 3, 1976; "By then I had given up on everything": interview with Timothy Owen; "Tim still strums his guitar": Donna to Joyce, April 19, 1977.

Page 173: "I swore a lot": interview with Mary Owen; "Mary's visits are briefer": Donna to Joyce, Nov. 25, 1977; "great tugs and pulls back": Donna to Joyce, April 19, 1977.

Page 174: "we relaxed to point of indecency": Donna to Joyce, Jan. 2, 1968; Hazel's quietness alarmed: Donna to Joyce, Dec. 28, 1968; "So Pop stayed in Iowa": Donna to Joyce, Feb. 7, 1973; "state's commitment to nuclear": Donna to Joyce, Dec. 3, 1976; "great interest in gardens": Donna to Joyce, Apr. 19, 1977.

Page 175: "I spend inordinate amounts of time": Donna to Joyce, Nov. 25, 1977; "it does not get easier": Donna to Joyce, Ibid.; wanted to produce film: Donna to Joyce, Jan. 9, 1969; modern version of *Doll's House*: interview with Grover Asmus, Oct. 1993; "Donna Reed Show" reunion plans: Donna to Joyce, Nov. 25, 1977.

Page 176: "can't imagine anyone else": Donna to Joyce, Ibid.; "think it's obscene": Donna to Joyce, Ibid.; "the endless negotiating before you start": Donna to Joyce, Ibid.; "a good placid marriage": Donna quoted in Cecil Smith, "Donna Reed: Back Where She Wants to Be," *Los Angeles Times*, Dec. 4, 1978.

Page 177: silently embracing: interview with David Miller; "Once you leave it": Donna quoted in *PSA California Magazine*, 1978; "darling, the last time": phone message to author from John Philip Law, Feb. 1995; silently recited Lord's Prayer during scene: phone interview with Jeff Corey, Dec. 5, 1994; "spirit of Helen Trent": review in *Variety*, May 25, 1979; "Oppressively chic": review by Howard Rosenberg, *Los Angeles Times*, May 26, 1979; "Stuffed with enough plot": Judith Crist, *TV Guide*, May 26 – June 1, 1979.

Page 178: "It feels very legitimate": Donna quoted in Robert Osborne, "On Location," *Hollywood Reporter*, Dec. 29, 1978; "their basic Midwest-ness": Donna to Joyce, July 12, 1979.

Page 179: "If one of us is ambitious": Donna to Joyce, Dec. 2, 1980; Grover wore dress uniform: interview with Carl and Friday Leonard, Tulsa, Oct. 15, 1993; "Power is very savage": Donna to Joyce, Dec. 2, 1980.

Page 180: "Isn't that a kick?": Donna to Joyce, July 12, 1979; "thought this might amuse": Donna to Karen Moreland, July 15, 1979.

Page 181: felt she was looking at herself: Donna to Joyce, between Thanksgiving and Christmas, 1982; "our family has been greatly extended": Donna to Joyce, Jan. 8, 1981; "great emotional loss": Donna to Joyce, Apr. 19, 1977; "greatly diminished mentally": Donna to Joyce, July 12, 1979; "I've been so sad ever since": Donna to Joyce, Ibid.

Page 182: "whatever turns you on": Donna to Joyce, Dec. 8, 1979; "I looked for more Mullengers": interview with Grover Asmus; "doing all four family lines . . . chess": Donna to Joyce, Dec. 2, 1980; "I shall be sixty": Donna to Joyce, Ibid.; "If I ever write a book about life in Tulsa": Donna to Opal Whiteing, June 1, 1981.

Page 183: "magical" hours at farm on funeral day: Donna to Joyce, Aug. 7, 1981; "Which gives me great pain": Donna to Joyce, Ibid.; Volvo breaks down outside Tulsa: Donna to Joyce, late 1982; "fiercely bonded" to old friends: Donna to Joyce, Mar. 4, 1979; experience with martinets in military: interview with Grover Asmus.

Pages 183–184: "working conditions in TV": Donna to Joyce, Mar. 25, 1983.

Page 184: mother less confident in new Hollywood: interview with Mary Owen; visit to Spago's: interview with Jody Watkinson and follow-up phone conversation May 1996; "Donna was incorruptible": interview with Karen Moreland.

Page 185: "I suppose I'm like my own dear mother": Donna to Betty Massman, Apr. 16, 1983; missed talking with Daisy Ellis: Donna to Betty Massman, Jan. 23, 1983; Mullenger farmhouse burned: Donna to Joyce, Mar. 25, 1983; last time she photographed well: interview with Lavone (Heidi) Flynn; shooting in Hong Kong described: Donna to Betty Massman, July 22, 1983; "my head on one side of room": Donna to Betty Massman, Ibid.

Pages 185–186: "thank my lucky stars": Donna to Joyce, Mar. 25, 1983.

Page 186: To paraphrase Willa Cather: Cather's observation about death raining around one as the years pass appeared in *Willa Cather in Person: Interviews, Speeches, and Letters*, selected and edited by L. Brent Bohlke (Lincoln: University of Nebraska Press, 1986), p. xxvii; "I really appreciate the way you raised the kids": Tony Owen quoted in Denison interview with Penny Stigers and Mary Owen; "he was very brave": Donna to Joyce, June 27, 1984; "Hurry!" to remake of *Wonderful Life*: Donna to Joyce, Dec. 13, 1983; Capra opposed to remake: Joseph McBride, *Frank Capra: The Catastrophe of Success*, p. 644; "I lost my head": Donna to Joyce, June 27, 1984; "book needed another chapter":

Donna quoted in Bob Thomas, "Ex-Iowan Sought Role as Farm Lady," *Lincoln (Nebraska) Star*, 1984; "quiet authority and simple elegance": Fred Rothenberg, "Donna Reed Makes the Move to Dallas," *Los Angeles Times*, August 31, 1984.

Page 187: "I'm creating Miss Ellie": Donna quoted in Jahr, "Great Hollywood Comebacks," *Ladies Home Journal*, pp. 162–63; "She wanted a desk": interview with Grover Asmus; "best part of whole thing": Donna to Joyce, Sept. 2, 1984.

Page 188: "cast for most part is": Donna to Joyce, Ibid.; "Can I call you Mama?": talk with Grover Asmus at Cronk's Cafe, Denison, June 28, 1987; Donna wanted to support him: interview with Asmus; hair printed to look bright gray: Donna to Joyce, Nov. 28, 1984; "I do not mind . . . look old": interview with Grover Asmus; "harsh side lighting": Donna to Joyce, Nov. 28, 1984.

Pages 188–189: "a gentleman's agreement": Donna to Joyce, Ibid.

Page 189: when Elizabeth Taylor appeared on soaper: interview with Norma Connolly; Donna gave cookies to cast: interview with Grover Asmus, and letter to author, July 24, 1997; "Wish I were doing more": Donna to Betty Massman, Jan. 21, 1985; "What a snakepit": Donna to Betty, Ibid.

Page 190: flulike symptoms: Donna to Opal Whiteing, May 4, 1985; "returning to the core cast": Donna to Joyce, May 21, 1985; "felt as if someone had opened a trapdoor": Donna interviewed by William Newcott, "Donna Reed: Why I'm Suing Dallas . . . ," *National Enquirer*, June 18, 1985; Grover feared brouhaha: interview with Grover Asmus; knocked down by thief while crossing street: Donna to Joyce, May 21, 1985.

Page 191: producers want her to issue statement: Robert Osborne, "Rambling Reporter," *Hollywood Reporter*, May 29, 1985; Lorimar's offer of twenty cents on dollar: interview with Grover Asmus, and letter from Donna to Opal Whiteing, May 4, 1985; "It's just a political thing": Donna to Opal Whiteing, Ibid.; "It's my stand to show": quoted by Newcott in *National Enquirer*.

Page 192: "Dallas/PR stuff . . . annoying": Donna to Joyce, May 21, 1985; "threw a monkey wrench": Donna to Joyce, July 24, 1985; "have felt God awful": Donna to Joyce, Ibid.

Page 193: "Pure misery": Donna to Joyce, Ibid.; "don't know what the good Lord": Donna to Betty Massman, June 9, 1985; "put life in perspective": Donna to Betty, Ibid.; "Soon all will be gone": Donna to Betty, May 22, 1985; Dr. Tom Shives a relative: Donna to Joyce, July 24, 1985.

Page 194: looking to buy weekend retreat at Oxnard: Donna to Joyce, Oct. 2, 1985; "Nor do I read things said about me": Donna to Joyce, Ibid.; "multiple duodenal ulcers": letter from Clyde Shives to author, Dec. 16, 1995; sorry she saw book on cancer: interview with Grover Asmus; "her usual . . . considerate . . . self": interview with Shelley Fabares.

Page 195: How big is your turkey? Ibid.; "I do need all your prayers": Donna to

Opal Whiteing, Dec. 6, 1985; "I just hate it when I can't think": interview with Penny and Mary in Denison; "All my life I've worried": interview with Karen Moreland; "We were pretending for her": interview with Penny and Mary.

Page 196: "God, am I going to be remembered for . . . Dallas?" interview with Norma Connolly; "She was a religious lady": interview with Timothy Owen; "doctors are very optimistic": *Variety*, Dec. 24, 1985.

Pages 196–197: "Oh no, I'm so jaundiced": letter from Pat (Mrs. Randolph) Scott to author.

Page 197: Tony Junior came by: interview with Tony Owen Junior, and letter to author, Aug. 22, 1997; "You've been a wonderful daughter": letter to author from Penny Stigers, Aug. 25, 1997; In the middle of the night: interview with Grover Asmus; "I think we've lost her": interview with Grover Asmus.

Page 198: "She was a woman of hope": "Friends Laud Donna Reed as Lady of Life," *Santa Monica (Calif.) Daily Breeze*, Jan. 18, 1986; "Anything life has to throw at me": interview with Timothy Owen; "It was the greatest catharsis": interview with Lillian Sidney.

Page 199: "the love of my life": Hugh Leonard, "A Long Affair with Donna Reed," *Sunday Tribune*, Jan. 19, 1996; poem by Tom Disch, "Donna Reed in the Scary Old House," *Paris Review,* vol. 37 (Fall 1995): 81–82.

Page 200: "Pretty girls often aren't as strong": interview with Lavone (Heidi) Mullenger.

Page 201: "I think it would take anyone meeting": letter from Steve Allen to author.

Page 202: young Donna playing piano at wedding: interview with Opal Whiteing; Donna's pecan pie: interview with Sandy Mullenger.

Index

3/99 4 12/98
added back 7/09 (last copy)